IDEAS
THAT
CHANGED
THE
WORLD

Authors
Julie Ferris, Dr. Mike Goldsmith, Ian Graham, Sally MacGill,
Andrea Mills, Isabel Thomas, and Matt Turner

Consultant
Roger Bridgman

LONDON, NEW YORK,
MELBOURNE, MUNICH, AND DELHI

Project editor Camilla de la Bédoyère
Editors Sally MacGill, Theresa Bebbington
Project art editor Ralph Pitchford
Art editors Sandra Doble, Steve Woosnam Savage

Senior editor Shaila Brown
Senior designer Spencer Holbrook
Designers Johnny Pau, Jane Thomas, Stefan Podhorodecki
Managing editor Linda Esposito
Managing art editors Diane Thistlethwaite, Jim Green
Category publisher Laura Buller

DK picture library Emma Shepherd
Picture researcher Karen VanRoss
Additional picture researchers Ria Jones, Jenny Faithful, Sarah Hopper
Production editor Marc Staples
Senior production controller Angela Graef
Jacket designer Laura Brim, Sophia M.T.T.
Jacket editor Matilda Gollon
Development team Jayne Miller, Laura Brim
Design development manager Sophia M. Tampakopoulos Turner

First published in the United States in 2010
This edition published in 2013 by
DK Publishing, 375 Hudson Street
New York, New York 10014

13 14 15 16 17 10 9 8 7 6 5 4 3 2 1
178385—08/13

DK books are available at special discounts when purchased in bulk for
sales promotions, premiums, fundraising, or educational use. For details, contact:
DK Publishing Special Markets, 375 Hudson Street, New York, New York 10014
SpecialSales@dk.com

A catalog record for this book is available from the Library of Congress

ISBN: 978-1-4654-1423-6

Hi-res workflow proofed by MDP, U.K.
Printed in China

**Discover more at
www.dk.com**

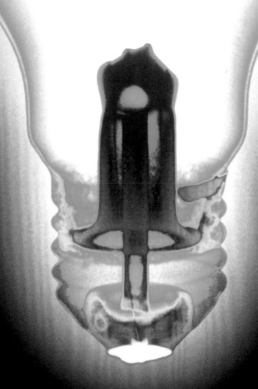

IDEAS
THAT
CHANGED
THE
WORLD

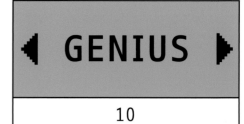

Contents

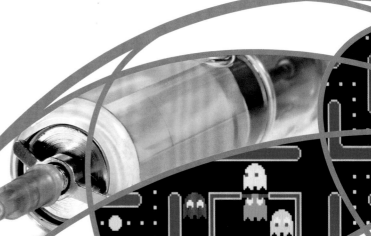

ON THE MOVE

144

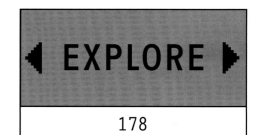

EXPLORE

178

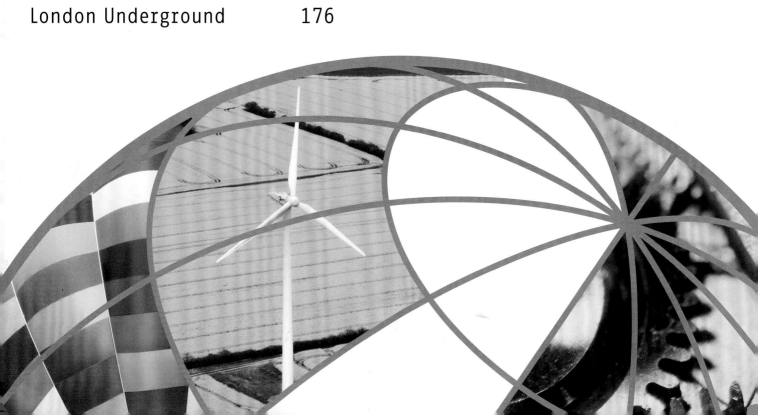

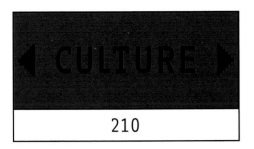

CULTURE

210

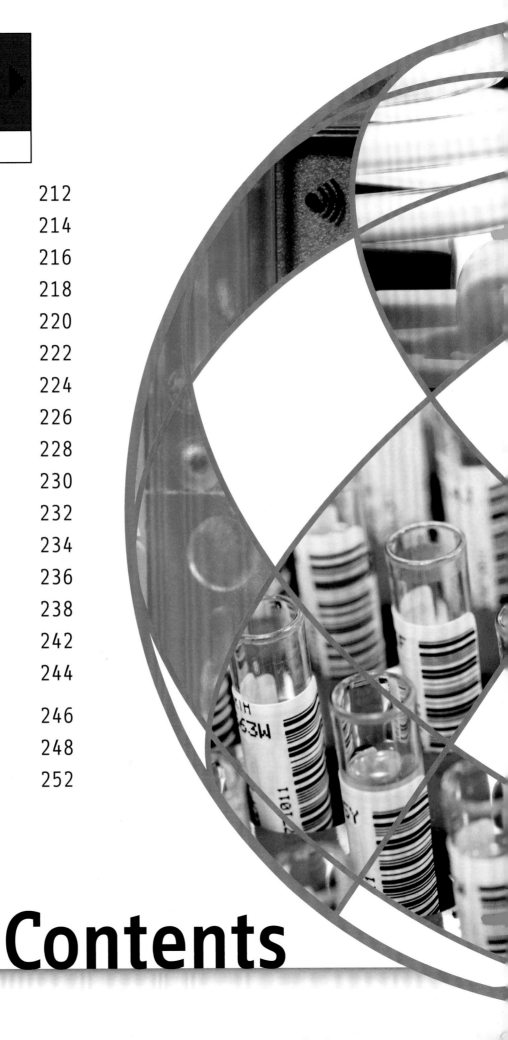

Contents

As Thomas Edison stated, **inventions are** mostly hard work. But without a big idea to begin with, they would never happen at all. And without these big ideas and the inventions they lead to, our lives would be very different. They have changed the way we live and think and changed the course of history.

Ideas in action

Just look around you—how many of the things you can see didn't have to be invented by someone? In fact, without inventions, many of us wouldn't even be alive— medicines and machines start keeping us safe and healthy even before we are born and continue protecting us throughout our lives. Some inventions keep us in touch with our friends, allow us to explore our world, or help solve the mysteries of the universe, while others simply help us enjoy ourselves.

Introduction

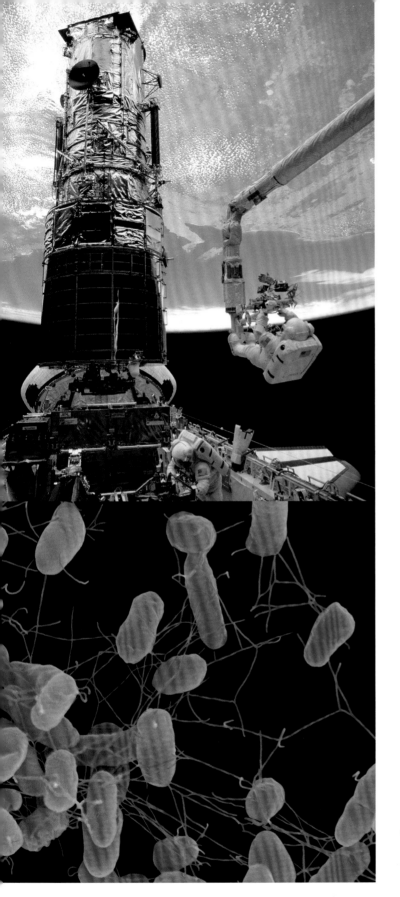

Changing the world

For many centuries, most inventions started as the big idea of a single person. That began to change around a century ago, and soon colleges, big companies, and even entire governments were helping develop new ideas and turn them into reality. When they work together, large groups of people can do amazing things, from wiping out diseases to flying to the Moon. It's said that more things were invented in the 1900s than in all the centuries that came before, and it's impossible to imagine just how many more things will be invented during this century.

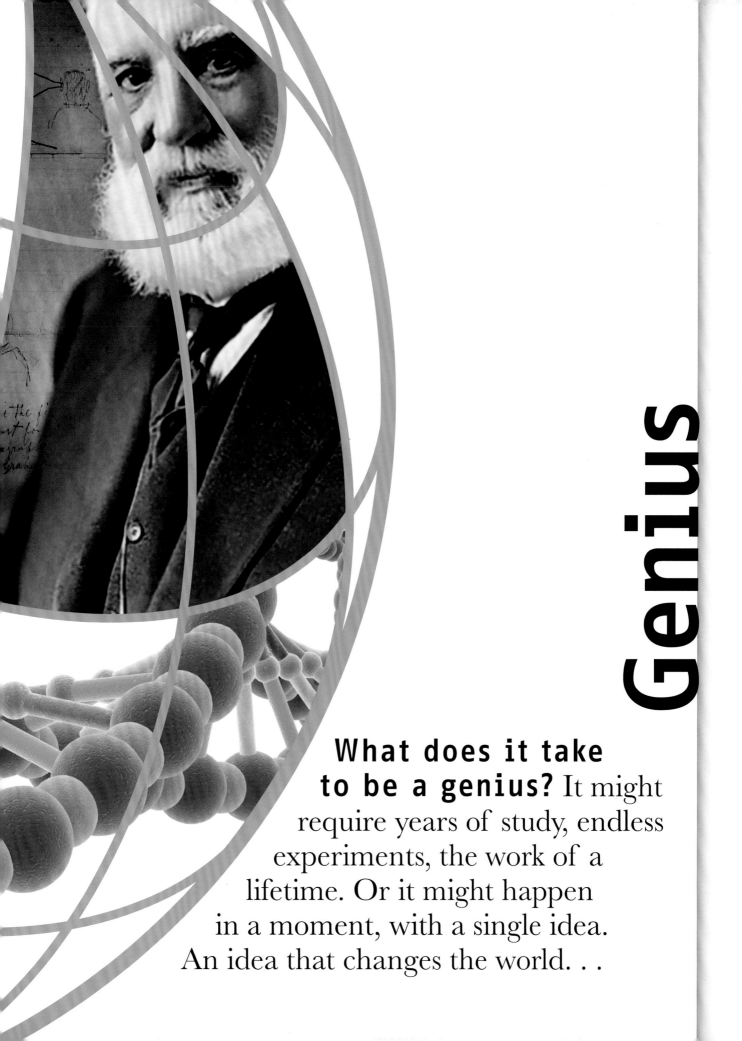

Genius

What does it take to be a genius? It might require years of study, endless experiments, the work of a lifetime. Or it might happen in a moment, with a single idea. An idea that changes the world. . .

The discovery of electricity sparked
a race to design electric lights that were small
and safe enough to be used at home. Englishman
Joseph Swan and American Thomas Edison hit
on the same bright idea: a glowing electric wire
sealed inside a vacuum. They teamed up to sell
their inventions, and in 1881, the first
commercial lightbulbs were produced. People
were no longer limited to candlelight to see in
the dark. For the first time, doctors, craftspeople,
and factory workers could see well enough to
work at night. Streetlights made traveling safer.
Miners no longer carried dangerous naked
flames. Within 25 years,
millions of homes were
lit by electric lamps.

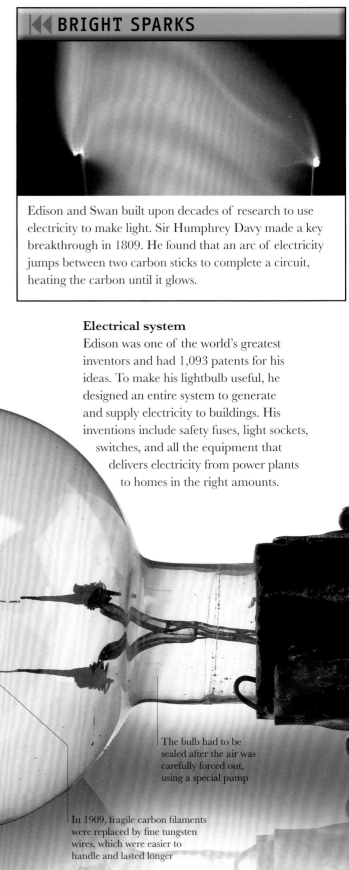

◀◀ BRIGHT SPARKS

Edison and Swan built upon decades of research to use
electricity to make light. Sir Humphrey Davy made a key
breakthrough in 1809. He found that an arc of electricity
jumps between two carbon sticks to complete a circuit,
heating the carbon until it glows.

Electrical system
Edison was one of the world's greatest
inventors and had 1,093 patents for his
ideas. To make his lightbulb useful, he
designed an entire system to generate
and supply electricity to buildings. His
inventions include safety fuses, light sockets,
switches, and all the equipment that
delivers electricity from power plants
to homes in the right amounts.

Edison and Swan both
created vacuums inside
their bulbs—with no
oxygen around it, the
filament can get white-hot
without catching fire

The gas argon
eventually replaced the
vacuum inside bulbs

Electricity passes through
the filament, heating it to
furnacelike temperatures

The bulb had to be
sealed after the air was
carefully forced out,
using a special pump

In 1909, fragile carbon filaments
were replaced by fine tungsten
wires, which were easier to
handle and lasted longer

Lightbulb

If you uncoil a lightbulb filament, it is 20 in (51 cm) long

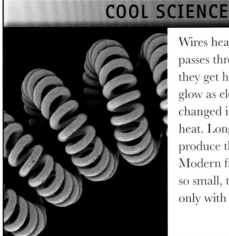

COOL SCIENCE

Wires heat up as electricity passes through them. If they get hot enough, they glow as electrical energy is changed into light as well as heat. Long, thin coiled wires produce the brightest light. Modern filaments have coils so small, they can be seen only with a microscope.

Warnings

At first, people were suspicious of the new technology. Warning signs were necessary to remind them not to light bulbs with matches. Customers had to be reassured that electric lamps would not damage their health or affect their sleep.

Popular light source

Lightbulbs made electric lighting affordable. Although they are more than 100 years old, Edison's original bulbs look very similar to today's incandescent bulbs. Easy to use, they have become the world's most popular source of light.

The term "lamp" originally referred to the bulb, but today we use it to refer to the fitting that holds it

Early Swan lamp

The bulbs slot into fittings that make contact with the electricity supply

Early bases, such as this wooden one, were eventually replaced by a screw-in base invented by Edison

A good source of light?

As countries around the world look for ways to reduce energy use, new types of lightbulbs are stepping into the spotlight.

More heat than light

Although cheap to produce, modern lightbulbs convert just 4–6 percent of their electricity supply into light. The rest is wasted as heat.

Energy-saving bulb

Compact fluorescent bulbs use one-quarter of the energy and last 10 times longer than filament bulbs. A coating on the glass glows as electricity passes through the gas inside.

Lighting the future

Light-emitting diodes (LEDs) produce little heat and have been used since the 1960s. New-generation LED bulbs are bright enough to light rooms and last for 25 years.

SEE ALSO X-ray 22 · Television 88

For most of human history,

disease-causing bacteria were our deadliest ▓▓▓▓▓▓▓▓▓▓▓▓▓▓▓, more soldiers ▓▓▓▓▓▓▓▓▓▓▓▓ting—even ▓▓▓▓▓▓▓▓▓▓be lethal. ▓▓▓▓▓▓▓▓▓▓al discovery of ▓▓▓▓▓▓▓▓▓teria without ▓▓▓▓▓▓▓▓▓▓ the course of history. Antibiotics have helped people live longer, healthier lives and transformed the way in which new drugs are developed.

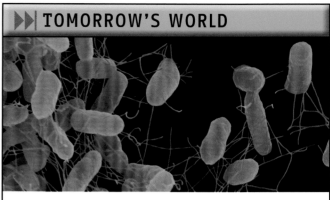

▶▶ **TOMORROW'S WORLD**

Bacteria, such as *Salmonella* (above), can rapidly change, making it difficult to treat the disease that they cause. Scientists are hoping to create new synthetic antibiotics that will target all types of bacteria even more effectively than natural ones can.

U.S. doctors prescribe 150 million doses of antibiotics every year

Deadly invaders

Bacteria are microscopic organisms. Many "friendly" bacteria live inside us without doing any harm, but disease-causing bacteria release chemicals that damage our cells. They cause some of the deadliest human diseases, including pneumonia, tuberculosis, and the plague.

Seek and destroy

Each antibiotic fights bacteria in a different way, stopping them from growing or reproducing normally. Penicillin, for example, stops bacteria from building their protective cell walls, so the bacteria are damaged or burst as they grow.

The first antibiotics were injected or used on skin wounds— most are now taken by mouth (orally)

Antibiotic capsules are made from gelatin or other digestible materials

Antibiotics

Miracle mold

Fleming discovered the first antibiotic when he left a dish of *Staphylococcus* bacteria uncovered for several days. Spores of *Penicillium notatum* mold, closely related to ordinary bread mold, drifted into the dish and began to grow. Fleming realized that the mold produced a chemical that was poisonous to bacteria—he called this penicillin.

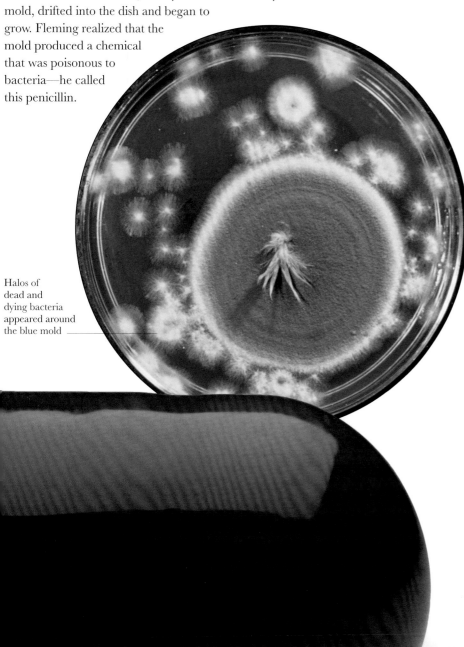

Halos of dead and dying bacteria appeared around the blue mold

Coatings can be added to capsules so that they dissolve in the intestine, protecting the penicillin from stomach acid

Your body breaks down penicillin after around four hours, so capsules must be taken frequently

The fight continues

Penicillin's success led to a scramble to find new antibiotics. In the 1950s, the discovery of streptomycin and other antibiotics made diseases—including tuberculosis—curable. People pictured a world free of infections, but bacteria began to fight back.

Viruses

Antibiotics don't harm viruses. However, they are vital to the development of virus-busting drugs. They are added to eggs, which are used to grow viruses for research and stop bacteria from infecting them.

A growing problem

The use of antibiotics is not tightly controlled—doctors prescribe them for virus infections, patients take incorrect doses, while farmers feed them to livestock. All of these things help new, antibiotic-resistant bacteria evolve.

SEE ALSO Vaccination 18

Penicillin

Alexander Fleming was the first person to investigate penicillin's bacteria-busting effects. However, it was the work of two lesser-known scientists that gave doctors the ability to fight bacteria with antibiotics. Ernst Chain and Howard Florey separated the antibacterial substance from the mold that produces it and used this to make a life-saving drug.

Purifying penicillin

Fleming tested his *Penicillium* mold on different types of bacteria and discovered that it killed those that caused pneumonia, syphilis, and diphtheria. It was also harmless to humans, unlike the antiseptics that were in use at the time—these chemicals killed bacteria but also damaged human cells. He published his research in 1929, pointing out that if penicillin could be extracted, it would be very useful in medicine. A decade later, Chain read Fleming's paper and suggested that he and Florey try to purify penicillin. By 1940, having tested it successfully on mice, they had extracted and purified enough penicillin to try it out on a human patient.

Ernst Chain
German-born Chain was an excellent biochemist who had left Berlin a few years before joining Florey's team in England.

Howard Florey
Florey led the Oxford University laboratory that rediscovered penicillin. Unlike Fleming, he did not like media attention.

Alexander Fleming
Fleming was a bacteriologist at Saint Mary's Hospital, in London, England. His first major discovery was that mucus from the nose has mild antibacterial effects. This work helped him see the significance of the moldy dish.

New sources

Florey and Chain had so little penicillin, they had to remove the drug from their first patient's urine and reinject him with it. Finding it difficult to extract enough penicillin from *Penicillium notatum*, Florey launched a worldwide search for a more productive strain of the mold. Finally in 1943, a lab worker brought in a moldy melon from a local market. This became the source of most antibiotics for the next decade.

Making an antibiotic

Florey and Chain's successful trials with penicillin helped persuade companies to produce the drug on a large scale.

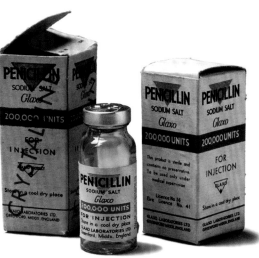

Penicillin for all

Production of penicillin was led by American companies, but it was not long before the technology was used by other countries, helping resolve the lack of supply.

Prizes and predictions

In 1945, Fleming, Florey, and Chain won a Nobel Prize for their work. Fleming made a speech predicting today's problems of antibiotic resistance—taking too little could expose bacteria to small, nonlethal quantities of the drug and allow them to become resistant. Few took notice of Fleming's warnings.

Military orders

The first penicillin stocks were sent straight to soldiers wounded on the battlefields of World War II. The "miracle drug" dramatically reduced deaths from infected wounds, and penicillin became a household name.

The cowpox virus is still used to make smallpox vaccines

Smallpox was once a common disease, killing most victims and leaving survivors with terrible scars. In 1796, Edward Jenner discovered that exposing people to the milder disease of cowpox prevented them from catching smallpox. He called his technique vaccination. A century later, Louis Pasteur figured out how to make vaccines for other diseases, triggering a massive advance in the fight against diseases. Vaccines have since been developed for many serious diseases, saving millions of lives.

The test

Jenner's work was remarkable at a time when no one knew that microorganisms, such as viruses and bacteria, could cause diseases. Working as a doctor, Jenner discovered that milkmaids who caught cowpox became immune to smallpox. He tested his theory by infecting an eight-year-old boy with cowpox. Two months later, Jenner transferred some pus from a smallpox victim into a cut on the boy's arm. The boy did not develop smallpox.

Metal syringes are often used to vaccinate animals—humans are vaccinated with smaller, disposable needles or syringes

Vaccination prevents more than two million deaths every year

Vaccines come in different forms—many are injected, but some are taken by mouth

Creating vaccines

In 1879, Pasteur decided to try and make milder forms of other diseases to use as vaccines. He heated anthrax bacteria to stop them from causing a deadly disease. The damaged bacteria were injected into animals. Later, the animals were injected with real anthrax and survived. Vaccines are still made from dead or weakened microorganisms using Pasteur's methods.

Vaccination

Fighting diseases

Pasteur's pioneering work prompted research into new vaccines. Once-common diseases like tetanus, rabies, measles, polio, and diphtheria can now be controlled and prevented by vaccination. Newer vaccines target the viruses that cause certain cancers.

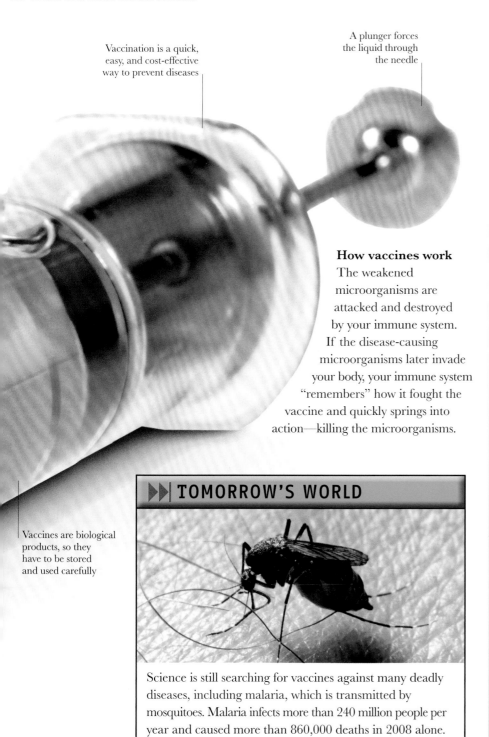

Vaccination is a quick, easy, and cost-effective way to prevent diseases

A plunger forces the liquid through the needle

Vaccines are biological products, so they have to be stored and used carefully

How vaccines work

The weakened microorganisms are attacked and destroyed by your immune system. If the disease-causing microorganisms later invade your body, your immune system "remembers" how it fought the vaccine and quickly springs into action—killing the microorganisms.

▶▶ TOMORROW'S WORLD

Science is still searching for vaccines against many deadly diseases, including malaria, which is transmitted by mosquitoes. Malaria infects more than 240 million people per year and caused more than 860,000 deaths in 2008 alone.

Milestones in medicine

Vaccinations have given scientists and doctors a greater understanding of the immune system and how it destroys invading microorganisms and viruses.

Protection on a large scale

Vaccination prevents diseases from spreading, protecting entire communities as well as individuals. Mass vaccination for children is now routine in many countries.

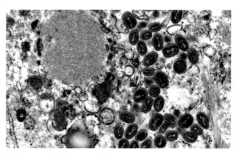

The end of smallpox

The last death from smallpox (above) was in 1977, following a huge program of vaccination that was coordinated by the World Health Organization.

Organ transplants

Immunology (understanding the immune system) made organ transplants possible. Doctors can stop the recipient's body from treating the new organ like a disease.

SEE ALSO Antibiotics 14 · Microscope 20

Microscopes zoom in on details that are invisible to the naked eye. They

are among the most useful of all scientific instruments, because they give us an insight into how things are structured and how they function. This 16th-century invention led to the discovery of cells and microorganisms and has unlocked many secrets of life, death, and diseases.

From spectacles to spectacular

In the 1590s, magnifying lenses were used widely in spectacles, so it's not surprising that a spectacle-maker invented the compound microscope. Hans Janssen and his son Zacharias realized that if one lens magnified a little, two could magnify more. A compound microscope is one that uses more than one lens to magnify (make bigger) an image.

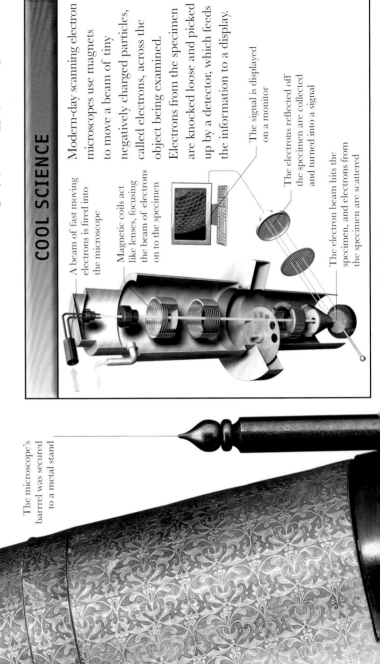

COOL SCIENCE

Modern-day scanning electron microscopes use magnets to move a beam of tiny negatively charged particles, called electrons, across the object being examined. Electrons from the specimen are knocked loose and picked up by a detector, which feeds the information to a display.

A beam of fast moving electrons is fired into the microscope

Magnetic coils act like lenses, focusing the beam of electrons on to the specimen

The signal is displayed on a monitor

The electrons reflected off the specimen are collected and turned into a signal

The electron beam hits the specimen, and electrons from the specimen are scattered

Robert Hooke (above) and Anton van Leeuwenhoek began microscope-based research in the 1600s

The microscope's barrel was secured to a metal stand

Hooke's compound microscope had three lenses—the eye lens was at the top

The barrel was made of wood, covered with thin leather

Hooke added a third lens inside this barrel to increase the visible area of the specimen

Microscope

Light and lenses
Lenses are pieces of glass with curved sides that bend light rays. The Janssens placed a lens at each end of a tube, creating a microscope that made objects appear 10 times bigger. In the 1670s, Anton van Leeuwenhoek made single-lens microscopes that could magnify objects 200 times.

The world's most powerful microscope magnifies 14 million times, revealing individual atoms

Hooke's drawing of thin slices of cork from trees revealed that plants were made up of tiny structures, which he called cells

Tiny worlds
Robert Hooke used a compound microscope to examine thousands of objects and living things. In 1665, he published a bestselling book, called *Micrographia*, which was packed full of drawings of the strange and exciting details that he'd seen. His most important discovery was the cell, which is the building block of plants and animals.

Specimens were mounted on this pin and lit by light from an oil lamp

The image could be focused using this screw

The barrel could be angled using a ball-and-socket joint

A magnifying lens was in the snout

Amazing discoveries
Better lenses led to more powerful microscopes. As microscopes improved, scientists delved deeper into the detail of life. Their discoveries were crucial to the development of science and medicine.

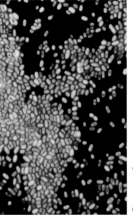

Modern microscopes
Electron microscopes were invented in the 1930s, becoming so powerful that they allowed scientists to see molecules for the first time. The latest models can reveal a specimen's physical and chemical properties.

Germ theory
Two hundred years later, Louis Pasteur used microscopes to study bacteria in diseased animals. His theory that microorganisms caused diseases revolutionized medicine.

Leeuwenhoek's microscope
In 1676, Leeuwenhoek used his simple microscopes to study plaque scraped off his teeth. He was amazed to see "tiny animals" moving around—he had discovered microorganisms.

SEE ALSO Vaccination 18 · Spectacles 114 · Hubble 182

The accidental discovery of x-rays,

a type of radiation, in 1895 astonished the world
and changed science, industry, and medicine
forever. Physicists, including Marie Curie, began
researching new areas, leading to the discovery
of radioactivity. Industry began using x-rays
to find faults in machines and materials. In
medicine for the first time, doctors could look
inside people's bodies without cutting them
open. X-rays are now used
worldwide to detect broken
bones, bad teeth, swallowed
objects, and even tumors.

Discovering the unknown

As Wilhelm Röntgen studied radiation from a
cathode ray tube, he noticed a mysterious green
light. He realized that unknown invisible rays had
penetrated a cardboard barrier and were making
a patch of fluorescent paint glow.

◄◄ BRIGHT SPARKS

In the mid-1800s, scientists
began pumping the air out of
glass tubes in order to study
glowing beams known as
cathode rays. In the 1870s,
scientist William Crookes
invented a better cathode ray
tube that led to amazing
breakthroughs in physics.
Crookes tubes were used to
discover electrons, plasmas,
x-rays, radioactivity, and even
led to the first television sets.

X-rays expose
photographic film in
the same way that light
does—the more rays
that hit the film, the
darker it gets

X-rays have more
energy than light, so
they can travel through
different materials

X-rays are a type
of electromagnetic
radiation, like light
and radio waves

The x-rays leave a
silhouette, or the shape,
of objects that they
can't travel through,
such as metal jewelry

X-ray

Penetrating power

Röntgen excitedly experimented with the new rays. He found that they passed straight through many objects. The most startling result came when he placed his wife's hand between the beam and some photographic film. He'd discovered a way to photograph the bones inside the body.

Bones let few x-rays reach the film—these show up as white "shadows," and help doctors see fractures

Soft tissues, such as flesh, let more x-rays through, so they appear gray

Invisible danger

By 1927, scientists realized that radiation could kill cells and cause cancer. Doctors began to use shields and small doses to protect themselves and their patients. The harmful effects have also been harnessed to treat diseases, by zapping cancer cells with x-ray beams.

X-rays were named after the mathematical symbol for an "unknown"

Looking inside

X-rays let us look inside things that are dangerous, difficult, or inconvenient to take apart—from the human body to gas pipelines and complex electronic equipment.

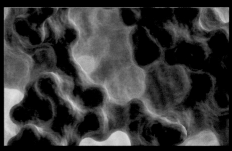

Probing proteins

An x-ray image can reveal the structure of miniscule molecules, such as this flu virus. This helps scientists design effective medicines.

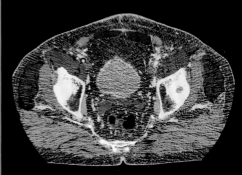

Peering into the pelvis

CAT scanners use multiple, moving x-ray beams to scan the body from every angle. A computer then builds detailed images, helping doctors find unhealthy tissue.

Catching criminals

X-rays are a quick and easy way to screen bags and luggage at airports and other places where both security and speed are important.

SEE ALSO DNA 24 · Radioactivity 28 · Television 88

FRANCIS CRICK AND
JAMES WATSON

Humans have always been interested in what gives living things their characteristics, and how this information is passed from one generation to the next. The unraveling of DNA and the science of genetics was one of the greatest achievements of the 1900s.

◀◀ BRIGHT SPARKS

In the 1860s, Austrian monk and scientist Gregor Mendel experimented with pea plants. He figured out that simple characteristics, such as flower color, are determined by two hereditary factors, one from each parent. Today, we call those hereditary factors genes.

Information carriers
Genes are carried on structures called chromosomes found in the nucleus of a cell. It was in the 1940s that scientists discovered chromosomes are made of long strands of tightly coiled deoxyribonucleic acid (DNA).

The four letters are different chemicals called bases—shown as four different colors

DNA is a simple four-letter alphabet that acts as a code, telling cells how to make proteins

What is DNA?
Scientists James Watson and Francis Crick discovered the structure of DNA in 1953, finally explaining how genes carry information. Each gene is a length of DNA that tells a cell how to make a specific protein. Humans, animals, and plants need many different proteins in order to live and grow.

DNA

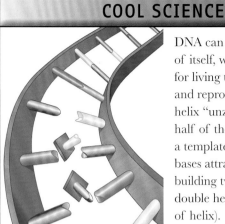

DNA can make copies of itself, which is essential for living things to grow and reproduce. The double helix "unzips," and each half of the ladder acts as a template. The separated bases attract new partners, building two identical double helices (plural of helix).

The bases pair up like rungs on a ladder, linking together two chains of DNA

A molecule of DNA is made up of two strands that twist around one another

Each backbone and its bases make one chain

The bases are linked together in long chains by a "backbone" made of carbon, hydrogen, oxygen, and phosphorus

The science of genetics

Genetics is the scientific study of genes—the hereditary factors in DNA. They affect almost everything about us, from how we look and behave to the illnesses that we might get as we grow older. Studying DNA helps us understand why some cells don't work properly and could lead to cures for many diseases in the future. Genetics has also given us DNA fingerprinting and genetic engineering (changing an organism's DNA to give it useful new characteristics).

The uncoiled DNA from a single human cell is almost 6 ft (2 m) long

Colonies of bacteria can be given genes that make them light up every hour or so. If conditions change, the timing changes. Putting these bacteria into patients could warn doctors when body conditions change, so that every patient gets their medicine when they need it.

SEE ALSO Antibiotics 14 · X-ray 22

Watson and Crick

The race to discover the structure of DNA

is one of the most exciting stories in the history of science. In the 1950s, Cambridge University scientists Watson and Crick were the first to show how this simple chemical can pack all of the instructions for building an entire living organism into a cell that is smaller than a speck of dust.

Rival teams
Watson worked on solving the mystery of DNA's structure with Crick, in Cambridge, England. In London, scientists Maurice Wilkins and Rosalind Franklin were trying to beat them to the finishing post. In 1951, Watson went to a lecture at King's College in London and saw Franklin's x-ray photographs of DNA.

Big puzzle
Watson (left) and Crick built 3-D models of DNA to figure out how the chemical fitted together.

Red herring

Franklin was an expert at using x-ray imaging to reveal the structure of molecules, and her pictures showed that the molecules have a helical (spiral) structure of some kind and a backbone. Back at Cambridge, Watson and Crick tried building a triple-helix model, linking three chains of DNA, but their idea for a triple helix was wrong.

"We have found the secret of life"

Francis Crick, 1953

Rosalind Franklin

Franklin came very close to discovering the structure of DNA on her own. She died in 1958, before the Nobel Prize was awarded to Watson, Crick, and Wilkins.

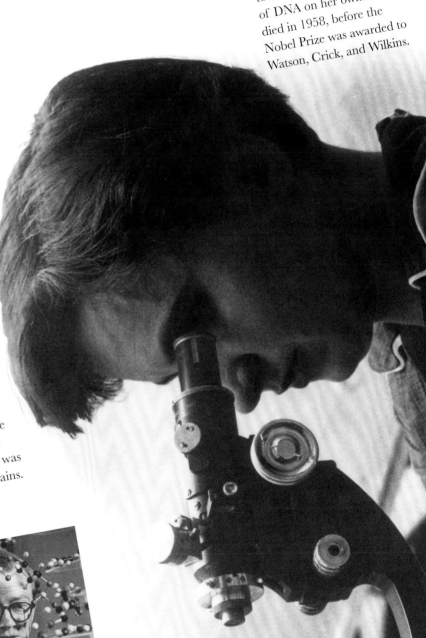

The breakthrough

Meanwhile, in 1952, Franklin took a better x-ray photograph of DNA, which Wilkins showed to Watson without her permission. Watson realized that the image showed a molecule with just two chains—a double helix structure. Using all the information they had gathered, Watson and Crick tried to build a model of a double-helix DNA molecule. They succeeded in the spring of 1953.

Photo 51

Franklin's famous x-ray photograph of DNA is known as Photo 51. The "X" of black stripes showed that the x-rays had passed through a helix. The missing stripe at the end of each arm revealed that the helix was made of two DNA chains.

Maurice Wilkins

Wilkins was annoyed that Franklin refused to publish her ideas until she had proved that they were correct. This is why Wilkins showed Photo 51 to Watson and helped him understand it. Wilkins is shown here with a detailed model of DNA.

As 19th-century scientists explored the nature of atoms, they discovered some materials with very special properties. Radiating (giving off) energy as tiny particles and rays, these radioactive materials have led to huge advances in medicine and scientific research. We have also learned how to release the enormous nuclear energy stored inside their atoms. There have been serious destructive consequences, but nuclear power now produces one-sixth of the world's electricity. It does so without releasing global-warming gases, using a fuel found in rocks all around the world.

Fuel rods contain pellets of uranium fuel

When lowered into the reactor, the bundle of rods will provide energy for three or four years

This French nuclear power plant produces enough electricity to boil 600,000 kettles at the same time

Radioactive elements
In 1896, the French physicist Henri Becquerel discovered that the metal uranium gives off radiation. Soon, other elements (substances that contain atoms of all one type) that are naturally radioactive were also found. In today's nuclear reactors, we can also make some elements become radioactive. Over time, all these gradually change into different chemical elements.

A uranium fuel pellet the size of a grape contains as much energy as three and a half barrels of oil

The Curies
French scientists Marie and Pierre Curie were interested in Becquerel's mysterious rays. In 1898, they discovered three new elements that give off radiation. Marie realized that radiation comes from the atoms of these elements. She called this property radioactivity. In 1903, Marie became the first woman to win a Nobel Prize, shared with Pierre Curie and Becquerel.

Radioactivity

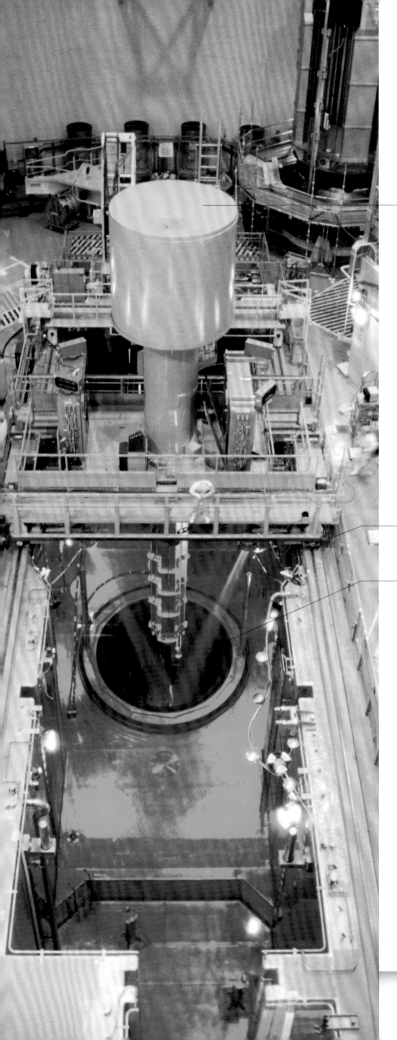

Nuclear power

Radioactive atoms are unstable. Bombarding them with even smaller particles called neutrons can split them apart. This process—called nuclear fission—releases huge amounts of energy as heat and radiation. A nuclear reactor harnesses this to create steam for generating electricity.

High-energy radiation is deadly, so power plant operators use machines to handle the fuel

Wider uses of radioactivity

We can detect even tiny amounts of radiation. Doctors use radioactive elements to trace the paths of chemicals inside the human body to study how the body works and diagnose diseases. Carefully targeted doses of high-energy radiation can also kill cancer cells. In industry, radioactive elements and sensitive detectors are used to check the thickness of materials like paper and plastic wrap as they are made. Scientists also use radioactive tracers. The amount of radiation given off by naturally radioactive elements tells us the age of ancient plant and animal remains.

The water's blue glow shows the strength of the nuclear reaction

The splitting of uranium atoms takes place inside the reactor's core

▶▶ TOMORROW'S WORLD

Rocks that contain uranium are taken from mines (left), but mining can contaminate land and water with radioactive waste. This is harmful to living things. Scientists are exploring ways to clean up this waste. One possible method is to use a type of bacteria that "eats" radioactive uranium and makes it safer.

SEE ALSO X-ray 22 · Solar cell 92

First used by sailors, soldiers, and explorers, tin cans can still provide life-saving food supplies. But since the 1920s, they have become essential, convenient, long-lasting food stock items in most households. Almost all foods can be canned, from the cheapest tomatoes to the finest caviar. Easily recycled and needing no refrigeration, cans are also one of the most environmentally friendly ways to preserve food. This means that people may still be using them in hundreds of years' time.

The first tin cans

In 1810, Englishman Peter Durand created tin cans by dipping sheets of metal into molten (melted) tin and connecting pieces together with a soldering iron. The first canning factory was built near London, England, in 1812, and by 1815 British troops were eating canned food at the Battle of Waterloo.

In 1813, a can of meat cost nearly one-third of a laborer's weekly income

A slow start

For years, production was very slow. Skilled tinsmiths made just six cans per hour by hand, which were then boiled for at least five hours. By 1846, machines could manufacture 60 cans per hour, but today's machines can make a thousand per minute. We now boil the food very quickly, at high pressures and temperatures.

◄◄ **BRIGHT SPARKS**

In the 1700s, many soldiers died of hunger while at war, so France offered a cash prize to anyone who could think of a new way to preserve food. In 1810, Nicholas Appert won the prize. It had taken him 14 years to find a method that worked—boiling food that was then sealed inside glass jars.

Gravy soup cans, 1899

Early cans were iron, but now most food cans are steel, and drinks cans are aluminum

Workers rolled metal rectangles to form the cylinders—some cans are still made in this way

A thin layer of tin stopped the inside from rusting

Tinsmiths soldered the ends of the can to the cylinder after hammering the edges down with a mallet

Tin can

Stopping the rot

For many years, people canned food without knowing how the process worked. In the 1850s, Louis Pasteur showed that boiling food killed the bacteria and mold that cause decay. Sealing the cans prevented more live microorganisms from reaching the food.

Old chicken

On their 2006 wedding anniversary, Les and Beryl Lailey opened a can of chicken 50 years after receiving it as a wedding present; it still tasted fine. Use-by dates are usually for two years, but if properly sealed, canned food may never go off.

A small hole, soldered closed afterward, let air escape while the food boiled

Opening cans involved a hammer and chisel until Ezra Warner invented the can opener in 1858

This gravy soup was for soldiers in the Boer War (1899–1902) to make beef tea

Much thicker than modern cans, early cans often weighed more than the food inside

Tinsmiths used lead solder (a mixture of melted metals) to seal cans, not realizing that it was poisonous

Preserving food

People have been trying to preserve food since ancient times. This means either killing bacteria and molds or stopping them from growing.

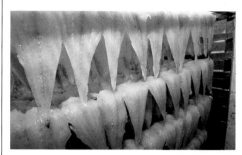

Traditional methods

The ancient Egyptians found that drying fruit in the sun made them last longer. For centuries, we have also smoked or salted meat and fish and pickled foods in vinegar.

Freezing

Microorganisms cannot function at freezing temperatures, and some die. But frozen food was not common outside cold countries until the invention of refrigeration.

Freeze drying

This method dries frozen food without damaging its structure. Adding water will return it to its original state, even years later.

SEE ALSO Microscope 20 · Refrigerator 64

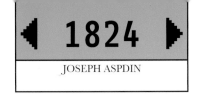

Much of the modern world is built from concrete, as it is cheap, hard-wearing, and does not burn. Almost all of this concrete has been made with Portland cement. Cement is a vital ingredient of most civil engineering structures, such as roads, bridges, and sewers. We also use it in mortar, to plaster walls, and to lay bricks. Ancient civilizations used natural cements, but Portland cement is consistently strong and easy to produce, which is why it has been such a massive success.

After water, concrete is the most widely used substance on Earth

Most concrete and mortar mixes have more than twice as much sand as cement

Cement, which makes up around 10 percent of concrete, is the glue that binds together sand and gravel

Concrete hardens because of a chemical reaction—called curing—between cement and water

Gravel gives concrete bulk and strength, but it is missed out when making mortar

Fibers or chemicals can make concrete even stronger

Fortune seekers

In the early 1800s, factories produced natural cements of limestone and clay. But their quality varied with the minerals found in the ground. Many people tried to make their fortunes with the perfect man-made cement. However, nobody understood the chemistry of concrete, so they could only experiment by trial and error.

Portland cement

To cast concrete, builders pour well-mixed cement, sand, gravel, and water into molds known as formwork

Success in the kitchen
In 1824, British bricklayer Joseph Aspdin burned crushed limestone with clay in his kitchen and then ground it into a powder. He had found the recipe for an artificial cement that reacted with water to become much stronger. It made gray concrete that looked like high-quality Portland stone, so he called it Portland cement.

Cables support the new concrete while the bridge is being built

From strength to strength
Aspdin's son William, who ran Portland cement factories, improved the recipe with higher temperatures and modified ingredients. French gardener Joseph Monier invented reinforced concrete in 1867. His concrete plant pots with steel mesh paved the way for today's massive reinforced concrete structures.

Its curved shape helps the bridge carry more weight

These are cast on site, but concrete blocks are often precast in factories

Without steel reinforcement bars, this 2,120-ft- (645-m-) long bridge would collapse

Early concretes
In ancient times, many people used mud or dung as natural cements. Some also made long-lasting concrete from materials available locally.

Concrete-tipped pyramids
Most scientists now agree that, rather than hauling huge stone blocks to the top of pyramids, the ancient Egyptians probably cast some in place using a clay-based concrete.

Ancient Roman ash
The Romans used ash from volcanos to make strong concrete. They changed its properties by adding blood, milk, and horsehair.

◄◄ BRIGHT SPARKS

In 1756, John Smeaton built a stone lighthouse off the U.K. coast. He noted that unlike ordinary mortars of limestone and sand, those that also had a high proportion of clay became harder in water and could withstand the pounding of the waves. Shown here is the lighthouse, which was rebuilt on land as a memorial.

SEE ALSO Stainless steel 38

Hoover Dam

Built in the 1930s during America's Great Depression, the Hoover Dam still stands as one of the most impressive feats of civil engineering ever. It took around 200 engineers and 20,000 construction workers to dam the Colorado River at Black Canyon. The concrete that they cast could have built a sidewalk 4 ft (1.2 m) wide all the way around the planet.

Camping in Ragtown

Months before dam building began in 1931, tens of thousands of men arrived at the site in search of jobs. They brought wives and children, but little money. Families camped in terrible conditions in a dry, barren spot that they called Ragtown. Diseases were rife, and the heat killed 25 people in the hot June and July of 1931. The following year, the government built Boulder City, where many of the workforce and their families lived until the dam was completed in 1936.

Monkeys, Puddlers, and Scalers

Work was far from easy, and 96 dam workers were killed in accidents. The men had specific duties: Powder Monkeys detonated dynamite, while Puddlers spread fresh concrete. High Scalers probably had the most dangerous job—they climbed down the cliffs on ropes to remove rocks.

Big blocks

The dam workers built wooden formwork to cast more than 200 huge blocks of reinforced concrete. These joined like giant building bricks to form the dam. They were stuck together with a strong cement and water paste.

> **I came, I saw, and I was conquered, as everyone would be who sees for the first time this great feat of mankind**
>
> U.S. President Franklin D. Roosevelt, 1935

A new landscape

Almost every year, the Colorado River had flooded in the spring, and then slowed to a trickle during the summer months. Farmers struggled to water crops, and much of the area was a desert wasteland. Hoover Dam transformed the landscape around Boulder. It also now provides a steady water supply to four states and electricity to 1.3 million people.

Taming the river

Upstream, the Colorado River (right) is still wild and unpredictable. In Boulder, the dam has blocked its flow to create a huge man-made reservoir, called Lake Mead (below). To build the dam, workers had to divert the river away from the site, by building temporary dams and blasting tunnels through the canyon rocks.

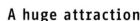

Producing power

The hydroelectric power plant sits at the dam's base. Water gushing through tunnels from Lake Mead turns massive turbine wheels 180 times per minute. These connect via shafts (pictured) to 17 electricity generators. Each can supply enough electricity for 100,000 homes.

A huge attraction

The curved Hoover Dam is an impressive 660 ft (200 m) wide and 730 ft (220 m) high and attracts more than seven million tourists per year. Half-buried deep underwater, the base is so thick that the concrete will probably continue to cure (harden) for hundreds of years.

Much lighter than glass, and virtually unbreakable, plastic bottles were obviously a very good idea. But making one for carbonated drinks was surprisingly difficult. The bottles that Nathaniel Wyeth designed were first used for Pepsi Cola in the 1970s. We now use them for all types of things, such as peanut butter and makeup. Unlike most plastics, polyethylene terephthalate (PET) can be recycled, so it is becoming more and more popular.

Lids are usually made from a different type of plastic and often cannot be recycled

In Africa, some people make their water safe to drink using only PET bottles and strong sunlight

An inquisitive man
Wyeth worked as an engineer for the American company DuPont. One day at work, his colleague told him that plastic bottles were useless for carbonated drinks. That night, Wyeth filled one with ginger ale and put it in the fridge. The next day, the swollen bottle was wedged in—it was too weak to cope with the pressure. He decided to make a stronger one.

Most water bottles are now made with PET

Ridges make bottles stronger, so they can be thinner and use less plastic

Hiding in the mold
Plastic molecules are long, thin chains. Wyeth's idea was to stretch these to line them up—a technique that made nylon thread stronger. Using air jets, he stretched hot plastic inside different shaped molds. After thousands of shapeless blobs, he found one mold empty. Then, looking closer at the sides of the mold, he spotted his first plastic bottle.

◀◀ BRIGHT SPARKS

Belgian chemist Leo Baekeland made the first synthetic plastic, called Bakelite, in 1907, which became fashionable in the 1920s for lamps, phones, and jewelry. PET, a type of polyester, was developed in 1941.

Unlike this modern PET bottle, early PET bottles had round bottoms, so they could not stand up without separate plastic bases

PET bottles

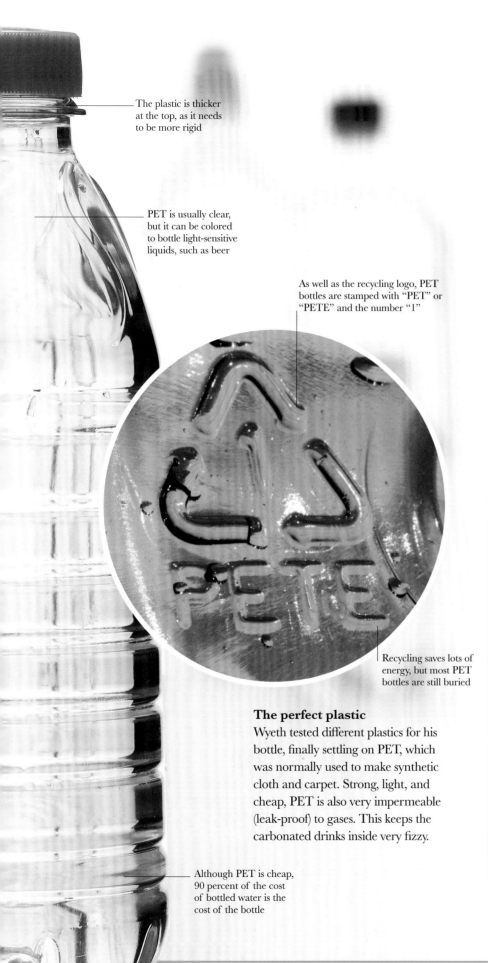

The plastic is thicker at the top, as it needs to be more rigid

PET is usually clear, but it can be colored to bottle light-sensitive liquids, such as beer

As well as the recycling logo, PET bottles are stamped with "PET" or "PETE" and the number "1"

Recycling saves lots of energy, but most PET bottles are still buried

The perfect plastic

Wyeth tested different plastics for his bottle, finally settling on PET, which was normally used to make synthetic cloth and carpet. Strong, light, and cheap, PET is also very impermeable (leak-proof) to gases. This keeps the carbonated drinks inside very fizzy.

Although PET is cheap, 90 percent of the cost of bottled water is the cost of the bottle

Recycling PET

PET comes from oil and takes centuries to degrade, but Wyeth did not really consider its environmental impact. Luckily, it is easy to recycle. The first recycled bottle became a new Pepsi bottle base in 1977. PET is now the world's most recycled plastic.

Piles of old plastic

PET recycling starts with sorting and squashing bottles into huge bales. These are sent to a recycling plant, where machines grind them into tiny flakes. After washing, the flakes are sold on to plastics factories.

Thousand uses

A surprising number of everyday things can be made from PET bottles. Most are turned into polyester fibers for carpets and fleece material. But we also make them into shoes, belts, bags, toys, ropes, containers, car parts, and, increasingly, new bottles.

SEE ALSO Tin can 30 · Nylon 50

1913

HARRY BREARLEY

Stainless steel uses

Most of us come across stainless steel many times each day—as nuts and bolts, exhaust pipes, saucepans, and even kitchen sinks. As well as being long-lasting, it is also hygenic.

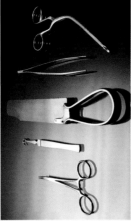

Surgical instruments

Doctors use stainless steel instruments in surgical operations. Despite being repeatedly sterilized (boiled to kill germs), they do not rust. They are also resistant to the chemicals in blood.

Storage and transportation

Stainless steel tanks do not develop leaks, even when they contain very corrosive (damaging) chemicals. So we use stainless steel to carry fuel, distil alcoholic drinks, and even carry household garbage.

Englishman Harry Brearley was trying to develop a type of steel for rifle barrels that wouldn't wear out quickly when bullets were fired.

To his amazement, among his many different steel samples was one that did not rust. It even resisted chemical attack from lemon juice and other acids. Unlike other steels, stainless steel lasts in most environments without having to be treated, painted, or renovated. It has revolutionized most modern industries, including food, medicine, and transportation.

Rust-free silverware

Living among the steel factories of Sheffield in the U.K., Brearley immediately saw the potential of his "rust-less steel" in the local silverware industry. In 1914, factories started making knives from stainless steel. During World War I, it was used in the engines of fighter planes.

The architect of the Chrysler Building had the 180 ft (55 m) finial (tip) added to make sure that it would be the tallest building in New York City

When stainless steel is damaged, it does not rust because chromium reacts with air to form a protective scar

Stainless steel is strong and can withstand wind and rain

Stainless steel makes the building one of New York's most stunning skyscrapers

Chrysler Building, New York, U.S.A.

◄◄ BRIGHT SPARKS

People have been making steel for thousands of years. In 1821, French mining engineer Pierre Berthier noticed that adding chromium metal made steel more resistant to chemical attack. But for years, scientists were not able to produce steel with enough chromium to make it stainless steel.

Stainless steel

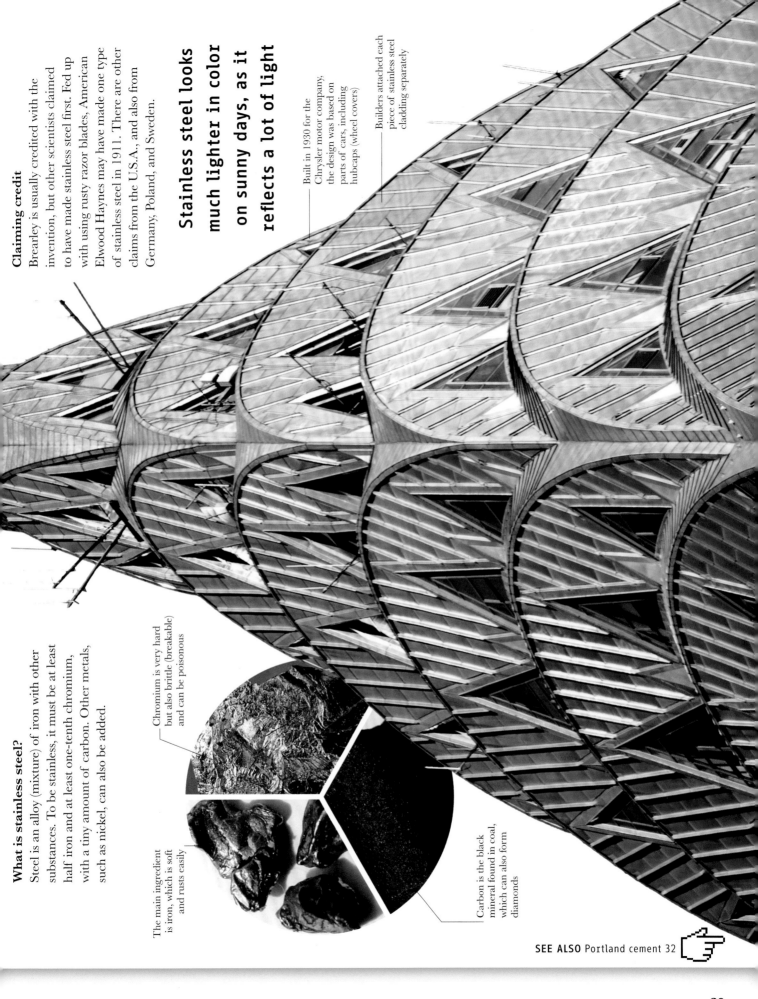

Claiming credit

Brearley is usually credited with the invention, but other scientists claimed to have made stainless steel first. Fed up with using rusty razor blades, American Elwood Haynes may have made one type of stainless steel in 1911. There are other claims from the U.S.A., and also from Germany, Poland, and Sweden.

Stainless steel looks much lighter in color on sunny days, as it reflects a lot of light

Built in 1930 for the Chrysler motor company; the design was based on parts of cars, including hubcaps (wheel covers)

Builders attached each piece of stainless steel cladding separately

What is stainless steel?

Steel is an alloy (mixture) of iron with other substances. To be stainless, it must be at least half iron and at least one-tenth chromium, with a tiny amount of carbon. Other metals, such as nickel, can also be added.

Chromium is very hard but also brittle (breakable) and can be poisonous

The main ingredient is iron, which is soft and rusts easily

Carbon is the black mineral found in coal, which can also form diamonds

SEE ALSO Portland cement 32

When the contacts touched, electricity passed along the telegraph wire

Operators tapped the key quickly or slowly to produce Morse code

The spring lifted the key to break the electrical circuit

The key acted like a switch in a large electrical circuit with the telegraph receiver

The receiver changed the key's electrical signals into dots and dashes on paper tape

Coils of wire wrapped around iron formed the electromagnets

Thousands of years ago, people sent signals using drums, smoke, and even pigeons. In the early 1800s, sending a letter was still the easiest way to contact someone far away. But telegraphs enabled people to send messages long distance along wires, with almost no delay. Kick-starting electronic communication, they paved the way for telephones, cell phones and even instant messaging.

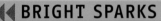

◀◀ BRIGHT SPARKS

French inventor and engineer Claude Chappe devised the first nonelectric telegraph network in 1794. It crossed France and even branched into other countries. Relay towers with armlike pointers spelled out messages in semaphore code (a flag-based alphabet). These were viewed by telescope from the next tower.

Paving the way

In 1830, American scientist Joseph Henry sent an electric current along more than 1 mile (1.6 km) of wire to strike a bell. His receiving device used an electromagnet. Many inventors then began designing telegraphs based on electromagnets, with varying success. In the U.K., railroads and post offices used telegraphs made by two British inventors, William Cooke and Charles Wheatstone.

Telegraph

Morse and Vail

In America, Samuel Morse was successful in improving Henry's device. Morse abandoned a career as a painter to develop a practical electric telegraph. In 1836, young engineer Alfred Vail saw Morse's crude device and offered to help improve it. They became partners, with Vail developing the working Morse telegraph seen here.

Simply clever

The Morse telegraph caught on, mainly because it was simple. It used just one telegraph wire to send messages, so the code was crucial. Using short and long electrical signals—dots and dashes—to make letters, Morse and Vail's code became the standard language of long-distance communication.

The most famous message in Morse code is the international distress signal, SOS (... --- ...)

A light metal arm moved down and up as the coils became magnetized and demagnetized

The other end of the arm rose to make small dents in the paper tape that fed through rollers

The tape came out here, embossed with Morse code

The clockwork mechanism kept the tape moving steadily

Telegraph wires carrying Morse signals connected to the coils of wire

Telegraph wires being laid across the Atlantic Ocean by the S.S. *Great Eastern*

Wiring the world

Built in 1844, Morse's first telegraph line ran between Washington, D.C. and Baltimore, Maryland. Twenty years later, telegraph lines spanned America and Europe and were soon to cross the Atlantic Ocean. Even after the telephone was invented, the telegraph business thrived for decades. The last telegram was sent in 2006.

SEE ALSO Cell phone 140

Who invented the telephone?

Scottish scientist Alexander Graham Bell is famous for inventing the telephone. But he was not the first person to transmit voices along wires. Nor was his telephone perfect—other scientists helped improve it. Many inventors also claimed to have invented the telephone before Bell, and some nearly beat him to receiving the recognition for this incredible device.

In first place

In 1874, Bell received funding to develop a telegraph that could send many messages down the same wire. But Bell and his assistant, Thomas Watson, also experimented with a talking telegraph. Bell applied for a U.S. patent for this on February 14, 1876. Three days after being given the sole right to make and sell telephones, he finally got the invention to work. Bell fought more than 600 lawsuits to defend his patent—the most valuable ever issued. But he won every case.

Alexander Graham Bell

Born in Scotland in 1847 to a deaf mother, Bell emigrated to Canada before settling in the U.S.A., where he taught deaf children to speak while investigating sound and electricity. A prolific inventor, he is shown here with the telephone sketch he drew in 1876.

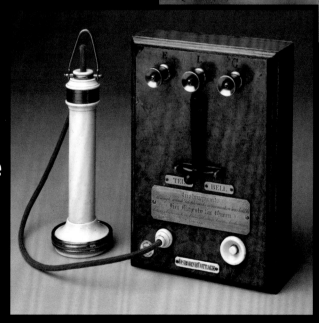

> ❝ **I then shouted into M [the mouthpiece], 'Mr. Watson, come here, I want to see you'** ❞
>
> Alexander Graham Bell, March 10, 1876

Bell's telephone

After forming the Bell Telephone Company in July 1877, Bell gave lectures to promote his invention. By the end of the year, he had sold 3,000 telephones. He used the receiver pictured here to show Queen Victoria of England how the device worked.

The outsider

Antonio Meucci beat Bell to the patent office by five years. But he could only afford temporary arrangements to prevent others from patenting the telephone. He stopped buying these in 1874—the year that his laboratory, which he shared with Bell, claimed to lose his telephone prototypes (working models). In 2002, the U.S. government recognized Meucci's work in the invention of the telephone.

Antonio Meucci

Meucci was an Italian inventor who moved to the U.S.A. in 1850. His wife suffered from crippling rheumatism, and in 1857 he built a telephone to talk to her from his basement laboratory.

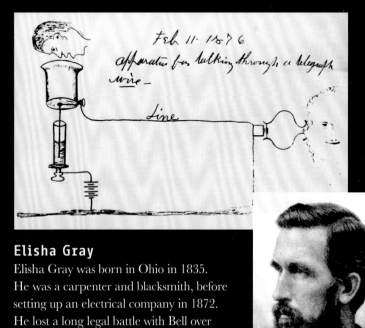

A photo finish

Among the scientists fighting Bell's patent in court was Elisha Gray. He also took a design to the patent office on February 14, 1876 and accused Bell of stealing his ideas to make a working receiver. Most people believe that Bell beat Gray to the patent office by a few hours. Yet a patent officer signed a legal document saying that he had been bribed to award Bell the patent—and that he even showed Gray's paperwork to Bell. Bell later denied that these events happened.

Elisha Gray

Elisha Gray was born in Ohio in 1835. He was a carpenter and blacksmith, before setting up an electrical company in 1872. He lost a long legal battle with Bell over his telephone design (above) but held 70 patents, including one for a fax machine.

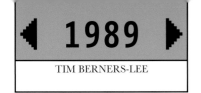

Tim Berners-Lee's colleagues

at the European organization for nuclear research (CERN) worked in many countries on different computer systems. He developed the World Wide Web to help them share scientific information. Now one quarter of the world's population can access billions of web pages over the Internet—a network of linked computers. This has completely transformed business, culture, politics, shopping, and even the way that we socialize.

A vague but exciting plan

In 1989, aged 24, Berners-Lee proposed that information stored on central "web servers" could be browsed by people on networked (linked) computers using the simple point and click system, called Hypertext. Writing "vague but exciting" on the proposal, his boss agreed to the project. Sitting at this NeXT computer, Berners-Lee put his ideas into practice. He developed HTML (Hypertext Markup Language) for writing web pages, HTTP (Hypertext Transfer Protocol), which is how servers and browsers talk to each other, and the very first browsing program, simply called WorldWideWeb.

The Internet network

CERN first used the web in 1991. But its network also linked to other institutes, via a network called the Internet. Soon, others connected to the Internet were setting up web servers. In 1993, CERN made its web development tools freely available. Six months later, there were 200 web servers, and the Internet itself had begun to grow.

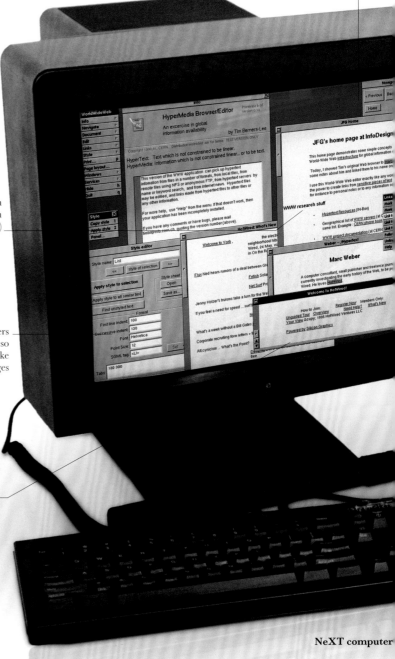

Berners-Lee worked on a black and white screen

Each page has its own address, called a uniform resource locator (URL)

The first web browsers were also editors, so people could make their own web pages

Pointing and clicking on a hyperlink directed the browser to another web page address

NeXT computer

The average Internet user visits more than a thousand web pages every month

World Wide Web

Easy browsers

The first web browsers were black and white and only worked on NeXT computers, but other versions were soon developed. Mosaic was the first to become popular with the general public. It was very slow, but it already had sound, video, and bookmarks.

▶▶ TOMORROW'S WORLD

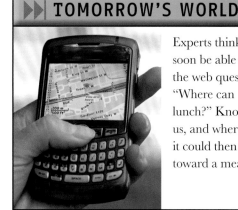

Experts think we will soon be able to ask the web questions like, "Where can I get some lunch?" Knowing about us, and where we are, it could then point us toward a meal.

Known as the Cube, this NeXT computer was the world's first web server

The Cube once stored all the pages and files on the World Wide Web

Computers linked via telephone wires or cables could browse the web

A sticker asked people not to turn off the computer—if they did, no one could access the web

The NeXT computer was powerful but expensive

Rather than a fixed hard drive, the computer had removable optical disks

A new world

The early web was for sharing information. But with the launch of Amazon.com in 1995, it also became a place to do business. Entire industries had to adapt to this. So even before broadband, mobile Internet, and countless web innovations like blogging, our world had already changed forever.

How the web has changed us

By making some things much easier, the web quickly changed people's habits. Many with Internet access would now struggle to do without.

Buying things

Online we can usually find exactly what we want to buy, at the best price. Without it, we can only buy what nearby shops are selling.

Finding things out

We all used to depend on asking each other or looking in books for answers. Now web pages cover almost every topic imaginable.

Networking with friends

Over the Internet, we can chat with friends, wherever they are, and also show them photos.

SEE ALSO Microprocessor 98

Based on a theory by physicist Albert Einstein, the invention of the laser was initially described as a solution looking for a problem. But people quickly found uses for its intense, narrow beam of light. Today lasers penetrate almost every aspect of life, from scanning bar codes to creating cancers, guiding missiles, and even replacing hair.

Masers and lasers

In 1954, Charles Townes built a maser. This used stimulated emission to amplify microwaves—similar to light waves, but with longer wavelengths. Adapting it for light waves was far from simple. In 1957, Townes' student Gordon Gould started making a laser. But failing to understand the patent process, he did not protect his invention and his work was exploited by others.

Laser machines often have two or three lasers, for different colored beams

To trace the Moon's path, scientists fire laser beams at mirrors that sit on the Moon's surface

Laser light is both bright and sharp

A laser produces light waves with the same wavelength, so they are a single color

Computer programmes can analyze a DJ's music and produce laser effects to go with it

The peaks and troughs of laser light waves are in step

Theory of a genius

We usually think of light as waves. Ordinary white light is a mixture of colored light waves, each one with a different wavelength. These are emitted (sent out) at random intervals in all directions. In 1917, Einstein theorized about making a much stronger light, using what he called stimulated emission. This would consist of waves with exactly the same wavelength that were perfectly in step, and all traveled in the same direction.

Moving mirrors make fast flashing laser beams look very dramatic

The beams only shine at the audience briefly, as they can damage people's eyes

Laser

Many dentists now use lasers rather than drills to whiten teeth, reshape gums, and remove decay. Surgeons also use lasers for delicate operations on the eyes and brain.

Light industry
Focused laser light can cut through most materials, including thick sheets of metal. Lasers can cut awkward shapes into delicate materials, and they never need sharpening.

Earth health check
Scientists use lasers to study the atmosphere and monitor greenhouse gases. Lasers are also used to monitor pollution in rivers.

SEE ALSO Bar code 128

COOL SCIENCE

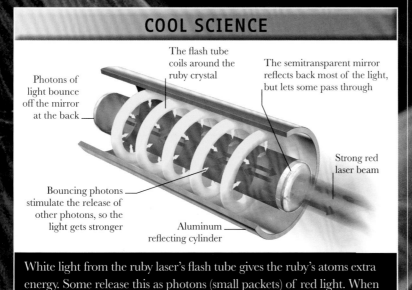

Photons of light bounce off the mirror at the back

The flash tube coils around the ruby crystal

The semitransparent mirror reflects back most of the light, but lets some pass through

Strong red laser beam

Bouncing photons stimulate the release of other photons, so the light gets stronger

Aluminum reflecting cylinder

White light from the ruby laser's flash tube gives the ruby's atoms extra energy. Some release this as photons (small packets) of red light. When photons meet other high-energy atoms, they make them release energy, too, as photons that are in step. As photons bounce between the two mirrors, the new laser beam strengthens and finally emerges through the semitransparent end.

Glass sandwich

LCD screens are layers of liquid crystal sandwiched between sheets of special glass, which—like sunglasses—polarizes (filters) light. They are thinner, lighter, and use less energy than the bulky cathode ray tubes of old-style screens.

The development of liquid crystal displays (LCDs) has been central to our increasingly digital lifestyle. These slim panels are used in most modern electronic gadgets. Many people contributed to the development of LCD technology. But the breakthrough that led to practical screens came in 1967, when American inventor James Fergason discovered a type of liquid crystal that could block or let through polarized light. Modern LCDs can display images, text, and video—and they are rapidly becoming smaller and more sophisticated.

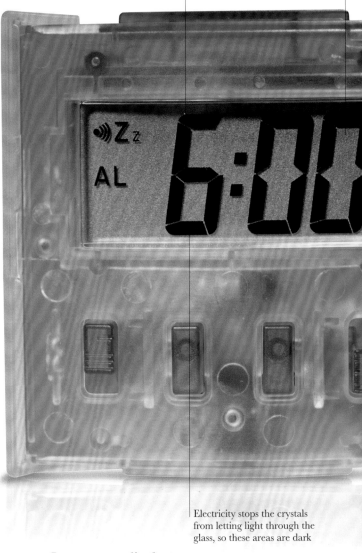

The liquid crystals are in segments, each with its own electricity supply

Reflected light makes the display appear gray

Electricity stops the crystals from letting light through the glass, so these areas are dark

◀◀ BRIGHT SPARKS

Liquid crystals were discovered in 1888, but few scientists looked into their uses. Interest exploded in 1963, when George Heilmeier (above) and Richard Williams suggested using them for displays. LCD screens appeared four years later.

Low-energy display

A black and gray LCD does not need a backlight, making it perfect for low-energy, battery-powered devices. Instead, surrounding light simply bounces off a mirror at the back of the display.

Liquid crystals are neither solid nor liquid; they exist in a state of matter between the two

LCD

Vertical polarizing filter

Liquid crystal twists light

Color filter

Glass

Electricity applied

Horizontal polarizing filter

Display

Light enters an LCD display and is polarized (to orient the rays in one direction) by a filter. When electricity is applied, the liquid crystals line up in a different direction, blocking light from passing through a pixel and making these sections appear dark.

A backlight makes color displays bright enough for us to see tones and details

The number of pixels in a display is known as its resolution

Touch-sensitive LCD screens are handy for everyone, but they also make it easier for people with language difficulties to communicate

Pixel pictures

More complex displays split the liquid crystals into millions of tiny elements called pixels. The more pixels a screen has, the more detailed its images. A computer screen can have more than one million pixels.

Each pixel (made up of red, blue, and green) can display more than 16 million different colors

Color filters cover the liquid crystals in each subpixel

Each subpixel has a variable electricity supply with 256 brightness levels

05:13

All

Send   Delete   More

SAMSUNG

Creating colors

Pixels are split into red, blue, and green subpixels, with liquid crystals controlling the brightness of each. They are so small that our brains see the combination of reds, blues, and greens as single colors.

SEE ALSO Television 88 · Digital camera 112 · GPS 190 · Sunglasses 236

In 1935, a patent was granted to the American chemical company DuPont for a new material called nylon. Products made from nylon reached stores in 1938. They were an instant hit with customers. At first, nylon fibers were used in toothbrushes. They also replaced silk in stockings, which became known as nylons. Today, nylon is used in a variety of products and textiles. As well as nylon fibers, solid nylon is used to make plastic products, including plastic pipes and some mechanical parts that used to be made from metal.

Why is nylon so useful?
Nylon is widely used because it is strong, tough, long-lasting, lightweight, easy to wash, resists scratches, and is not damaged by oil or a wide variety of chemicals. It can also be easily dyed different colors.

COOL SCIENCE

Nylon is a polymer. A polymer is a long chain of units made of groups of atoms. Nylon is made in a laboratory, but there are polymers in nature, too. Cellulose, found in the cell walls of plants, and natural rubber are polymers.

The bottom of the balloon is made of fireproof material because nylon is sensitive to heat

Nylon

The downside of nylon

Nylon has some disadvantages. If it gets too hot, it melts and burns. When it burns, it gives off poisonous fumes (gases). Once it is made, it is difficult to dispose of. Unlike natural fibers, such as cotton and wool, nylon does not rot in the ground when it is thrown away.

Nylon is made from petroleum—it was developed to be a substitute for silk, a more expensive material to make

The balloon fabric is made from nylon panels stitched together

The nylon fabric is coated with chemicals to make it more airtight and waterproof

Nylon balloons

Most hot-air balloons are made from nylon. It was first chosen for this job because it had already proved to be a very good material for making parachutes. A type of fabric called ripstop nylon is used. Extra threads are woven into the material to stop tears from spreading.

The very first parachute jump using a nylon parachute was made in 1942

A versatile material

Nylon can be made into different forms, making it a good material for products found in industry, sports, and the home.

Pipes

Nylon can be molded and formed into different shapes. Nylon pipes and hoses are used in car engines. Water and drainage pipes are also often made of nylon.

Rope

Nylon is used to make strong and flexible ropes. In fact, nylon ropes are the strongest type in common use. They are used in mountaineering and to pull heavy loads.

Woven and stitched

Nylon fibers are used in all types of products that are woven or stitched together, including clothing, carpets, upholstery, and tents.

SEE ALSO PET bottles 36 · Umbrella 214

Wallace Carothers

The story of nylon began when DuPont opened a new research center in the 1920s. They chose a brilliant young scholar and chemist, Wallace Carothers, to run it. Carothers was born in Iowa on April 27, 1896. After obtaining a science degree in 1920, he earned a doctorate at the University of Illinois. Carothers went to work at Harvard University in 1926, and two years later he moved to DuPont.

> " Nylon can be fashioned into filaments as strong as steel, as fine as a spider's web, yet more elastic than. . . natural fibers "
>
> DuPont Vice-President Charles Stine, 1938

Leaving Harvard

When Carothers was offered the chance to run his own laboratory at DuPont, at first he was unsure of whether or not to leave Harvard. He would have more research assistants of higher quality at DuPont, but he might be freer to follow the research that most interested him at Harvard. DuPont reassured him that he would be given all the support he needed to carry out his research. They also offered him nearly twice as much money as he was earning at Harvard.

Wallace Carothers

Carothers and his team of scientists at DuPont made new materials by combining different chemicals. They tried scores of combinations, searching for one that would produce a successful new material.

An unhappy life

Sadly, Carothers did not live to see the great success of the materials that he created. He rarely went out and hated the public speaking that he had to do as part of his work. He also had bouts of depression. In 1936, Carothers married Helen Sweetman, another DuPont worker, but his depression continued and he spent some time in a hospital. On April 29, 1937, at the age of 41, Carothers killed himself by taking poison—one year before the first nylon products went on sale to the public.

Neoprene

Nylon wasn't the first new material to be made in Carothers' laboratory at DuPont. In 1930, it developed neoprene, the first successful mass-produced synthetic rubber. Wetsuits worn by divers are made of neoprene.

First products

The first nylon product that people could buy was a toothbrush with nylon bristles. Until then, bristles had been made of animal hair.

Mass production

Nylon is ideal for making thousands of copies of the same product by forcing liquid nylon into molds. This DuPont worker is surrounded by 10,000 nylon combs, the number that one worker could make in a single day in the 1950s.

Dynamite

Dynamite was the first powerful explosive that was safe to handle. It transformed construction, mining, and quarrying, blasting a path into the 1900s. We use explosives to build railroads, roads, and tunnels. We blast through rocks to build dams and crack them open to extract coal. Alfred Nobel's discovery also ignited research into more powerful explosives. These help us free up even more of Earth's resources—the rocks and minerals used to make cars, computers, cell phones, and even medicines.

Killer chemical

Italian chemist Ascanio Sobrero first made the liquid nitroglycerin—dynamite's explosive ingredient—in 1846. It was much more powerful than gunpowder, but deadly to handle. Even the tiniest knock could make it explode. It caused many fatal accidents, including one that killed Nobel's younger brother, Emil.

Health and safety

Nobel developed devices called blasting caps. These could be used to detonate (trigger) nitroglycerin explosions from a distance. But he also discovered that mixing nitroglycerin with kieselguhr (a chalky sand) made it much safer. He called this substance dynamite.

Pushing the plunger sent a powerful electric current down a wire

Invented in 1878, blasting boxes used electricity to set off a blasting cap

TOMORROW'S WORLD

Scientists are developing new explosives that will make firework displays even more spectacular. Mixing chemicals in miniscule quantities—literally a few molecules at a time—makes them more powerful, so even more explosive.

Firefighters use dynamite and other explosives to put out fires in oil wells

The fuse triggers a small explosion in a blasting cap attached to its end

The shock from the exploding blasting cap makes the dynamite explode

The fuse allows explosions to be set off from a distance—this type burns

Dynamite can be shaped into tubes and safely packed in paper

Dynamite does not have to contain kieselguhr—sawdust and other absorbent materials can also be used

Detonating dynamite
Dynamite was so stable that it could be dropped, hit, or burned without exploding. But it still exploded powerfully when detonated by a blasting cap. Demand for dynamite grew quickly, and Nobel eventually owned 90 dynamite factories in 20 countries.

Nobel Prize
Dynamite made Nobel a wealthy man, but he was sad that people used his inventions for war. In his will, Nobel left his fortune to set up the Nobel Prize. Since 1901, this has been awarded every year for work that most benefits humankind.

An inventive man
Nobel started his dangerous experiments with explosives in 1860, continuing them long after he invented dynamite. When he died, aged 63, he held 355 patents—for inventions such as synthetic rubber as well as for other explosives. Shown here is his laboratory in Sweden.

Alfred Nobel
Born in Sweden in 1933, Nobel grew up in Russia, where his father made land mines for the Czar. He learned to speak five languages and developed wide interests. Although chemistry was his greatest passion, Nobel also wrote poetry in his spare time.

SEE ALSO Hoover Dam 34

Great Gizmos

A single amazing invention, like the clock or the printing press, can change people's lives all over the world. Often, great gizmos like these go through many versions over the years, getting better and better all the time.

1860

ÉTIENNE LENOIR

Tiny explosions

There are two types of internal combustion engines: those in cars and motorcycles are intermittent, which means that fuel burns in short bursts. Jet planes and rockets have engines in which the fuel burns constantly.

Engines are machines that burn fuel to make things move. The first successful engines were all steam engines, which use steam from a boiler to move a piston in a cylinder. In internal combustion engines, the fuel is burned inside the cylinder. This makes them lighter and more efficient than steam engines, so they quickly replaced steam engines in machinery and vehicles.

Modern engines are more than 100 times as powerful as Lenoir's engine

Lenoir's gas engine

In 1860, Belgian engineer Étienne Lenoir built the first successful internal combustion engine (right). It was also the first to be built in large numbers. Lenoir's engine mixed gas with air inside the cylinder and was ignited (set alight) with a spark. The gas exploded, thrusting out the piston, which then turned the wheel.

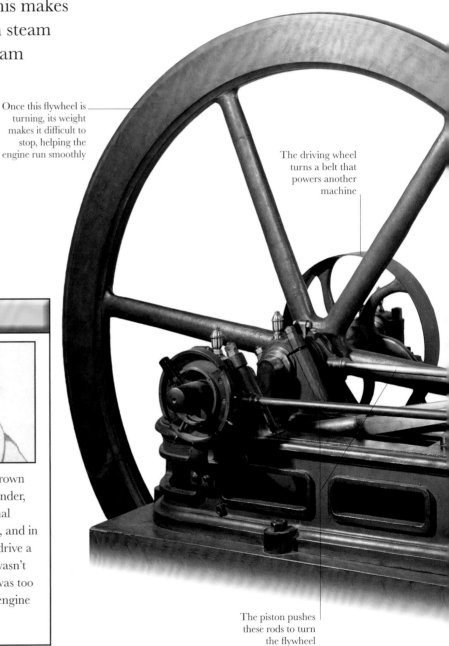

Once this flywheel is turning, its weight makes it difficult to stop, helping the engine run smoothly

The driving wheel turns a belt that powers another machine

The piston pushes these rods to turn the flywheel

◄◄ BRIGHT SPARKS

In 1823, Samuel Brown patented a two-cylinder, gas-powered internal combustion engine, and in 1825 he used it to drive a vehicle, though it wasn't very successful. It was too similar to a steam engine to work well.

Engine

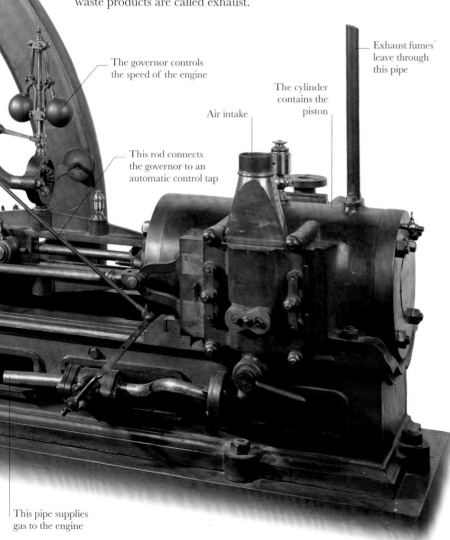

Tiny internal combustion engines can be used instead of batteries to produce electricity to power equipment such as computers. (Batteries need to be recharged about five times as often as these engines need to be refueled.) They are made of steel, but the scientists who made them want to use silicon to build much smaller versions, which will be the size of pinheads.

From fuel to fumes

Internal combustion engines convert the energy that is contained in fuel into other forms of energy, including motion and heat. They produce pollutants, including gases and tiny particles, during the process. These waste products are called exhaust.

The governor controls the speed of the engine

Exhaust fumes leave through this pipe

The cylinder contains the piston

Air intake

This rod connects the governor to an automatic control tap

This pipe supplies gas to the engine

The engine evolves

Over the years, engineers have worked hard to build engines that are reliable, quiet, light, run smoothly, and use fuel efficiently.

Gas to liquid

Nikolas Otto made an improved version of Lenoir's gas-fueled engine. Then, in 1885, Daimler modified it to run on liquid fuel, and used it in the world's first motorcycle.

Speed machine

The Harley-Davidson company has been making motorcycles for more than a century. This one is from 1942—by then, engines were extremely efficient and powerful.

Built for sport

Today, supersport bikes perform well because they have "high revving" engines, which means their components move very quickly, producing a great deal of power.

SEE ALSO Ford Model T 148 · Helicopter 160 · Electric car 172

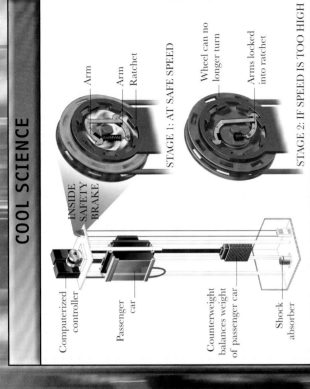

INSIDE SAFETY BRAKE

Arm
Arm
Ratchet

STAGE 1: AT SAFE SPEED

Wheel can no longer turn

Arms locked into ratchet

STAGE 2: IF SPEED IS TOO HIGH

Computerized controller

Passenger car

Counterweight balances weight of passenger car

Shock absorber

Four sets of rollers engage with a pair of rails that run up the side of the building

Walls and ceiling are made of toughened glass that is treated to keep out the Sun's heat

Elevators are equipped with very reliable safety systems. If the elevator starts to fall, its cable spins the wheel inside the safety brake faster than usual, and the two arms inside the brake swing outward and interlock with a ratchet. This prevents the wheel from turning, bringing the elevator to a halt.

Elevators

The first elevators were invented thousands of years ago in ancient Greece. For a long time they were not a very safe way to travel, and it was only after 1852—when Elisha Otis designed and demonstrated one that was equipped with a safety device—that people began to trust them. Without safe elevators, there could be no skyscrapers, and modern cities would look very different.

Clever machinery

Today's elevators are comfortable, fast, and safe. Many are connected to computer systems to ensure that they are in the right place at the right time. This is done by keeping elevators close to busy floors when not in use, and making sure that they stop more often on downward journeys when it's time for people to leave the building.

Metal rails provide extra safety.

Ventilation, as well as heating and cooling systems, automatically keep conditions comfortable inside the elevator

Elevators everywhere

It's not just people who use elevators: they are often used for moving goods around, and some multistory parking lots have vehicle elevators, too. Aircraft carriers have huge versions, each large enough to hold two jet planes and able to lift more than 150,000 lb (70,000 kg). Special types of elevators, called stair lifts, can also be fitted into the homes of people who find it difficult to walk up stairs.

Cool views

Occasionally, skyscrapers have external elevators that travel up and down the outside of their walls. This saves space inside the building and gives people amazing views as they travel. As these elevators are exposed to the weather, they have to be fitted with special heating and cooling units.

The world's fastest elevators are in the Burj Khalifa skyscraper in Dubai, United Arab Emirates—they travel at 40 mph (64 km/h)

▶▶| TOMORROW'S WORLD

One day, it may be possible to travel into space in an elevator! There are already thousands of satellites in orbit around our planet. Some orbit at the same rate that Earth turns, which means that they always remain above the same location. In theory, an elevator could take people up to these satellites, as shown in this artist's impression.

SEE ALSO GPS 190

Elisha Otis

Many cities are dominated by huge and beautiful skyscrapers and famous landmarks. Skyscrapers allow huge cities to be built using only small amounts of land, and they provide safe, sheltered, and comfortable places for people to live and work. But without Elisha Otis's big idea, we would not have these incredible buildings today.

Global safety

American inventor Elisha Otis installed his first passenger-carrying safety elevator in a New York department store in 1857 and kept improving his invention until his death in 1861. His sons, Charles and Norton, then started the Otis Brothers Company, and by 1873 more than 2,000 Otis elevators had been installed. Their use in famous buildings helped make them popular, and there are now 1.7 million in use all over the world.

Elisha Otis
In 1853, Otis staged a dramatic demonstration of his safety elevator in an attempt to gain public confidence. He cut the rope of an open elevator. Luckily, his safety system worked and led to the development of high-rise buildings.

Eiffel Tower
Otis elevators were installed in the curved legs of the Eiffel Tower in France. Completed in 1889, it was the world's tallest structure until 1930. It is still the tallest in Paris and is one of the most recognizable buildings in the world.

Statue of Liberty
In 1886, the Statue of Liberty was given to the U.S.A. by the people of France. It has 324 steps, but in the early 1900s an Otis elevator was installed, making going to the top a lot easier!

The sky's the limit

What people call a skyscraper has changed over the years. In the 1880s, the Home Insurance Building in Chicago, Illinois, seemed amazingly high, but its 10 stories would not be very impressive today. However, it introduced the building technique that, together with the elevator, is key to skyscraper construction: it was built using a metal "skeleton" of iron and steel to support the weight of the building rather than its external walls. Later skyscrapers used all-steel frames.

Burj Khalifa

Dubai's Burj Khalifa (which means "Khalifa Tower" in Arabic) is the tallest structure in the world. Completed in 2010, it is 2,717 ft (828 m) high and has 208 floors. The building contains 57 Otis elevators. Two of these are double-decked elevators (one cab mounted above the other) that take people to the 124th floor observation deck.

> **" A skyscraper is a boast in glass and steel "**
> Mason Cooley, American author

Milan Cathedral

For centuries, the highest city buildings were often cathedrals. This one in Milan, Italy, was started in 1386 but not finished until 1965! In 1997, a new Otis elevator was installed inside one of the 135 spires.

Mori Tower

Opened in 2003, the Roppong Hills Mori Tower is an important landmark in the Japanese city of Tokyo. People can work, shop, and play under one roof. There are 12 Otis elevators in this 54-storey building, all of which are double-decked elevators.

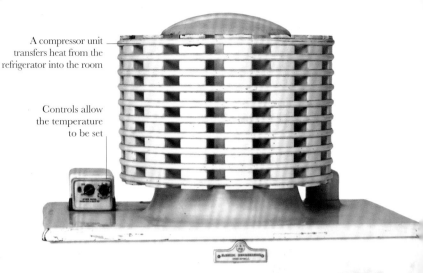

A compressor unit transfers heat from the refrigerator into the room

Controls allow the temperature to be set

Many people helped develop the refrigerator, but they only became really useful machines when people could afford to buy them for their homes. The price of the General Electric all-steel model was what made it into a household item. Chilling food slows down the growth of bacteria that cause food poisoning, so food in a refrigerator lasts longer before going bad. It also means that less food is wasted, people suffer fewer health problems, and shopping no longer has to be a daily chore.

The icebox is the coldest part of the refrigerator

A cheaper chiller

Christian Steenstrup worked for the American company General Electric, and designed the first affordable refrigerator in 1927. At $525, it was still expensive, but it cost half the price of its competitors. Just three years later, it was by far the most popular refrigerator in the U.S.A.

◀◀ **BRIGHT SPARKS**

Until the mid-1900s, people moved natural ice from cold parts of the world to warmer areas and stored them in underground "ice houses." Chunks of ice from the ice houses were used to cool "iceboxes," which were like unpowered refrigerators.

GE monitor-top refrigerator, 1927

Refrigerator

Put to good use

Another advantage of the all-steel refrigerator was that it didn't have the strong smell of ammonia that some other types had, so it could be kept in the kitchen. Since then, refrigerators have become common items—but they aren't only used for food storage in homes. They are vital in hospitals to keep medicines cool, and every air-conditioner unit contains one. Refrigerators that can cool to below freezing point are called freezers and are used to store food for even longer.

COOL SCIENCE

A coolant gas circulates in coils, absorbing heat

An expansion valve converts liquid coolant into cold gas

The condenser coil releases heat from the coolant

The motor drives the compressor

Compressor

If you blow on wet skin, it feels cold. This is because the liquid water is changing into vapor—and it is using heat energy to do it. Refrigerators work in the same way: inside them liquid changes to gas, cooling the interior. The gas changes back to liquid in pipes outside the unit, releasing warmth into the air.

Purple cold areas

Green cool areas

Seeing heat

All objects send out infrared rays, which we can sometimes feel as heat. Although we can't see these rays, special cameras can detect them and make heat-pictures of things, like the inside of this refrigerator. These heat pictures are called thermograms—in this one, the hottest objects are red and the coldest are purple. It's important that refrigerators do not have hotspots, where food would go off, or cold spots, where it might be damaged by being frozen. A thermogram of the refrigerator could be used to check for warm or cold spots.

The latch ensures that the door closes tightly, so that cool air does not escape

Red warm areas

The single-door refrigerator was the most popular model, but there were models with two doors—and even some with three doors

A thick, insulated door stops the refrigerator from warming up

A refrigerator warms the room that it is in, and if you open its door, the room will soon become even warmer

Magnetic attraction

In the future, refrigerators may be cooled by using magnetism. Some materials contain tiny structures called magnetic domains, which form patterns when a magnetic field is present. When the field is turned off, the domains become jumbled, which cools the material as part of the jumbling process. The cold material can then be used to cool a refrigerator.

SEE ALSO Vaccination 18 · Tin can 30

Machines powered by wind have been in existence for thousands of years. Windmills have long been used to grind grain into flour to make bread and to pump water. Yet it was not until 1887 that the wind was first used to generate electricity. Scottish inventor James Blyth used a horizontal windmill to generate enough electricity to light his own house, and, coincidentally, American inventor Charles Brush built a similar machine for his Ohio home. By the 1930s, there were wind-powered generators all over North America, mostly supplying electricity to remote farms.

Generating interest

James Blyth realized how useful his invention could be and offered to build a machine that would provide enough power to light the streets of his village. His neighbors, however, were not so easily persuaded. They thought electricity was the work of the devil and refused his offer. Eventually, Blyth's invention was put to good use when wind-powered generators provided an emergency electricity supply for his local hospital.

Turbines today

Today, electricity-producing wind machines are called wind turbines. Each one produces only a little electrical power, so hundreds are needed to supply as much as a power plant. As a result, they are often built in groups, called arrays or wind farms. As the wind changes direction, the tops of the turbines turn to face the wind.

Doubling the length of a wind turbine's blades produces not just double, but four times as much electricity—so the best wind turbines are large ones

Most wind turbines are painted gray to blend in with the color of the sky

A ladder allows access to the nose for maintenance

The world's largest wind turbine has a rotor 410 ft (125 m) across

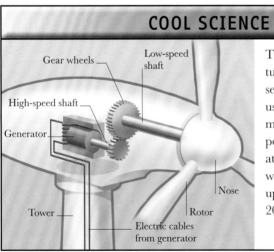

COOL SCIENCE

Gear wheels

Low-speed shaft

High-speed shaft

Generator

Tower

Nose

Rotor

Electric cables from generator

The blades of a wind turbine turn only once per second or two. Generators use electromagnets to turn motion into electrical power. They only work well at high turn speeds, so gear wheels are used to "step up" the rotation to around 20 turns per second.

Above the waves

The wind blows more strongly out at sea, because there are no hills, trees, or buildings to slow it down. So, many wind farms are built offshore, even though this is much more complicated and expensive than building them on land. However, it does mean that people are not bothered by the noise that they make.

Wind turbine

The generator turns the motion of the blades into electricity. The turbine shuts down automatically at very high wind speeds to avoid damage

The wind turbine's tower is a huge steel tube, up to 300 ft (90 m) high

Good or bad?

Wind turbines are often regarded as one of the solutions to the energy crisis: unlike fossil fuels, wind energy will never run out. However, there are fierce disagreements about whether their benefits are worth the problems that they cause.

Advantages of wind energy

Wind turbines occupy only small areas and can share fields with crops or cattle. Unlike power plants that burn coal or oil, they make no waste gases, so they are considered a source of "green" energy.

Disadvantages of wind energy

Some people think that wind turbines are ugly and pose a threat to flocks of birds that might fly into them. When turbines are in remote places, it is expensive to transmit the electricity that they make to the people in towns and cities who will use it.

SEE ALSO Solar cell 92 · Helicopter 160

**Michael Faraday's groundbreaking
work with magnets** and electricity led
to simple electricity generators. The discovery by
Zénobe Gramme that generators could also be
used in reverse as electric motors gave people a
new source of power for industry. Before electric
motors were available, machines were powered
by steam, water, or animals. Today, electric
motors are used in a huge number of household
items and are essential for industry.

Faraday's motor

In 1821, Faraday showed that electricity
and magnetism could produce motion
when he invented a simple electric motor.
Modern motors use electricity and
magnetism, too. A motor contains coils of
wire wound around pieces of iron. When
electricity flows through the coils, they
become magnets. These "electromagnets"
and other magnets push and pull each
other to turn the motor.

Electromagnets hug the
rotating iron ring in the
middle of the machine
to intensify the magnetic
forces acting on it

Two metal arms
transfer direct
current electricity to
the metal barrel

The barrel supplies
electricity to the wire coils,
alternating the direction of
the current so that the
motor keeps turning

**Gramme
machine**

▶▶ **TOMORROW'S WORLD**

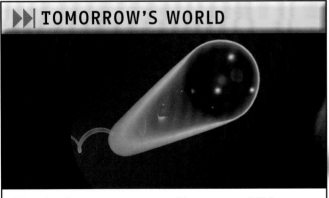

Tiny electric motors open up exciting new possibilities.
The prototype Proteus motors are just 2½ times the width
of a hair and small enough to travel through blood vessels.
Surgeons will equip them with cameras so that they can be
used to repair damage to the circulatory system.

The coils of wire are wrapped
around an iron ring that can rotate
freely between the electromagnets
above and below it

When electric currents flow
through the wire coils,
magnetic forces turn
the iron ring

Electric motor

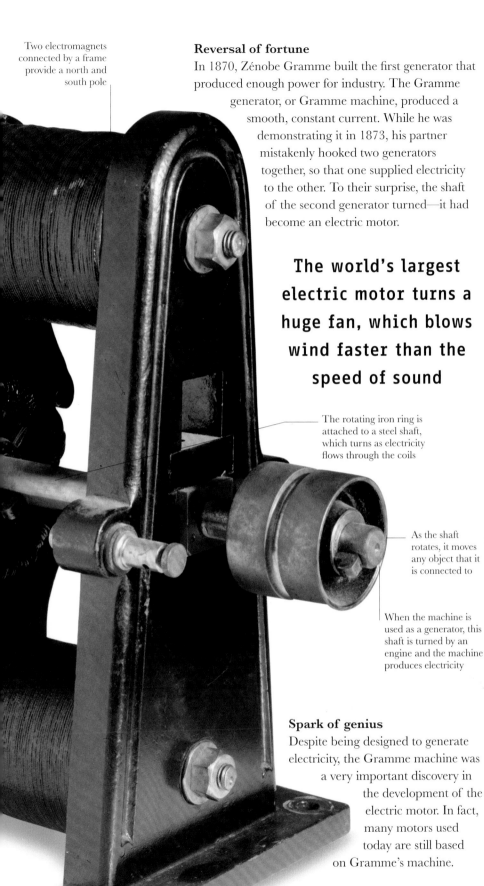

Two electromagnets connected by a frame provide a north and south pole

Reversal of fortune

In 1870, Zénobe Gramme built the first generator that produced enough power for industry. The Gramme generator, or Gramme machine, produced a smooth, constant current. While he was demonstrating it in 1873, his partner mistakenly hooked two generators together, so that one supplied electricity to the other. To their surprise, the shaft of the second generator turned—it had become an electric motor.

The world's largest electric motor turns a huge fan, which blows wind faster than the speed of sound

The rotating iron ring is attached to a steel shaft, which turns as electricity flows through the coils

As the shaft rotates, it moves any object that it is connected to

When the machine is used as a generator, this shaft is turned by an engine and the machine produces electricity

Spark of genius

Despite being designed to generate electricity, the Gramme machine was a very important discovery in the development of the electric motor. In fact, many motors used today are still based on Gramme's machine.

Driving the world

Almost every electrical object with moving parts contains a motor, from vibrating cell phones to large industrial machines. Electric motors can be as small or large, as the job demands, and can be started and stopped with the flick of a switch.

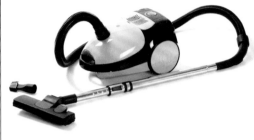

Alternating current

Most large machines in the home have motors that can use alternating current (AC)—a type of current that is supplied to wall outlets and constantly changes direction. In 1883, Nikola Tesla invented another type of AC motor, which is used to operate heavy machinery in factories.

Direct current motors

Batteries supply constant, direct current (DC), and many battery-powered gadgets, such as electric toys, use DC motors fitted with permanent magnets. We use another type—the stepper motor—in complex electronic equipment like computer disk drives, where movement needs to be precisely controlled. Laptops and other gadgets have adapters that convert AC electricity into a DC power supply to run these motors.

SEE ALSO Battery 96 · Steam locomotive 162

The father of electricity

From luxury gadgets to lifesaving machines, today's electrical equipment depends on the discoveries made by the genius known as the "Father of Electricity"— Michael Faraday. His groundbreaking inventions include the first electric motor and a method of generating electricity that lies at the heart of all power plants. Faraday's ideas inspired other scientists to explore electricity and magnetism, sparking a golden age of invention that changed the world.

Michael Faraday

Faraday, an English Chemist, came from a poor family and left school at 13. In the 1800s, it was very difficult for someone like him to become successful. Yet Faraday achieved so much that, in 1858, Prince Albert awarded him a house at Hampton Court Palace, in southern England.

Teaching science

Faraday loved to share his excitement about science with everyone. In 1825, he began to give entertaining Christmas lectures for young people at the Royal Institution in London, Engand. The lectures continue today and are shown on television.

Using electricity

In the early 1800s, electricity was a laboratory novelty rather than a practical source of energy. Faraday changed this when, in 1821, he showed that electromagnetic energy could be used to produce motion—creating the first electric motor. In 1831, he discovered that electricity begins to flow in a conductor when it is moved between the poles of a magnet. Within weeks, he used this idea to invent the electric transformer and generator. For the first time, electricity could be produced without a battery and in much greater amounts.

Motor

Faraday was inspired by the discovery of electromagnetism—the fact that a current passing through a metal wire produces a magnetic field around the wire. His simple motor used this idea. He suspended a wire in a small cup of mercury with a magnet at the bottom (left). When a current was passed through the wire, it swung around the magnet in a circle. This was the first time anyone had produced continuous movement from electricity.

Transformer

Transformers turn high voltages into low ones and vice versa. They are used in electrical gadgets, and to change the high-voltage electricity from power plants into safer voltages for our homes.

Faraday made the first transformer by coiling two lengths of wire around an iron ring

Passing electricity through one coil made an electric current flow briefly in the other coil

Diary

Faraday researched many other areas of chemistry and physics. In 1822, he wrote in his diary (above) "Convert magnetism into electricity!" However, he was so busy that almost 10 years passed before he tried doing it.

Generator

Faraday's generator uses magnets and motion to generate electricity. The copper wheel is turned by hand so that its rim passes between the poles of a permanent magnet. This continually cuts the magnetic force lines, causing an electric current to flow in the copper. The current is led off through a wire and today can power a small lightbulb.

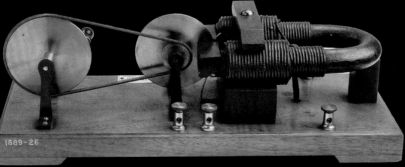

1889-26

1764

JAMES HARGREAVES

James Hargreaves never meant to change the world—his invention, the spinning jenny, was simply a machine that made it quicker and cheaper to produce yarn from the fluffy covering of cotton plant seeds. But cheap yarn was bad news for other yarn makers in the area, and they smashed his machine. Hargreaves fled to Nottingham, England, and continued to work on automation, the process of replacing human labor with machines.

"Jenny" was the name of Hargreaves' daughter, who knocked over a spinning wheel and gave Hargreaves his big idea

Moving the bar stretched the yarn

The worker spun the wheel with one hand and the bar with the other

These helped twist together the fibers

Cottage industry
Before the invention of the spinning jenny and other textile machines, textiles were made at home. This is known as a cottage industry. Spinning was mostly done by women, while weaving—making finished cloth—was generally seen as men's work.

◄◄ BRIGHT SPARKS

Some of the earliest spinning machines were spinning wheels, and they were probably invented in India. Spinning wheels were used to turn natural fibers, such as wool and cotton, into a thread that could be woven or knitted into a textile.

Spinning jenny

Yarn was wound around a row of spinning spindles

Child labor

One of the reasons for the success of the spinning jenny was that it could be operated by a child, unlike spinning wheels, which were more difficult to use. Hargreaves died in 1778, and by then more than 20,000 spinning jennies were in use all over Great Britain.

These cords attach the wheel to spindles

The worker rotated the wheel with this handle

A row of bobbins held the loose cotton fibers in place, ready to be fed through the bars to the spindles

Although early spinning jennies had sloping wheels, later models had upright ones, which were more efficient

Time for change

The spinning jenny, and other machines used to make textiles, changed the way in which people lived and worked. Their use sparked the time known as the Industrial Revolution— a period when large factories were set up and people moved from the country to towns. Its effects spread from Europe and throughout the world.

Slow progress

The invention of the spinning jenny was part of a slow process of developing textile machines, in which many inventors were involved.

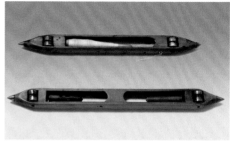

Kay's flying shuttle, 1733

John Kay's flying shuttle, which was a device for holding thread, speeded up the process of weaving. Machines with these shuttles were faster at making more fabric, of greater width, and with fewer workers.

Arkwright's water frame, 1768

Richard Arkwright's invention was an important improvement on the spinning jenny. It made stronger cotton threads, and was powered by a water mill.

Crompton's mule, 1779

The next significant improvement was Samuel Crompton's spinning mule; it could make many types of threads quickly and easily.

SEE ALSO Robots 74 · Jeans 226

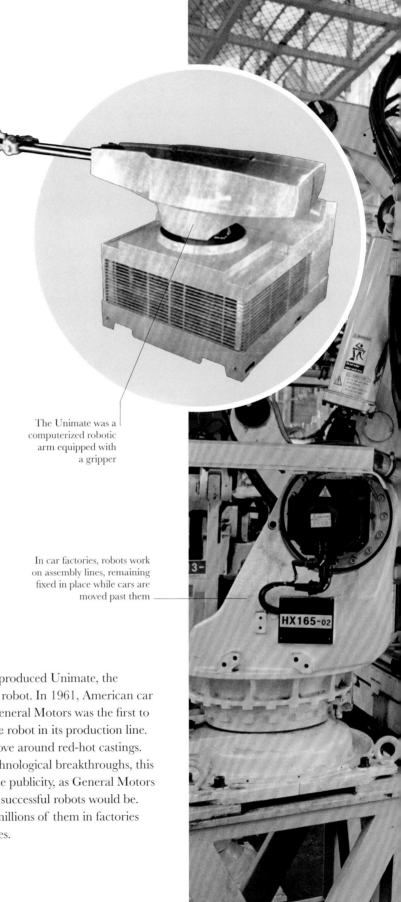

For centuries, people have been fascinated with the idea

of building lifelike machines. Until the 20th century, these were just clever toys, but, in the 1950s, engineers began to work on the idea seriously. Some of them wanted to build a machine that would be a step beyond the highly sophisticated factory machines that were in use at the time. They wanted to build an adaptable, flexible machine that could do a range of tasks, just like a human being can—they wanted to build a robot.

The Unimate was a computerized robotic arm equipped with a gripper

Pioneers of robotics

Robots had been popular for many years in science-fiction magazines and movies when American engineers George Devol and Joseph Engelberger were inspired to change science fiction into science fact. In 1954, Devol patented his idea of a "general purpose machine:" a robot that could be programmed to transfer items from place to place in a factory. In 1956, he and Engelberger met, and they formed a company called Unimation Inc. (Unimation is short for "universal automation").

In car factories, robots work on assembly lines, remaining fixed in place while cars are moved past them

In just a single year, one car factory replaced 200 workers with 50 robots and increased production by 20 percent

Unimate

Unimation Inc. produced Unimate, the world's first true robot. In 1961, American car manufacturer General Motors was the first to install a Unimate robot in its production line. Its job was to move around red-hot castings. Unlike other technological breakthroughs, this one received little publicity, as General Motors was unsure how successful robots would be. Now, there are millions of them in factories in many countries.

Robots

◄◄ BRIGHT SPARKS

Like a robot, the Jacquard loom followed coded instructions, but while modern robots receive instructions from computers, the loom was controlled by cards with holes punched in them. These directed the positions of the threads, so different patterns could be woven automatically. It was invented in 1801 by Joseph-Marie Jacquard.

By using a series of joints, the robot's arm can be moved in any direction

Perfect people

Many car factories now use teams of industrial robots—often, there is not a human to be seen. Robots are ideal for tasks in which exactly the same operations are repeated over and over. They are tireless, never make mistakes, and don't get bored. For jobs like this, robots are much faster, cheaper, and more reliable than humans—and they can cope easily with hot, dark, noisy, or hazardous conditions.

Robotic arms can have a range of end effectors (tools) attached to them, including grippers, hooks, or welding apparatus

►► TOMORROW'S WORLD

Many research scientists are working to make robots intelligent. This would make them even more adaptable and easier to instruct than today's robots and enable them to cope with unexpected problems, too. This prototype robot is called a Robonaut. One day, real versions may work alongside humans, both in factories and in space.

SEE ALSO Ford Model T 148 · Mars rovers 188

Robots in our world

Robots aren't only found in factories. Today, they are used for exploring space and cleaning homes, fighting fires and dealing with bombs, exploring sunken ships and patrolling the skies—they are even used to operate on people and star in movies. Some are larger than trucks, while others are small enough to travel inside the human body! As they develop further, robots will become even more essential to our lives.

Robotic reactions

All robots contain "feedback" mechanisms, so they can react to the world around them. Basic mechanisms may simply detect walls and other obstacles, but more complicated ones allow robots to see, hear, or feel. Fire-detecting robots can even "smell" fumes. After decades of research in many countries, robot senses are now quite sophisticated and, in some ways, better than our own.

Playing with robots

Robotic toys have been popular since the mid-1900s, and for a while Sony's Aibo—a robotic dog that could be trained—was popular. Human-size versions are new. To play Ping-Pong, robots need to combine balance, speed, and feedback.

In safe hands

No human's hands are as steady as a robot's can be, so robot surgeons can outperform humans when very complicated operations are needed, such as in brain surgery. Tiny medical robots can even enter the body to track down problems.

Help in the home

Houses are difficult environments for robots to work in: full of obstacles, delicate objects, and stairs. So developing household robots is a challenge. At present, automatic vacuum cleaners are the most successful type.

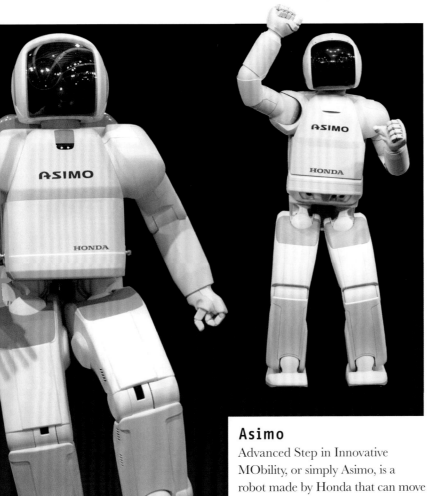

Asimo

Advanced Step in Innovative MObility, or simply Asimo, is a robot made by Honda that can move in incredibly human ways. It can shake hands, climb stairs—and even pour tea! Asimo robots can run at speeds of up to 4 mph (6 km/h).

> **I visualize a time when we will be to robots what dogs are to humans**
>
> Claude Shannon,
> American mathematical engineer

Machine intelligence

The main obstacle that limits the use of robots is that, although they react to things, they are not intelligent in the way that people are, so it is difficult for them to cope with unfamiliar places or unexpected problems. This is why artificial intelligence is a major area of research. The latest robots can recognize human faces and figure out routes over rough ground. In the future, intelligent robots will be able to understand human speech, which will make them simpler to control. It's even possible that, one day, robots will be smarter than people.

Animatronics

Robots that look like animals and monsters are known as animatronics. They are often used in movies. Some museums, such as the Natural History Museum in London, England, have animatronic dinosaurs, which move and roar like the real ones might have.

Planes without pilots

The first experimental robot planes were invented nearly a century ago, and some were used during World War II. Today, many robot planes, including this MQ-1 Predator, are used for spying. It is also equipped with laser-guided missiles.

River robots

Scientists have built robotic fish to explore rivers. They swim like real fish and can "sniff" out chemical pollution, helping in the battle to keep rivers clean. They send the data back to shore by WiFi technology.

Each swing of the pendulum raises and lowers metal fingers, which are called pawls

When the upper pawl rises, it lifts a lever, allowing one tooth on the rim of the small wheel to "escape," so the wheel turns at a constant rate

As this small wheel turns, the spikes push down on the lower pawl (metal finger), nudging the pendulum to keep it moving

This gear wheel links the movement of the small wheel and the large gear wheel

A tightly wound spring in this brass drum uncoils, providing the energy that drives the gears and turns the clock hands

Each swing of the pendulum allows the spring to unwind by a set amount

Pendulum clock

Modern living depends on knowing the time. Accurate clocks help us catch buses, turn up at work or school, and tune into television shows. They tell household and industrial machines when to turn on and off. They make sure power plants meet peak demand. Pendulum clocks were the first clocks that could keep time to within minutes and seconds. Their invention in the 1600s brought timekeeping into homes and businesses, changing daily life and opening up new possibilities in science.

The smallest modern clocks are the size of a grain of rice and fit on a microchip

A timely theory
A pendulum is a string or rod with a weight at the end. Around 1637, Italian scientist Galileo Galilei noticed that the swings of a pendulum measure out equal time intervals, even as the swing becomes smaller. He realized that this regular motion could be used to control a clock. Galileo designed this clockwork mechanism in 1642 but died before he had a chance to build a working model.

The length of the pendulum rod determines the time it takes to complete each swing

Moving the weight up and down the rod makes the clock go faster or slower

COSTRUITO A FIRENZE
L'ANNO 1883

M.S.C.H.I.A.B
337

Atomic clocks

Atoms and molecules vibrate at specific rates, which can be harnessed to keep time. The first atomic clock used ammonia molecules that vibrated 24,000,000,000 times per second. Atomic clocks enable scientists to time events to one-millionth of one-trillionth of a second.

Quartz crystals

Most modern clocks and watches contain quartz crystals. When placed in an electronic circuit, these little crystals oscillate (move backward and forward) in a very regular way. As they oscillate, they send out tiny electric pulses that drive a motor to turn the hands.

Time marches on

Pendulum clocks helped the world run on time for 270 years. In the 1900s, more accurate—and smaller—methods of timekeeping were developed.

BRIGHT SPARKS

Chinese engineer Su Song designed and built an incredible water-powered clock in 1094. The 39-ft- (12-m-) tall device was constructed on three levels, and was the most advanced clock of its time. Shown here is a modern model of Song's clock tower.

The first pendulum clock

Dutch scientist Christian Huygens made the first working pendulum clock in 1656. His design linked a pendulum to weights falling under gravity. The falling weights turned the clock hands. The pendulum precisely controlled the rate at which this happened. Huygens' clock was accurate to the nearest minute, instead of the nearest hour like other weight-driven clocks of the time.

SEE ALSO Microprocessor 98 · Electric motor 68

The master of time

Finding an accurate way to tell the time at sea challenged the greatest scientists of the 1700s. Englishman John Harrison devoted most of his life to solving the problem and eventually invented a marine timepiece that kept time almost as well as a pendulum clock did on land. Almost every 19th- and early 20th-century ship carried one. By making navigation more accurate, the device saved dozens of vessels and thousands of lives.

The longitude problem

To navigate, sailors needed to know the time back home, but clocks of the time could not cope with the rocking, rolling, and temperature changes of a sea voyage. Poor navigation led to shipwrecks, killing thousands of sailors. So in 1714, the British government offered a £20,000 prize (worth about $3,500,000 today!) to the person who could solve what became known as "the longitude problem." John Harrison, a skilled clockmaker, began working on a marine clock in 1728.

Harrison's prize-winning chronometer, 1759

John Harrison

The explorer Captain James Cook had taken a chronometer to sea and declared it his "trusty friend." Harrison, shown in this painting holding his chronometer, died soon after Cook's return and perhaps never knew of this success.

Solved with a watch

Harrison's first three designs were large timepieces that were based on pendulum clocks, but they could compensate for motion and temperature changes at sea. They were not quite accurate enough. In 1759, he made a completely different design. This chronometer was based on a pocket watch. After 47 days at sea, it was just 39 seconds off. Thinking that the result was a fluke, the prize's judging panel was unconvinced, so Harrison had to appeal to the king for support. It wasn't until 1773 that Harrison finally received recognition for solving the problem that had outfoxed both Galileo Galilei and Sir Isaac Newton.

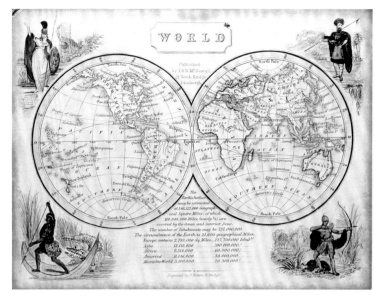

Where in the world

The lines of longitude on this early map run from the North Pole to the South Pole, dividing up the world like segments of an orange. Each line represents a new time zone. By comparing the local time with the time back home, sailors could tell where they were. They calculated local time from the position of the Sun, but they needed a clock to know the time where their journey began.

" By God, Harrison, I will see you righted! "

King George III
of England

Workings of chronometers

At 5 in (13 cm) in diameter, this chronometer looks like a very large pocket watch. It is driven by the energy from a tightly wound spring. A balance wheel swings back and forth to regulate the spring, carrying out the same job as a pendulum. When the temperature rises, the wheel's rim expands, cleverly canceling out variations in the strength of the balance spring.

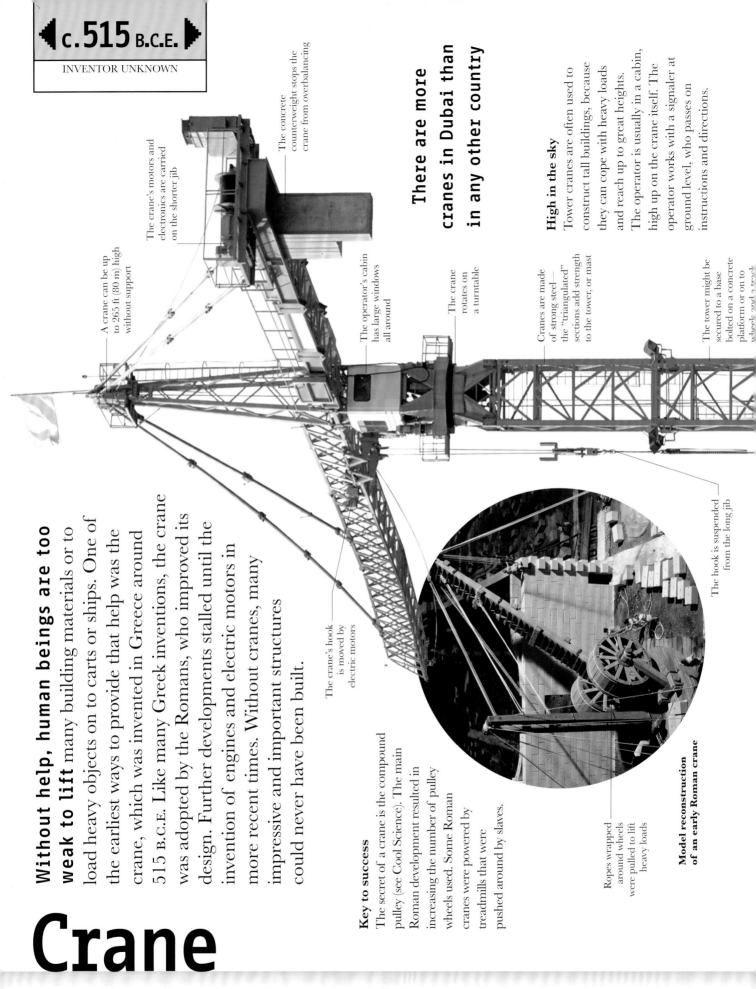

Crane

Without help, human beings are too weak to lift many building materials or to load heavy objects on to carts or ships. One of the earliest ways to provide that help was the crane, which was invented in Greece around 515 B.C.E. Like many Greek inventions, the crane was adopted by the Romans, who improved its design. Further developments stalled until the invention of engines and electric motors in more recent times. Without cranes, many impressive and important structures could never have been built.

Key to success

The secret of a crane is the compound pulley (see Cool Science). The main Roman development resulted in increasing the number of pulley wheels used. Some Roman cranes were powered by treadmills that were pushed around by slaves.

The crane's hook is moved by electric motors

Ropes wrapped around wheels were pulled to lift heavy loads

Model reconstruction of an early Roman crane

The crane's motors and electronics are carried on the shorter jib

The concrete counterweight stops the crane from overbalancing

A crane can be up to 265 ft (80 m) high without support

The operator's cabin has large windows all around

The crane rotates on a turntable

There are more cranes in Dubai than in any other country

Cranes are made of strong steel — the "triangulated" sections add strength to the tower, or mast

High in the sky

Tower cranes are often used to construct tall buildings, because they can cope with heavy loads and reach up to great heights. The operator is usually in a cabin, high up on the crane itself. The operator works with a signaler at ground level, who passes on instructions and directions.

The tower might be secured to a base bolted on a concrete platform or on to wheels and a track

The hook is suspended from the long jib

Rising up

Today, many cranes are so huge that moving them from place to place in one piece would be impossible. Self-erecting cranes overcome this problem. They use jacks (lifting devices) to raise their upper sections and add new parts. This also means that a crane can get taller alongside the structure that it is building.

Cranes for the job

Tower cranes for erecting tall buildings are not the only cranes used. Over the years, cranes of many types have been invented, each one designed for a specific type of job.

Fixed cranes

Gantry cranes and overhead cranes have trolley sections that travel in only one direction along a beam, which is attached to either walls or tall columns. These cranes are used to lift especially heavy objects in large industrial areas and factories. Container cranes are a type of gantry crane used for lifting cargo containers.

On the move

At dockyards, cranes are vital for loading and unloading ships, but they need to be mobile. They often move on caterpillar tracks because these spread the great weight of the crane—and its loads—over a wider area than wheels could and help the moving crane stay stable.

SEE ALSO Portland cement 32 · Elevators 60

For thousands of years, people have been writing to preserve their stories, thoughts, and discoveries. If they wanted their writings to be read by more than a few people, each copy was written out by hand, a task that took a long time and led to mistakes. Sometimes people paid a scribe, a professional writer, to do this, or short works could be carved into blocks of wood. When Johannes Gutenberg introduced his printing press, copies of work could be made quickly and cheaply, and became available to more people than ever before.

A secret invention

Gutenberg was born in Mainz, Germany, around 1398, the son of a rich merchant. Little is known of his life until he announced his great invention, which he had been working on in secret: the printing press.

This press was made in 1811, but it works in a similar way to Gutenberg's

When the press is lowered, the forme and tympan are pressed together and the page is printed

Metal letters are arranged in a tray called a forme and then covered in ink

◄◄ BRIGHT SPARKS

Sometime before 200 C.E., carved blocks of wood were first used in China to print patterns on to fabric. Then in 1045, Pi Cheng invented movable type that could be used to print text. However, the Chinese language has so many characters that the process was very complicated, and the idea did not catch on.

Printing press

Printing breakthrough

Gutenberg's press was the first in Europe to use movable type. This means that, instead of carving a new block for each page, letters were simply slotted into place in a tray, or forme. As many pages as required were printed from this, and then the letters were taken apart and used again. This Bible is one of the first books that Gutenberg produced with his printing press.

Gutenberg's Bible had elaborate hand-painted decoration

The lever turns a screw to raise and lower the press

Paper is placed in a wooden frame called a tympan

The tympan is on hinges, so that when it is pushed down, the paper it holds is pressed on to the inked metal letters in the tympan

Once the tympan has been folded down on to the forme, both are moved under the press

Changing the world

At the time, individual wooden print blocks were carved laboriously by hand, but with Gutenberg's press entire books could be printed cheaply and quickly. Suddenly, knowledge and stories could be copied easily. As a result, there were rapid advances in education and a great sharing of knowledge and ideas.

The spread of the press

Gutenberg's idea quickly caught on, and printing presses appeared rapidly all around Europe. By 1500, 236 towns in Europe had at least one, and around 20 million books had been printed: a staggering number, given that there were only around 70 million people in Europe.

Printing presses could produce as much material in one day as a scribe could in one year

The need for speed

A faster press means cheaper books, so over the centuries many people have worked on ways to speed up Gutenberg's invention.

Steam power

In 1811, Germans Friedrich König and Andreas Bauer demonstrated a high-speed press driven by steam. It could print more than 15 pages per minute.

Setting the type

Invented by Ottmar Mergenthaler in 1886, the Linotype machine had a keyboard that allowed its operator to assemble letters into lines of words (typesetting) automatically, rather than having to do this by hand.

Printing today

Modern printers are computer-controlled and fully automatic. Paper is moved, folded, and stapled entirely by machine.

SEE ALSO World Wide Web 44 · Money 120 · Newspaper 224

Whatever name it goes by, the smallest room in the house is also one of the most important. Today's flushing toilets and massive sewage systems are much more hygienic than the chamber pots and other hazardous waste removal habits they replaced. By removing human waste safely, toilets have saved countless lives. Our modern toilets also tend to be more convenient, more private, and a lot less smelly than their predecessors.

Royal flush

Sir John Harington's 1596 Ajax is usually considered the first modern flushing toilet. It used levers and weights to pour water from a cistern, and to open a valve that let waste flow away. Harington installed one for his godmother, Queen Elizabeth I of England, who found it rather noisy. Few people saw any point in the toilet, so it did not catch on.

Water was held in a cistern and flowed into the bowl through this inlet

The lip spread the water around the pan

Waste was piped to a sewer or other drainage system

The Unitas, 1883, produced by Thomas Twyford

The Unitas model was so popular in Russia that *unitaz* became a Russian word for toilet

Twyford's stunning toilets were all ceramic—earlier toilets were encased in wood

◀◀ BRIGHT SPARKS

Toilets built over dug pits were around long before flushing toilets and are still common in some parts of the world. But, although most toilets would have been basic, archaeologists have found a 2,000-year-old flushing toilet in the tomb of a Han Chinese king.

Flushing toilet

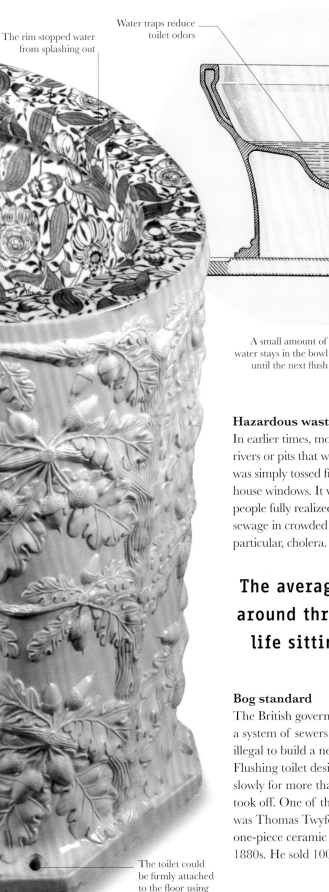

The rim stopped water from splashing out

Water traps reduce toilet odors

Gases are trapped behind the water

A small amount of water stays in the bowl until the next flush

Toilets can drain straight down, like this, or feed into gently sloping pipes

The toilet could be firmly attached to the floor using bolts or screws

Hazardous waste

In earlier times, most human waste went into rivers or pits that were emptied by hand. Much was simply tossed from chamber pots out of house windows. It wasn't until the 1850s that people fully realized the connection between sewage in crowded cities and diseases—in particular, cholera.

The average person spends around three years of their life sitting on the toilet

Bog standard

The British government began building a system of sewers and in 1875 made it illegal to build a new house without a toilet. Flushing toilet design, which had advanced slowly for more than two centuries, suddenly took off. One of the most successful inventors was Thomas Twyford, who made the first one-piece ceramic (pottery) toilets in the 1880s. He sold 100,000 in the first five years.

Sewage solutions

Toilets and sewage systems date back to some of the world's earliest cities. The people of the Indus Valley built the world's first-known drainage system, which connected every house to the central drains. Ancient Rome also had a complex sewage system similar to those of today.

Drain away

Around 5,000 years ago, city-dwellers in Pakistan's Indus Valley probably poured water down toilets to flush them. Drains carried waste away from where people lived, keeping their cities much cleaner and protecting them from some diseases.

At your convenience

The ancient Romans built excellent sewage systems, although their shared toilets may have been too public for our tastes. After the collapse of the Roman Empire, the technology was abandoned for centuries.

SEE ALSO Antibiotics 14 · Vaccination 18

From the late 1800s onward, inventors all over the world struggled to make the same dream come true: they were searching for a way to transmit moving pictures into the home. Working systems did not appear until the 1920s, and Scotsman John Logie Baird gave the first public demonstration of television in 1925. However, his success didn't last long.

Baird's "Tin Stove" Televisor went on sale in 1930—only around 1,000 sets were sold

The disk gave the Baird Televisor its distinctive shape

This knob switched on the disk and roughly controlled its speed

This control adjusted the speed exactly to steady the image

This spinning disk, invented by Paul Nipkow in 1884, was at the heart of Baird's invention

Early pioneers

In the 1920s, inventors all over the world were building television systems. In the U.S.A., Charles Francis Jenkins built a mechanical system, while American Philo Farnsworth and Russian Vladimir Zworykin worked separately on electronic versions, as did Isaac Schoenberg in Great Britain and Kenjiro Takayanagi in Japan.

Television

How Baird's TV worked

The signal the TV receives makes the brightness of a bulb change very quickly. The viewer watches the bulb through a spiral pattern of holes in a rapidly spinning disk, and the moving holes and changing brightness combine to form a tiny moving image. A lens makes this image bigger.

▶▶ **TOMORROW'S WORLD**

This Cell Regza television can show many channels on its screen at the same time. In the future, televisions are likely to be much more "interactive," allowing viewers to zoom in and track favorite actors or athletes, or even automatically record them when they are transmitted.

This small screen displayed the moving images

Baird's defeat

Baird's televisions were mechanical devices, based on spinning disks. For a while, the BBC sent broadcasts both to them and to competing electronic TV sets. The Baird system was abandoned in 1937, and the superior electronic system became widespread.

Televisor images were in color—red: the red light came from the neon bulbs that Baird used

The first public TV broadcasts could be watched and listened to—but not at the same time

A separate radio receiver was connected to the Televisor to pick up TV broadcasts

The logo of the Baird Company was Earth in a cloud

Television today

In less than a century, televisions have developed from unreliable devices, showing fuzzy black and white images, to big, bright panels with clear images in full color. In many countries, there is a television in almost every home.

SEE ALSO LCD 48 · Radio 116 · Kinetoscope 230 · Video games 234

From script to screen

Turning a script into a television show is a complicated operation involving many people and places. But it is also a very expensive process, so it is vital that it is completed in time and on budget. The executive producer—the person in charge of the entire operation—decides who will work as part of the team that puts the show together and is responsible for the finished product.

Bringing stories to life

We all see the cast of actors who appear in a television show, but there are also people, known as the crew, who work behind the scenes to plan and film it. The director's job is to guide the cast and crew as they make a writer's script come alive on the screen. A script editor is also needed, to rewrite words or change scenes that are too long or expensive. When the filming is complete, editors turn the filmed scenes into a show fit for television.

Planning and scripting
The first stage is to write the script and agree how it will be filmed, as well as who will be working on it.

Pre-production
Next, the filming of each scene is carefully planned, sets are built, actors are cast, and stunts and special effects are prepared.

Production
Most of the filming takes place in the production phase—part in studios and part on location, as shown here.

TV shows for all

There are many types of television shows. Scripted shows include soap operas, dramas, documentaries, and many children's shows. Others, such as sports coverage and chat shows, are unscripted, although presenters and researchers plan and prepare topics and questions in advance. News and magazine shows tend to mix scripted material with live interviews. While some TV channels offer a range of shows, others specialize in just one type, such as cartoons or music. Most TV channels make money by charging companies to advertise during commercial breaks.

Television studio

Set designers change the look of a studio to suit a particular show. Using scenery and props they can recreate almost any environment, from colorful jungles to kitchens or caves.

TV control room

From the control room, the director compares and changes views from different cameras, with the help of a technical director. Sound is also monitored, and instructions are given to the cast and crew.

Post-production

In post-production, the film segments are cut and joined together. Music is added, along with other sound and visual effects.

Broadcasting

Finally, the show is broadcast by a TV channel. Many are also sold abroad and may be released on DVD later.

> **Television enables you to be entertained in your home by people you wouldn't have in your home**
>
> David Frost, British television presenter and producer

The discovery that some materials produce electricity when light falls on them was made in 1839, but the first solar cell was not built until 1883, when American inventor Charles Fritts made one from gold and selenium. But, because it did not work well, it was not very practical, and it took almost a century before really effective devices could be developed.

◀◀ TOMORROW'S WORLD

In 2008, Chinese scientists copied the patterns of ridges on butterfly wings and used them to make light-absorbing electronic devices. They found that the patterns allowed more light to be captured, so solar cells built in this way should be more efficient (better at turning sunlight into electricity).

Sun power

All materials contain electrons, which are tiny particles that each carry an electrical charge. Solar cells are made of materials called semiconductors, in which some electrons are only loosely held in place. The electrons move when light shines on the cell, and this produces electricity.

Solar challenge

There are two main challenges to making an effective solar cell: it needs to absorb as much light as possible and then to turn it into as much electricity as it can. Hot deserts can make ideal settings for solar cell arrays like this one, as the land is empty and barren and of little use for other purposes.

These arrays are angled to catch maximum sunlight

Each solar cell only produces a tiny amount of electricity, so they are usually used in large numbers

Each of the individual rectangles is called a module—a solar cell array is the entire set of rectangles

Solar cell

Made to measure

Solar cells are clean and quiet and are especially useful where only a little electricity is needed because, unlike power plants, it is as easy to build a small array as it is to build a large one. They are also so light and tough that they can be used even on movable objects such as backpacks and briefcases.

Catching the Sun

Not all solar-powered systems use solar cells. Curved mirrors are sometimes used to concentrate the Sun's heat and use it to boil water. A generator then uses the steam to produce electricity.

Solar cells are very reliable so they need few repairs, but they do need to be kept clean to work well

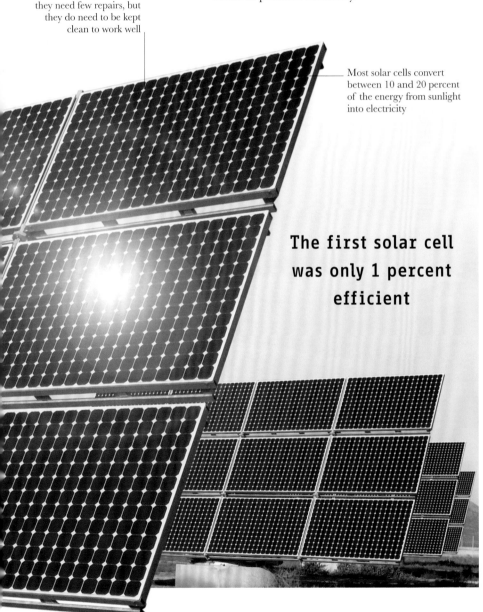

Most solar cells convert between 10 and 20 percent of the energy from sunlight into electricity

The first solar cell was only 1 percent efficient

Cheaper and better

Over the last few years, solar cells have become cheaper and more efficient and are now used in many applications.

Phone top-ups

Solar power is ideal for charging cell phone batteries when there is no electrical outlet available. Laptops can be charged in the same way.

Cheaper meters

Parking meters are sometimes fitted with solar cells. This is because they are used outside where there is plenty of sunlight and need very little electricity to operate.

Flying by light

This experimental remote-controlled plane uses solar power to fly. It contains batteries so that it can keep flying for a while even after sunset.

SEE ALSO Cell phone 140

Clean energy

Today, most of the energy that runs our homes, cars, and factories comes from burning coal, gas, or oil. These are called fossil fuels, because they are the remains of plants or animals that were buried underground millions of years ago. There are two main problems with these fuels: when they burn, they produce gases and tiny particles called pollutants, which damage our health, other living things, and our planet, and they are running out.

Looking for alternatives

Scientists have been searching for different ways to meet our growing demands for energy. Nuclear power, for example, is one alternative. However, nuclear power plants are expensive to build, and their hazardous waste is difficult to dispose of safely. Renewable energy sources, such as solar power, are ones that will not run out, although they may be expensive to set up, and often have other disadvantages.

Planet power

Earth is hot inside, and in Iceland the heat is so close to the surface that it warms surface water. Shown in this picture is a geothermal power plant that uses the heated water to generate electricity. Most of Iceland's energy comes from under the ground.

Tidal energy

The water levels at coasts and estuaries (river mouths) rise and fall with the twice daily tides. Tidal barrages, such as this one on France's Rance River, have turbines that are driven by the flow of falling tide water. The movement is then converted into electricity.

Hydroelectricity

Most of the world's renewable energy comes from hydroelectric systems, which make electricity from the power of falling water. These are reliable, clean, and cheap to run. However, building a large hydroelectric system usually requires a huge amount of concrete (which releases greenhouse gases) and also disrupts the local environment for both wildlife and people. China currently produces more hydroelectricity than any other country.

Arrowrock Dam

Water pours through the Arrowrock Dam in Idaho. When it was built in 1915, it was the world's tallest dam.

> **"Someday we will harness the rise and fall of the tides and imprison the rays of the Sun"**
>
> Thomas Edison, American scientist and inventor

Biogas

In certain conditions, rotting plants and manure produce methane gas that can be burned, or stored, and used to run special cars. Biogas digesters, like this one in India, also provide the ideal conditions for methane to be produced and used for cooking and lighting.

Electricity was an exciting and mysterious phenomenon in the 1700s, and scientists argued about what it really was. Some thought that it was closely connected with life itself, but when he built the world's first battery, Italian physicist Alessandro Volta proved that electricity could be made using chemicals. It was to be some years before people found practical uses for electricity, but when they did, batteries became vital.

The first battery

Alessandro Volta's invention was soon called the Voltaic Pile—and that's what it was, a pile of copper and zinc disks, each one separated by a piece of cloth soaked in salty water. The more disks used, the higher the voltage produced. It wasn't until 1896 that batteries went on sale to the public.

Glass rods supported the column of disks

Electric current flowed along this wire

Copper and zinc disks

Voltaic Pile

Modern batteries are standardized—this AA battery produces 1.5 volts

Alkaline
Mignon LR6 AA AM3
MN 1500 1.5V

Dead but moving

In the 1790s, Italian Luigi Galvani made the legs of dead frogs twitch by touching the nerves with metal instruments. He said there was "animal electricity" in the frogs. But Volta showed that the twitches were caused by using different metals, as in the Voltaic Pile.

How batteries work

Like a heart pumping blood around the human body, a battery uses the energy stored in chemicals to "push" electrical currents around a circuit. The voltage of a battery is a measure of how hard this pushing force is.

Battery

These organic radical batteries are bendable, less than $^1/_{25}$ in (1 mm) thick, and are fully charged in less than 30 seconds. They do not use harmful metal chemicals to make electricity, so they can be safely thrown away.

Storing batteries in the fridge makes them last longer

The chemicals inside batteries are harmful and can cause pollution, so batteries should be recycled

Modern batteries are coated in steel

This is the positive (+) terminal

This is the battery's negative (–) terminal

This is a nine-volt battery

Rechargable batteries
After a while, batteries go flat, which means that they run out of energy and can no longer produce electricity. Some batteries can't be used again, but many can be connected to a source of electricity and recharged.

All types of batteries
Today, there are many types of batteries, which use different chemicals to produce electricity. These have different practical uses.

Lead-acid
Cars use lead-acid batteries. Although heavy, they are very powerful and can be recharged by the car's engine.

Zinc-air
Tiny zinc-air batteries are used to provide the power for hearing aids. They need oxygen from the air in order to work.

Lithium-ion
These batteries are often used in laptops, cell phones, and electric cars. They are rechargeable, lightweight, and long-lasting.

SEE ALSO Telegraph 40 · Electric motor 68 · Solar cell 92 · Electric car 172

Microprocessors are all around you—in your iPod, phone, television, and digital watch. Cars use dozens of microprocessors, and our lives would be very different without them—many gadgets would be much larger, more expensive, and less reliable. Some would not exist at all. In fact, this little device may have had a bigger impact on our daily lives than any other scientific discovery of the last 50 years.

The first microprocessor was the size of a fingernail and had the same computing power as most computers of the time, which filled large rooms

All cell phones contain microprocessors

Thin wires connect the chip to other equipment

Microprocessors and other components are wired together on a circuit board

Up to 30 layers of different materials are laid over pieces of pure silicon

Some modern microprocessors have 291 million transistors

Chips and processors
A microprocessor is a type of microchip (silicon chip)—a piece of equipment made mostly of silicon and so small that its details can only be seen with a microscope. Microprocessors work like tiny computers, controlling equipment, carrying out calculations, processing data, and making decisions. This is an Intel 8086 microprocessor, introduced in 1978. The 8086 was used in NASA's space shuttles.

▶▶ TOMORROW'S WORLD

One day, surgeons may implant microprocessors into people's brains to take over the jobs of damaged cells. Conditions like blindness and deafness, and diseases that attack brain cells, could all be treated with this technology.

Microprocessor

Speedy developments

If vehicles had been developing since 1960 as quickly as microprocessor technology, today's cars would be extraordinary. They would have engines less than 0.1 in (3 mm) long and be capable of speeds of more than 240,000 mph (390,000 km/h)—while being so cheap that you could buy one with your allowance!

There are around 300 steps to making a single microprocessor

World's first

The first commercial microprocessor, the Intel 4004, was designed by Intel engineers Federico Faggin and Ted Hoff, of the American company Intel, and Masatoshi Shima of Busicom, a Japanese company. The Intel 4004 went on sale in 1971. It measured around 0.02 sq in (13 sq mm) and contained 2,300 transistors (a transistor is a device that controls and changes the flow of electricity).

SEE ALSO Robots 74 · Apple computer 102 · Cell phone 140 · GPS 190 · Video games 234

From valves to microprocessors

Many important electrical devices, including electric motors and generators, were invented in the 1800s. However, it was the development of electronics in the 1900s that has led to most of today's technology. Electronic parts control the movement of tiny particles called electrons to change the direction and strength of electric currents. A key development was the invention of the transistor. The first working version was built by American engineers Walter Brattain and John Bardeen in 1947. Together with project leader William Shockley, they were awarded the 1956 Nobel Prize in Physics for their breakthrough.

Thermionic valve
These were vacuum tubes that could change or halt the flow of electricity. They contained small heaters and glowed like lightbulbs. Shown above is the first thermionic valve.

Early devices
One of the first electronic inventions was the triode (a type of thermionic valve), patented by American Lee De Forest in 1908. It was an amplifier—a device that increased the strength of an electric signal—and was used to boost weak radio transmission. The first electronic devices were large and rather unreliable. Being hand-built, they were also expensive. Their modern equivalents are designed with the help of computers and built by machines.

> **We are in an electronic technology age now and it's about time we put away the old stuff**
>
> Monica Edwards, English author of children's books

Then and now
Until the middle of the last century, the use of electronics was mainly limited to radio, recording, and movies. Now it is an essential part of most technology. Many early devices contained vacuum tubes—containers with the air sucked out. We now make most electronic parts from silicon, a substance that we can alter to use in controlling electric current. Tiny in comparison to vacuum tubes, they are also much better at their jobs.

Early computer
Many early electronic computers, like this one, had thousands of thermionic valves. The valves needed to be replaced frequently, as they often burned out.

Transistor

Transistors do the same job as valves but are much smaller, tougher, and use less power. This is the first working transistor, created by Brattain, Bardeen, and Shockley in 1947.

Microchip

This is the first microchip—an integrated circuit with different electronic components on the same piece of silicon. It had just five components; today's chips have hundreds of millions. Microchips went on sale in 1961.

Microprocessor

Launched in 1971, this is the first commercial microprocessor, the Intel 4004. In an area the size of a fingernail, it could carry out 92,000 operations per second and perform many of the functions of a computer.

Transistor radio

Radios were very popular in the 1900s, but they only became really portable with transistors. In the 1960s, radios were often called transistors.

Pacemaker

Microchips are small and reliable. As a result, pacemakers like this one could be developed. Pacemakers are implanted into people's bodies to help their hearts beat properly.

Cell phone

The first cell phones were developed in the 1970s, but now around half the people on Earth have at least one. They all contain microprocessors.

Unlike most computers of
its time, the Apple I used
a television set (connected
here) to display its results

The owner of this Apple I
was eager to let the world
know that it was an Apple

Ready-made machine

Most low-cost computers were sold
in the form of dozens of components
that had to be wired together. The
Apple I was a complete circuit board,
which only needed to be connected to
other units. Hand-built by Wozniak
and Jobs, only around 200 Apple I
computers were made.

The Apple I had
no mouse, color,
sound, or graphics

These clips would hold
a small television set

A BASIC language

The Apple I was popular partially
because it could be programmed in
BASIC. This has simpler rules than most
other computer languages, which makes
it easy to learn and use. Users wrote their
own programs—often text-based games.
A tape recorder could be plugged into the
Apple, so that the programs could be
saved on cassette tapes.

**In 1976, there were many large
computers in offices** and factories but
very few computers in people's homes. Steve
Jobs and Steve Wozniak helped change all that
when they came up with a simple design for making
computers. Their first computer, Apple I, didn't sell
well. However, their next model, the Apple II, was
very successful, and soon it was being used in homes
all over the world.

Only capital
letters were used

Apple computer

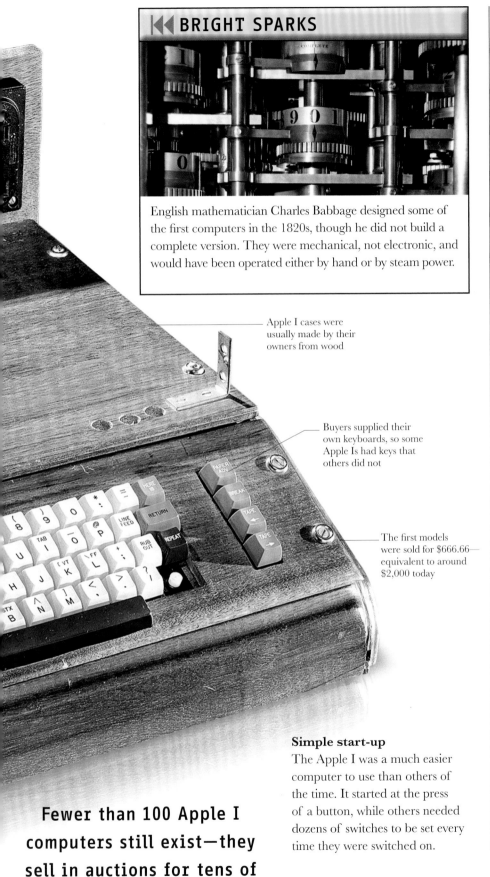

BRIGHT SPARKS

English mathematician Charles Babbage designed some of the first computers in the 1820s, though he did not build a complete version. They were mechanical, not electronic, and would have been operated either by hand or by steam power.

Apple I cases were usually made by their owners from wood

Buyers supplied their own keyboards, so some Apple Is had keys that others did not

The first models were sold for $666.66— equivalent to around $2,000 today

Simple start-up
The Apple I was a much easier computer to use than others of the time. It started at the press of a button, while others needed dozens of switches to be set every time they were switched on.

Fewer than 100 Apple I computers still exist—they sell in auctions for tens of thousands of dollars

Milestones in computing
It is less than a century since the first electronic computers were built, and since then they have developed at an amazing speed.

Pilot Ace, 1950
The Pilot Ace was one of the world's first successful computers. It was built by English computer pioneer Alan Turing. Users would buy time on it to carry out their calculations.

IBM 5150, 1981
The IBM Personal Computer was very popular, and other manufacturers soon built similar machines, with separate keyboards, monitors, base units, and printers.

Handheld devices
Today, many people use small devices that combine the functions of a computer with a cell phone, camera, and MP3 player.

SEE ALSO World Wide Web 44 · Microprocessor 98

Wozniak and Jobs

Steve Wozniak and Steve Jobs built the Apple I for fun—but Jobs also loved the idea of starting a company, so together they set up the Apple Computer Company in 1976. At first, they only expected to sell the Apple I at their local computer club—but a $50,000 order from a local computer store was the start of bigger things.

Jobs and Wozniak meet

Wozniak and Jobs joined the Homebrew Computer Club in 1974. There, they were inspired by computer systems built by fellow hobbyists, such as this one.

Homemade Homebrew computer system

Garage company

Deciding to develop their own computer and sell its circuit boards, they started designing the Apple I in Jobs' bedroom, and then built it in the garage.

The Jobs' family home

Apple I

The pair ended up producing these Apple I circuit boards—they couldn't afford the parts, so they promised to pay later, when they sold the boards.

Apple I boards

Apple II

Jobs and Wozniak learned so much from building and selling the Apple I that their follow-up computer, the Apple II, was a much greater success.

Apple II computer

Success

Wozniak and Jobs became rich, successful, and famous, and they continued to develop new Apple computers for many years.

Jobs (left) and Wozniak (right) in 1984

Going global

Apple computers are used throughout the world. The Apple company is so successful that it now has offices in many countries.

Apple iMac

A successful brand

When Wozniak (far left) and Jobs asked an advertising company for advice, the agency thought that "Apple" wasn't the right name for a computer. But Wozniak and Jobs disagreed—apples are healthy and found in the home, just like their computers should be. Now, the Apple brand is one of the most successful in the world.

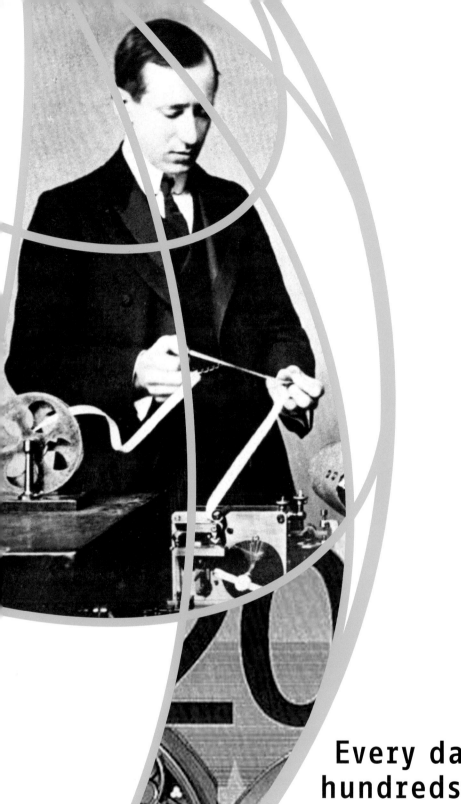

Handy Gadgets

Every day, we use hundreds of amazing inventions that make our lives easier. Some are so familiar and easy to use that we hardly even think about them. But imagine life without the things in this chapter. . .

The door is coated
with a metal mesh to
prevent microwaves from
escaping into the kitchen

The interior of the cooking chamber is
lined with a conductive material, such as
metal, which bounces the microwave
energy back into the oven and food

The turntable rotates
to ensure that food
is evenly cooked

Food may be cooked
in a bag, which is
made from a material
that remains stable at
high heat

One of 20th century's most useful gadgets, the
microwave cooks or heats food in a fraction of the time taken by a
conventional oven. It also reduces waste, since we can reheat food in
convenient amounts. But the microwave is more than simply a time-saver
for people with busy lives: it can also provide a healthier way of preparing
food, since it preserves more nutrients during the cooking process.

Microwave

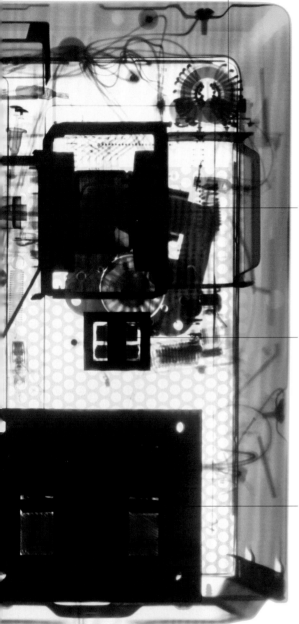

This coil helps prevent interference from the oven getting into the electricity supply

The magnetron tube uses the voltage to emit a stream of microwaves, which are directed by a wave guide into the cooking chamber

The fan prevents the magnetron assembly from overheating

A high-voltage transformer raises the household voltage to a very high level, which is then supplied to the magnetron tube

Making microwaves

At the heart of the microwave oven is the magnetron, which has positive and negative electrodes between the poles of a strong magnet. Electrons (negatively charged particles) from the negative electrode are attracted to the positive electrode by a high voltage. The magnet makes the electrons spiral around the positive electrode, creating microwaves.

The latest microwave ovens connect to the Internet—so you can browse recipes or e-mail while you wait

Catch that wave

An antenna in the magnetron picks up the microwaves and sends them along the waveguide (a metal tube) into the oven chamber. A rotating paddle in the ceiling helps spread the waves evenly. The metal-lined walls reflect waves back into the food.

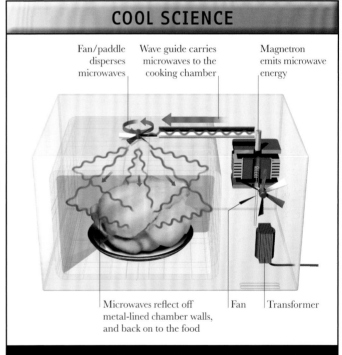

COOL SCIENCE

Fan/paddle disperses microwaves

Wave guide carries microwaves to the cooking chamber

Magnetron emits microwave energy

Microwaves reflect off metal-lined chamber walls, and back on to the food

Fan

Transformer

The microwave oscillates 2.45 billion cycles per second. In the cooking chamber, each water molecule in the food tries to remain "lined up" with the wave; it does so because a water molecule is naturally dipolar—positively charged at one end and negatively charged at the other.

Cooked by waggle

Food only cooks properly in a microwave if that food contains water. Caught in the microwave field, the water molecules "waggle" as they try to keep up with the waves. They do so very fast, and it's the speed of the waggle that raises the temperature, which cooks the surrounding food.

SEE ALSO Refrigerator 64

The first microwave

The microwave oven basically works rather like a radar transmitter—which is not surprising because its inventor, Percy Spencer, had helped to design and manufacture the ground-, ship-, and aircraft-based radar sets that helped the Allies win World War II. Microwave ovens have come a long way since Spencer's first inventions of the 1940s—and they're a lot smaller, too!

Inspired by chocolate

Spencer hit on the oven idea during a radar-related research project in 1945. While testing a magnetron tube, he found that a chocolate bar in his pocket had melted. He decided to investigate. First, he tried popcorn, which duly popped. Then he cut a hole in a kettle, placed an egg in it, and pointed a magnetron at the hole. The egg exploded in the face of a colleague who was watching the experiment!

Percy Spencer

As an inquisitive teenager, American Percy Spencer taught himself the basics of electrical engineering, later picking up radio telegraphy skills in the U.S. Navy. He began making wireless equipment and in the 1920s joined the new Raytheon Company.

" When the chocolate bar melted. . . Flash! The light went on "

Laurence K. Marshall, cofounder of Raytheon Company

The first microwave

Spencer saw that the magnetron could be used as a heat source, and his research led to the first Raytheon microwave ovens. Early models were huge and impractical: they cost $5,000 and became so hot that they required water-cooling. By 1947, the company was offering the first Radarange; this was still the size of a fridge and cost $2,000–3,000, but people had begun to take an interest in its potential. In 1967, Amana (a company owned by Raytheon) released the first truly domestic Radarange model. It cost less than $500 and fit on a kitchen countertop.

Fridge-size microwave

Though innovative, Raytheon's original microwave oven was too bulky to find a market. It was also very expensive, so initial sales were disappointing.

Countertop microwave

The first Amana Radarange microwave oven used ordinary home electricity and had just two buttons, "Start" and "Light." It also included two control knobs, one for cooking times up to five minutes and the other for longer cooking times up to 25 minutes.

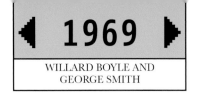
Digital cameras have transformed the way in which the world takes pictures. The technology at the heart of digital cameras has almost entirely replaced photographic film in science and industry and enabled astronomers to see objects in space that were once invisible. Back on Earth, sharing digital photographs using cell phones, e-mail, and websites has become so easy that it is changing the way we record our daily lives—and even shapes the news and politics.

The user looked through this lens to line up the picture

Chemical to digital
Conventional cameras, such as this 1901 Eastman Kodak, use chemical film to record images. In the mid-1900s, governments wanted to take pictures from spy satellites, but sending film to Earth wasn't possible. A new technology was needed to record images on a computer and send them as digital signals.

The lens focuses the incoming image on to light-sensitive film

All digital cameras need electricity to work

Eastman Kodak

Chemicals in the film react to the light, creating a record of the image

NASA's PS1 telescope uses a 1,300-megapixel camera to search for nearby asteroids

COOL SCIENCE

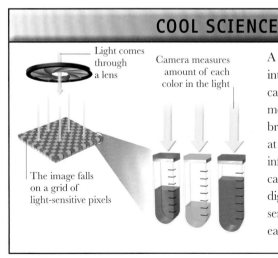

Light comes through a lens

The image falls on a grid of light-sensitive pixels

Camera measures amount of each color in the light

A CCD breaks pictures up into millions of tiny squares called pixels. The camera measures the color and brightness of light arriving at each pixel and stores the information so a computer can recreate the image. A digital photograph is really a series of numbers describing each pixel that it holds.

Digital camera

Silicon steps up

The breakthrough came when Willard Boyle and George Smith invented the charge-coupled device (CCD) in 1969. They realized these light-sensitive silicon chips could record images electronically. In 1973, a Kodak engineer used a CCD to make the first digital camera. It was as big as a toaster and took almost one minute to record and display a 0.01-megapixel photo.

Many cameras can also record moving images

CCDs are made of silicon, a material that can respond to light

Most digital cameras have a liquid crystal display instead of a viewfinder

The focus-assist lamp helps the camera focus in low light

This button controls the many functions of the camera

The flash brightens the image when there is not enough light

The display does the opposite of the CCD—changing a digital code into thousands of pixels to make an image

Unlike film, the photographer can see the images immediately by pressing this button

A 12.1-megapixel camera has 12.1 million pixels in its CCD

The camera adjusts the shutter speed and aperture size to control the amount of light reaching the CCD

Digital imaging

Today's digital cameras are smaller and faster, with more pixels and larger memories—but they still use CCD technology. CCDs are 100 times more light-sensitive than film, transforming the way that scientists study the Universe. They are also used in scanners, photocopiers, bar code readers, and digital video cameras.

This camera has a zoom lens, which makes an object or person seem closer

These figures indicate the range of possible distances from the lens to the sensor

SEE ALSO LCD 48 · Microprocessor 98 · Bar code 128

Until glasses with magnifying lenses were invented in the early 1200s, it wasn't possible to correct bad eyesight. By enabling scholars, writers, and craftspeople to work into old age, glasses brought about huge advances in science, the arts, and engineering. In the 1450s, with the invention of the printing press, cheap mass-produced reading glasses became popular. Glasses with lenses for seeing distant objects were also developed.

Benjamin Franklin

COOL SCIENCE

People didn't know how glasses worked until Johannes Kepler explained it in 1604. Magnifying lenses (top) help far-sighted eyes by bending light inward, to focus on the back of the eye. Near-sighted eyes focus too strongly, so they need lenses that bend incoming light outward (bottom).

Double vision
Different lenses are needed for seeing near and distant objects. The American statesman and inventor Benjamin Franklin disliked switching glasses when he wanted to read. So he used some "double spectacles," with both types of lens in one frame: they became today's bifocals.

Nose pinchers
The first glasses had no arms—and were held in front of the eyes. Others, called pince-nez (nose-pinchers), perched on the nose. People had to try different pairs of lenses until they found ones that worked. In the 1800s, doctors and glasses makers began examining eyes to prescribe lenses of the correct strength.

Plastic or glass lenses are often coated with chemicals to improve performance

Glasses

Plastic fantastic

During the last century, new materials transformed glasses from medical aids into fashion accessories. Plastics enabled us to make light, colorful frames, and frameless glasses with lenses held by nylon cords. Memory metals were developed, which make frames spring back into shape when squashed. People began buying expensive designer models, and some people who had perfect eyesight even began wearing glasses with plain glass instead of lenses.

Glasses with arms that rest on the ears first appeared around 1730

The frame holds the lenses at the right height and distance from the eyes

Nosepads spread the weight of the glasses, making them more comfortable

High-tech lenses

We now use plastic to make lenses as well as frames. Plastic lenses are thinner, lighter, and more robust than glass. They can be coated with special chemicals to make them scratch proof and even to become self-darkening, so that they protect eyes from the Sun's harmful ultraviolet (UV) rays.

Improving eyesight

For around 600 years, glasses were the only way to correct many vision problems. However, some people find glasses inconvenient or prefer not to change their appearance by wearing them. So eye specialists began to develop new ways to improve eyesight.

Invisible lenses

Lenses that sit in contact with the eye were invented in 1887. But these were thick, heavy glass and couldn't be worn for long periods. More than 100 million people now wear the more comfortable plastic contact lenses.

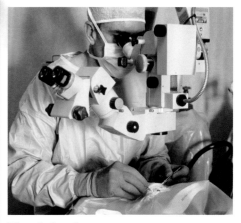

Plastic implants

In just 20 minutes, a surgeon can replace a natural lens with a plastic one while the patient is awake! This has helped millions of people with cataracts (cloudy lenses) to see.

Around 150 million Americans—almost half the U.S. population—wear glasses

SEE ALSO Microscope 20 · Printing press 84 · Sunglasses 236

Radio began in 1888, when Heinrich Hertz produced and detected invisible electromagnetic waves that could travel through space just like visible light. In 1901, Italian Guglielmo Marconi captured the world's attention by using these radio waves to carry a Morse code message across the Atlantic Ocean. A flood of uses followed, from ship-to-shore communication to public broadcasting, radar, and space satellites. Today's wireless gadgets, such as games consoles and cell phones, use radio.

Radio waves carried words spoken on the Moon 238,900 miles (384,400 km) into homes

The receiver inside the radio decodes radio waves that are captured by the metal antenna

Scientists have developed tiny "intelligent" radio systems to monitor hospital equipment, such as blood bags. Signals sent to a central unit can warn doctors if the blood gets too warm or if the bag has the wrong blood type for the patient.

Sending signals

A radio transmitter generates radio waves using electrical currents. It then alters the waves so that they carry information. The height or the length of the waves is varied to represent sounds like speech or music. Changing the height is called amplitude modulation (AM), and changing the length is called frequency modulation (FM).

Radio

Receiving signals

Like all electromagnetic radiation, radio waves travel at the speed of light—around 186,400 miles (300,000 km) per second. Thousands of radio signals are passing you right now. Radio receivers decode the signals and reproduce the sounds that are transmitted. Inside a receiver, devices called transistors change and amplify electrical signals. They convert radio signals into currents that activate a loudspeaker.

Digital signals can carry extra information, such as the name of the radio station you are listening to

Clockwork radios are powered by winding them up, bringing radio to poor and remote communities that don't have a reliable source of electricity

Millions of radio signals arrive at a radio every second—the tuner selects just one frequency, or signal, at a time

Electric currents make the loudspeaker move, producing sound waves that we can hear

Radio in our world

Many types of information are carried by radio signals. At first, they were used for private communication. In the 1920s, signals began to be broadcast to the public.

Listening in

A radio broadcast is a one-way transmission, bringing news and entertainment to our homes, cars, and wireless gadgets. Radio waves carry pictures as well as sound to televisions.

Over and out

Two-way radios send as well as receive signals, so users can have a conversation. They are ideal for communicating with planes, boats, and emergency vehicles.

Radio control

Radio-controlled toys receive signals from a transmitter in the handset. Rather than coding for sounds, pulses of information activate motors to make the toys move.

SEE ALSO Television 88 · Cell phone 140

117

Marconi

Guglielmo Marconi was not the first person to send signals using radio waves, but he proved that radio worked over long distances and developed practical applications that changed the world. By devoting his life to improving wireless technology, Marconi brought us ship-to-shore communication, radar, and public broadcasting—becoming rich and famous in the process.

Record keeper
Marconi (left) shared his experiments and triumphs with George Kemp (right), his chief assistant and friend. Kemp kept an excellent diary of their work.

Tuning signals

As radio signals were sent over longer distances, a problem emerged. Signals sent from different places could overlap and interfere with each other. Marconi developed transmitters (left) and receivers that could be tuned to send and receive radio waves of just one wavelength.

> ❝ Every day sees humanity more victorious in the struggle with space and time ❞
>
> Guglielmo Marconi

Early experiments

Marconi's radio experiments began in his parents' attic in Italy, where he built equipment to send simple Morse code signals up to 1¼ miles (2 km). Later, Marconi worked in the U.K., capturing media attention with a series of demonstrations. In 1897, Marconi formed a business to use his technology, and in 1901 he sent the first radio signal across the Atlantic Ocean.

Success story

Marconi, who had left school with no qualifications, won the Nobel Prize for Physics in 1909. His success continued, and his company played a vital role in both World Wars and helped develop radar. Marconi continued to improve wireless communication until he died in 1937. As a mark of respect, thousands of people lined the streets for his funeral, and the world's radio transmitters fell silent for two minutes.

Disaster at sea

Marconi's equipment allowed ships to stay in radio contact all the way across the Atlantic Ocean. In 1912, the *Titanic* disaster showed how important this was. After the ship struck an iceberg, radio operators sent distress calls to nearby ships, saving 700 lives.

Long-distance message

Marconi's patented tuning technology helped him achieve his dream of sending a radio signal across the Atlantic Ocean. On December 12, 1901, a Morse code signal from a huge transmitter in the U.K. (left) reached Marconi as he sat 1,800 miles (2,900 km) away in Canada.

Birth of broadcasting

By 1920, radio waves could carry speech and other sounds as well as Morse code. Marconi's company organized the world's first live music broadcast—a concert by the famous singer Dame Nellie Melba (left). The age of public broadcasting had begun.

People have used animal fur, coconuts, salt, dogs' teeth, and even human skulls as money

Ancient coins

The ancient kingdom of Lydia (now western Turkey) stamped coins from around 650 B.C.E. Called staters, these were made from gold, silver, or a mixture of the two, in a range of values. Soon, neighboring civilizations also began to use coins.

The Lydians authorized staters with stamps—often of animals—and shapes punched into the back

Lydian stater

This spade-shaped bubi could be threaded on to a necklace

Lady Liberty bears a torch and olive branch—symbols of enlightenment and peace

A bubi's markings included a clan name, place name, or weight

Tokens of the East

The Chinese also invented a system of coins, but how it developed is still a mystery. Chinese dynasties may have been making and using bubi—bronze castings shaped like miniature farming tools, such as spades and knives—as far back as the 700s B.C.E.

Ancient Chinese bubi

Gold Double Eagle, 1933

The coin is 97 percent gold and 3 percent copper

Money has been around in some form or other for more than 6,000 years. Early civilizations traded possessions for goods. But it was not always easy to pay with a barrel of barley or a cow, so instead people began to use lumps of rare metals or other precious objects as tokens of value. Around 2,500 years ago, these became standardized metal coins. We still use coins today, together with banknotes. One day we might spend and receive all money electronically, and cash could become a thing of the past.

20 Euro banknote

The flag of Europe is printed on the front of the note

BCE ECB EZB EKT EKP

Euro users speak many languages, so values are only shown as numbers

20

Money

Paper money

The Chinese also invented paper money, beginning with credit slips—pieces of paper that the holder could use to pay taxes on tea and salt. They first printed official paper money in the 10th century. It was another 500 or 600 years before banknotes caught on in the Western world.

◄◄ BRIGHT SPARKS

Many ancient cultures used shells as money. Native American tribes shaped clam shells into wampum—beads that were then traded for goods. Wampum were precious because they took so long to make.

Collecting money

Coins tell us about other cultures, so numismatics (studying or collecting coins) can be fascinating. However, rare coins are usually expensive. The $20 Double Eagle coin seen here recently sold for $7.59 million, making it the world's most valuable coin.

These coins were melted down by the government, so only around 20 still exist

The note is part of a set of Euro banknotes picturing European architectural styles—this one has a Gothic design

The Euro is used in 16 different countries of the European Union (EU)

Paper engineering

In 1295, the explorer Marco Polo wrote that Chinese paper notes got so tattered that people often threw them away. Modern banknotes are much tougher. They are also packed with antiforgery devices.

Foiling the forgers

A hologram and a rainbow stripe appear when ultraviolet light is shone on this Malaysian banknote. Notes have had watermarks since the 1600s, but they may also have tiny letters that are only visible through a powerful lens or hidden pictures that change if they are photocopied.

Plastic cash

Most paper money is made from cotton and linen fibers. But Australia, New Zealand, and several Asian nations now print banknotes on a type of plastic. Tough and waterproof, the notes stay clean and last up to five times longer than paper ones.

SEE ALSO Credit card 122 · Cash register 124

Credit cards have changed how the world uses money, and few people now carry around large amounts of cash. Instead, thin pieces of plastic allow people to buy goods, pay bills, and take money out of banks almost anywhere in the world. Modern cards even have computer chips that are designed to keep the card holder's money and personal details safe.

In 2004, Californian Steve Borba jokingly applied for a credit card for his dog, Clifford, and received one

The name of the company that issues the card is printed on the front

A unique card number identifies the issuer and the card holder's account number

A smartcard's computer chip is always in the same position, so machines can read details from it

Buy now, pay later
From the 1910s, before credit cards were invented, U.S. businesses offered their customers storecards. They permitted valued customers to pay for goods at a later date. Storecards were a popular way to pay for fuel and hotel bills.

Charga-Plate

Personal details used to be printed on slips, as in the Charga-Plate system

Metal money
Stores began to club together and accept cards from others in their group. Devised in 1929, the Charga-Plate was a metal tag with the card holder's name, city, and state. It was used to print a record on a paper slip.

The date when the card expires (runs out) may be used as an extra security measure

Credit card

COOL SCIENCE

Holograms are pictures that appear in 3-D (three-dimensional). Making a hologram involves lasers, beam splitters, lenses, mirrors, and special film. Holograms make it very difficult to produce fake copies of credit cards.

Holograms are one of the many security systems used by banks

All credit cards are the same size: 3.37 x 2.13 in (85.60 x 53.98 mm)

A logo on the front shows the brand of the credit card

The plastic age
The first modern credit cards were introduced by Diners' Club, Inc. in the 1950s. Credit cards are issued by banks and allow people to pay over many months, or even years. As more businesses accepted cards, and banks worked together to electronically transfer money, plastic payments spread across the world.

Stripes or chips?
Modern credit cards still have details on the front. But they also store personal information in magnetic stripes and microprocessor chips. Stripes and chips enable machines to read information about the card holder's account.

Magstripes
Introduced in 1960, magnetic stripes store data, such as personal details. The data is stored by lining up tiny magnetic particles on plastic tape. The stripe is read by swiping it through a card reader.

Smart card chips
The chip is a microprocessor: it can handle digital information, just like a tiny computer. Card readers usually need a personal identification number (PIN) to access this personal information. This system is widely used in Europe.

SEE ALSO Laser 46 · Microprocessor 98 · Money 120 · Cash register 124

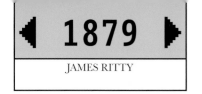

◄ 1879 ►

JAMES RITTY

In earlier times, store owners had little idea of how much stock they owned, how much they were selling, or which products customers actually wanted to buy. It was also too easy for cash to disappear from the drawer. James Ritty's invention, patented in 1879, changed all that, and as cash registers became more sophisticated, they made purchases easier, reduced theft, and put useful facts at owners' fingertips. Today's checkout machinery is one of the key tools used by manufacturers and retailers to keep customers happy. . . and to sell more goods!

The open cash drawer

Before registers were invented, money from sales went into the cash drawer. However, all too often dishonest cashiers simply stole cash or they gave credit and forgot to record it. In short, owners seldom knew whether they were making a profit or a loss and whether staff were honest.

◄◄ BRIGHT SPARKS

The abacus, or counting frame, has been used for at least 4,500 years. After the Sumerians first developed it, usage spread to the Egyptians, Greeks, and other ancient civilizations. This Chinese abacus may look simple, but it can perform multiplication and even square roots, as well as basic addition or subtraction. It dates from 2,200 years ago.

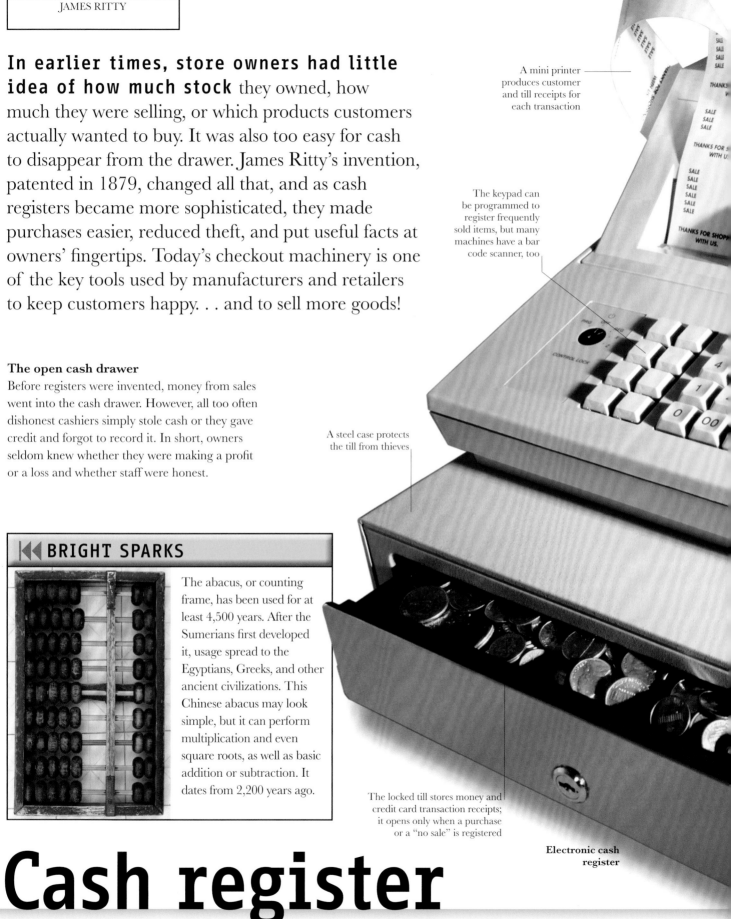

A mini printer produces customer and till receipts for each transaction

The keypad can be programmed to register frequently sold items, but many machines have a bar code scanner, too

A steel case protects the till from thieves

The locked till stores money and credit card transaction receipts; it opens only when a purchase or a "no sale" is registered

Electronic cash register

Cash register

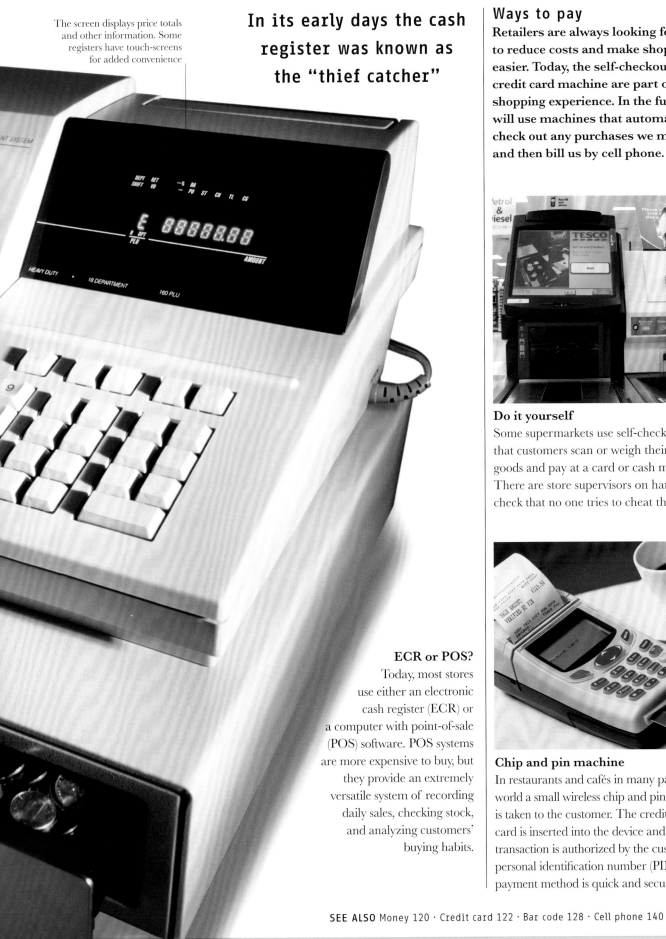

The screen displays price totals and other information. Some registers have touch-screens for added convenience

In its early days the cash register was known as the "thief catcher"

Ways to pay

Retailers are always looking for ways to reduce costs and make shopping easier. Today, the self-checkout and credit card machine are part of the shopping experience. In the future we will use machines that automatically check out any purchases we make and then bill us by cell phone.

Do it yourself

Some supermarkets use self-checkouts so that customers scan or weigh their own goods and pay at a card or cash machine. There are store supervisors on hand to check that no one tries to cheat the system.

ECR or POS?

Today, most stores use either an electronic cash register (ECR) or a computer with point-of-sale (POS) software. POS systems are more expensive to buy, but they provide an extremely versatile system of recording daily sales, checking stock, and analyzing customers' buying habits.

Chip and pin machine

In restaurants and cafés in many parts of the world a small wireless chip and pin machine is taken to the customer. The credit or debit card is inserted into the device and the transaction is authorized by the customer's personal identification number (PIN). This payment method is quick and secure.

SEE ALSO Money 120 · Credit card 122 · Bar code 128 · Cell phone 140

James Ritty

American James Ritty was worried. He ran a saloon bar in Dayton, Ohio but he never made much money because his dishonest staff kept stealing from the cash drawer. How could he stop them? The problem led him to invent Ritty's Incorruptible Cashier—the world's first cash register. Sadly, he made little money from his idea but sold it to others. . . who developed it and went on to make a fortune.

One good turn

Ritty had his big idea in 1878. Thieving at the bar was so serious, he became sick with worry and had to take a vacation. While voyaging to Europe, he saw a gauge that recorded how many turns the steamship's propeller made. Could he use this technology for counting sales? As soon as the ship docked, he hurried back home again and got to work. After a few false starts, Ritty eventually came up with his now-famous Incorruptible Cashier, the world's first cash register.

James Ritty
Ritty was born in Dayton, Ohio, in 1836 to French parents who had emigrated to America. He briefly studied medicine before joining the army. He later ran a saloon bar business, which he continued until he retired in 1895.

> **I'll prove that I can sell honesty to the world**
>
> John H. Patterson, founder of the National Cash Register Company

Incorruptible Cashier
Ritty's first cash register had two rows of keys, each marked with an amount of money. When they were pressed, the total appeared on the clocklike dial.

Ritty's workshop

Ritty bought this workshop in Dayton to make his new machine, but he found it all too difficult and decided to stick to running bars. So he sold the patent.

A new direction

John H. Patterson was an Ohio grocery store owner and, like Ritty, had been losing money badly—around $50,000 per year. He had bought a couple of Ritty's Incorruptible Cashiers to try them out. They were a success, returning him a profit. Delighted, he bought the patent from Ritty and trained up staff to sell machines to stores all over the country. He named his firm the National Cash Register Company. Today, known as NCR, it continues to sell machines throughout the world.

Bold as brass

Patterson's machines, mostly cast in brass, had hundreds of moving parts and performed sophisticated calculations. By 1906, they ran on electricity; this is an early hand-cranked model.

127

1949

JOSEPH WOODLAND AND
BERNARD SILVER

Bar codes are small, simple, and useful—and they help the modern world stay organized. They work like identity badges, giving access to data about the objects that they are attached to, from goods in factories and stores, to human beings and medical supplies. Around five billion bar codes are scanned every day, keeping track of mail and people's buying habits.

Doodling in the sand

In 1948, American students Joseph Woodland and Bernard Silver were researching a device that could identify products for a local food chain. Woodland was thinking it over on a beach, wondering if he could use Morse code, when he absentmindedly drew lines in the sand with his fingers. The answer was staring him in the face: suddenly, he realized that he could use a code of bars and spaces. In 1949, the two men filed their patent.

Each digit contains a total of seven units (slim bars or spaces)

4 = 1011100 =

The bars of a UPC appear in three different widths—thicker bands contain more units than thinner ones

The Start Digit has the arrangement 101 (where 1 is a bar and 0 is a space)

This is the UPC number: the first six digits are called L-codes, and the final six digits are called R-codes

0 3 6 0 0 0   2 9 1 4 5 2

These Guard Bars separate the two blocks of six digits and are always arranged 01010

Bar code

Cracking the code

However, it was a long time before there were lasers to read bar codes or computers powerful enough to process the data. The two men spent many years improving the idea, but, tragically, Silver died in 1963. By the early 1970s, Woodland was working for IBM and had developed the Universal Product Code (UPC), the basic bar code that is still in use today. Bar codes were first used on products in supermarkets in 1974.

The first product checked out in a supermarket using its bar code was a pack of chewing gum

Bar codes are cheap and easy to put on various objects

UPCs are everywhere

All products have a number, which is converted into a bar code and clearly printed, so it can be read by an optical scanner. This saves an operator from having to punch numbers in and risk an error. The number is printed in numerals beneath the bar code, so it can be entered manually if the scanner isn't working.

The medical sample tubes are bar coded so they can be easily identified

▶▶ TOMORROW'S WORLD

Radio frequency identification (RFID) is likely to take over some of the tasks that bar codes perform today. This image shows how the system might work: a radio-tagged salmon is being checked out on a "smart" supermarket trolley.

SEE ALSO DNA Laser 46 · Cash register 124

Staples provide a tough and tidy alternative to keeping paper together with glue, tape, paperclips, or tags. The "golden age" for inventing staplers lasted from about 1870 to 1900, when industry was booming, city populations were growing, and companies were producing mountains of paperwork. Several American inventors raced to produce a practical machine that would help office clerks cope with their filing. Today's staplers have many uses, from bookbinding and dressmaking to surgery and even building construction.

The plunger was pressed down upon the staple

A built-in spring brought the plunger back up again after use

The body was made from cast iron and measured 4½ in (11.4 cm) high

The clinching anvil turned the staple ends inward to hold together the pieces of paper

The lever arm could also be used as a carry-handle

McGill Single-Stroke Staple Press, 1879

One at a time

With the earliest staplers, you loaded one staple at a time. The first such model to be patented, in 1877, was designed by American Claus Boerdine. Two years later, Englishman C. H. Gould patented his McGill Single Stroke Staple Press. This inserted and clinched (turned the ends of) the staple in a single stroke—hence the name. It sold well.

A single staple at a time, measuring ½ in (12 mm) wide, was loaded into a slit beneath the plunger; it was stout enough to bind several sheets together

The magazine contains a row of staples

Modern stapler

Channels in the anvil close the staple arms in on one another

Strips and spools

One-at-a-time staplers were slow and awkward, and soon makers were producing staplers that carried several staples, which were formed from one long metal strip and had to be detached by forcefully pressing down on the plunger. Others carried spools of wire, from which the machine would cut a staple and then bend it into shape and drive it in—all in one hit.

Stapler

Pinning it together

For more than 100 years, surgeons have been using staples to close wounds and hold them together, both inside the body and on the skin. Stapling is a lot quicker than stitching with thread.

Ants to the rescue

Army ants can be used in a medical emergency. Their jaws pull the wound together as they close. The ant is then removed, leaving the head and jaws in place.

Speedy surgery

Surgical staples are made from titanium, steel, or plastic and are quickly inserted with a special tool. They are later removed and can be reused.

Stitching a book

Staples are not just used in offices, they are put to use in industry, too. Booklets, for example, are stapled using specialized stapling machines. First, pages are assembled on a saddle-shaped support. Then, stitchers cut staples from spools of wire and run them through the spine of the booklet. This process is called saddle-stitching, or wire-stitching.

The plastic casing of a modern stapler provides a comfortable grip

The arm is hinged with a pin and sprung so that it opens again after each use

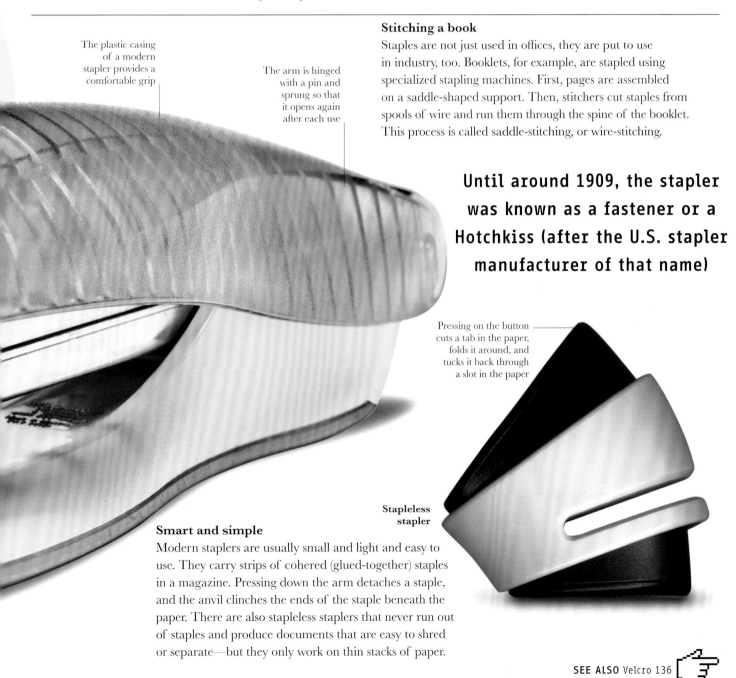

Until around 1909, the stapler was known as a fastener or a Hotchkiss (after the U.S. stapler manufacturer of that name)

Pressing on the button cuts a tab in the paper, folds it around, and tucks it back through a slot in the paper

Stapleless stapler

Smart and simple

Modern staplers are usually small and light and easy to use. They carry strips of cohered (glued-together) staples in a magazine. Pressing down the arm detaches a staple, and the anvil clinches the ends of the staple beneath the paper. There are also stapleless staplers that never run out of staples and produce documents that are easy to shred or separate—but they only work on thin stacks of paper.

SEE ALSO Velcro 136

Before stamps were invented, sending letters and packages was a difficult, expensive, and unreliable process. In the 1830s, Rowland Hill, an English teacher, realized that a better system was needed and began to reform the British postal system. His changes—including the invention of the first sticky postage stamp—meant that ordinary people could afford to use the postal services, and businesses thrived. Soon other countries began to use postage stamps, too.

Stamps are marked with their country of origin

The white edge of a stamp is called the margin

A postmark shows the date, time, and place of collection

Time for change
Until the 1840s, the person who received a letter had to pay for postage, rather than the sender. Rowland Hill believed that the cost of sending a letter should be calculated according to its weight rather than the distance it traveled—and that prepayment, by means of a stamp, would be a fairer and more efficient system.

◀◀ BRIGHT SPARKS

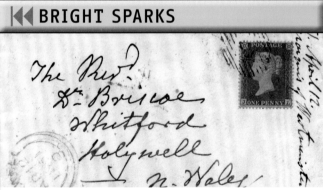

The first British Penny Blacks were sold in sheets, and each stamp was cut out with scissors. In 1848, Henry Archer invented a perforating machine that punched tiny holes around the edges, so stamps could be torn apart by hand.

Fourpenny post
Rowland Hill's plans to improve the British postal system were welcomed by business owners. In 1839, Hill was asked to start running the new system, and a cheap flat rate of fourpence per letter was quickly introduced.

Stamp

Sticky stamps

In early 1840, customers could buy a sheet of letter paper for one penny, which included the cost of the postage. A few months later, Hill's first adhesive postage stamps went on sale. They were called Penny Blacks.

The British Penny Black carried a profile of Queen Victoria and the postage price

Some stamps have security measures, such as watermarks, to prevent forgery

Stamps are perforated along their edges

Used stamps are postmarked, to stop anyone from using them again

High-price hobby

Some philatelists (stamp collectors) will pay big money for beautiful or unusual specimens; even misprints have a high value. Very rare stamps, such as the Mauritius 1d orange and 2d blue or the Swedish Treskilling Yellow, can change hands for millions of dollars.

Great Britain is the only country in the world that doesn't have to carry the name of the country on its stamps

Staying in touch

People have used different ways to transmit messages to one another for thousands of years—from carrier pigeons to e-mails and instant messaging. Postal systems are still popular, though—even underwater!

Message in a barrel

In 1793, whaling captain James Colnett set up the Post Office Barrel in Floreana, one of the remote Galápagos Islands, for use as a mail-drop by passing mariners. The old barrel is still used today.

Underwater mail

Tourists to the Pacific island of Vanuatu can dive undersea to send their mail. The underwater post office accepts waterproof postcards for an hour everyday and dispatches them all over the world.

SEE ALSO Telegraph 40

The wonder of Post-It® Notes is that they can be removed and repositioned again and again, so they can be placed almost anywhere and used for countless purposes. Post-It® Notes were the result of teamwork at 3M, an American company: one scientist invented the low-stick glue, another dreamed up the paper notes and their ideas came together. As with so many trail-blazing inventions, it took the scientists and their company several years to make the idea "stick."

First steps

In 1968, Spencer Silver, a senior chemist at 3M's research laboratories, came up with a not-very-sticky glue that allowed paper to be repositioned. But he couldn't see exactly how to use it—on a message board? In a spray can? He asked 3M to develop it, but for years they couldn't see the point of it; all they wanted was ever-stronger glues!

It was Art Fry who came up with a practical use for Spencer Silver's glue

The first Post-It® Notes were canary-yellow to match the color of legal notebooks

Post-It® Notes have adhesive applied to the back of the paper and only along one edge

Putting glue and paper together

Another 3M worker, Art Fry, was a singer in his church choir and was annoyed at how his hymnbook markers always fell out. In 1974, he heard about Silver's low-tack glue and realized what he needed: notebooks backed with the glue. Art built a machine to make his own sticky notes and showed them to 3M.

The highlighter pen contains fluorescent ink

Post-its

Press and peel

3M eventually developed Fry and Silver's idea. At first, the product was named "Press 'n' Peel" and it was a hit with the public. By 1980, the name had changed to Post-It® Notes, and they went on sale all over the U.S.A. One year later, they were sold in other countries. Today, many other companies also make sticky notes.

New products have been developed using the not-so-sticky adhesive

The glue isn't very sticky, so the note can be used several times

Sticky flags are used to mark pages in a book without damaging it

The 3M "Flag+" pen contains a highlighter and sticky flags, making it easy to mark text and find the page again

Post-It® Notes now come in more than 60 colors and all types of shapes

COOL SCIENCE

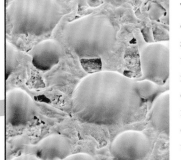

The glue contains billions of tiny sticky acrylic spheres; the gaps between the spheres prevent them from sticking too well. A coating on the back of the notes makes the glue stay on them and not transfer to the other surface.

Sticky stuff

Quick, slow, weak, or strong, there are now glues available for every imaginable purpose, ranging from open-heart surgery to cutting-edge crime detection.

Body glue

Today, surgeons may use glue, instead of stitches, to close wounds in body tissue. The latest high-tech glues often come in two tubes and are mixed directly on the cut or wound, hardening in seconds. To fix a cracked tortoise shell, a vet uses a slow but very tough glue, such as epoxy resin.

Criminal chemistry

Superglue is used to reveal fingerprints, which contain chemicals such as acids and proteins. When heated, superglue reacts with these chemicals. They turn white and can be photographed.

SEE ALSO Stapler 130

Velcro, or hook-and-loop fastener, is used on many things from shoes to space shuttles and provides an easy-to-use alternative to buttons, zippers, and press studs. The inventor, a Swiss engineer, got the idea in 1941 when he spotted fuzzy seedheads from a burdock plant clinging to his dog's coat after a hunting trip.

Inside the helmet of every space shuttle astronaut is a patch of Velcro "hooks"—it's used to scratch an itchy nose

On one surface there are thousands of loops, made of nylon or polyester thread, which catch the hooks

The other surface is coated in tiny hooks

Burdock is a European wildflower; when it has finished flowering, a dry seedhead, covered in hooks, develops

Inspired by nature
Looking at his dog's coat, George de Mestral saw how the tiny, hooked spines all over the plant burs (seedheads) got caught in loops of fiber or fur, like hook-and-eye clothing fasteners. He wondered how he could put this natural stickiness to good use.

Velcro

One backing surface is packed with countless tufts of fine nylon loops. On the other surface, there is a heavier grade of nylon, which is sewn and then cut under hot infrared lights to form hooks. Each piece can be used again and again, because there are so many hooks and loops, which fasten to form a bond.

Loopy nylon

De Mestral used nylon to make the hooks and loops, because it is tough but flexible. But it took him a number of years to figure out how to weave the material. Stitching more than 300 hooks and loops into an area the size of a postage stamp was no easy task.

The backing fabric is usually made of nylon or polyester

Ripping Velcro apart is still very noisy—and inventors are trying to create a silent version

Rip and stick

Finally, in 1955, de Mestral had a product: Velcro. Its name came from the combination of the French word for velvet (*velors*) and hook (*crochet*). Velcro is now used for many products, from clothes to luggage and military equipment. It was even used to help hold together the first artificial heart!

Copying nature

Scientists and inventors often look to nature to help them solve everyday problems—it is a process called biomimicry. Blue mussels and geckos, for example, have been studied extensively by scientist to solve some sticky problems!

Sticky and steadfast

Blue mussels are able to stick themselves to rocks so they can withstand the force of crashing waves. They have inspired the development of new glues that are toxin free and work under water.

Gripping geckos

Geckos are lizards that have millions of tiny hairs on the sole of each foot. The hairs create weak electrical forces that work like a sticky glue, enabling geckos to climb upside-down. Scientists are hoping to use a similar system to create glues that we can use.

SEE ALSO Nylon 50 · Post-its 134

Most of us use zippers every day on our clothes,

bags, or sports equipment, so it may seem strange that this toothed fastening device took 40 years to catch on. Whitcomb Judson, an inventor in Chicago, Illinois, came up with the basic idea in 1893, but it wasn't until the zipper hit the fashion world in the late 1930s that this handy little fastener became really popular.

Snaps and sliders

Originally, footwear and clothes were closed with fiddly hooks and eyes or with snaps. Judson tried to make things easier: he designed a row of hooks and eyes that were linked and unlinked by a slider. Known as the clasp locker, the device worked, but it often jammed, too.

◀◀ BRIGHT SPARKS

Sometimes more than one person can come up with the same great idea. In the 1840s, American Elias Howe was a coinventor (along with Isaac Singer and others) of the sewing machine, which made him a millionaire. In 1851, he also patented an early type of zipper fastener but was too busy to develop the idea.

Zipper

Each tooth has a dimple on one face and a nib (point) on the other

The slider has a Y-shaped channel that brings the teeth together at an angle, and in an alternating pattern, to lock them together

When the teeth run through the slider, they are locked into place

The pull tag makes it easy to operate the slider

A slow start

A wealthy investor, Colonel Lewis Walker, set up the Universal Fastener Company to back Judson's invention. But despite several attempts, none of them really worked, and in 1904 Judson gave up.

The world's longest zipper was made in 1985 and measured 60 ft (18.3 m)

Next steps

Walker hired a Swedish engineer, Gideon Sundbäck, who ditched hooks and eyes, and in 1913 came up with the Hookless No. 2. It was much like a modern zipper, with two rows of metal scoops mounted on stout tape and operated by a Y-shaped slider.

Tough woven backing tape carries the two rows of teeth

Zips catch on

When the fashion industry finally accepted zippers in 1937, they really took off. In 1939, zipper-makers sold around 300 million units, twice as many as in the previous year. By 1950, annual sales hit one billion.

The bottom of the zipper is fitted with metal stops (not shown), which prevent the slider from falling off

Extreme zippers

Today, the versatile zipper has been adapted to be used in many types of special clothing and devices that need to be both watertight and airtight.

Safe at sea
Diving suits have heavy-duty zippers, made from materials such as nickel silver and bronze alloys, designed to stay secure under very high pressure.

Good to blow
Even bagpipes have high-tech zippers on their air bags, which need to be airtight and watertight, but also need to be opened for cleaning and moisture control.

Action zips
Spacesuits are fitted with special zippers for airtight action. NASA has also worked with Speedo to produce low-drag zippers on Olympic swimsuits.

SEE ALSO Stapler 130 · Velcro 136

Cell phone

One third of the global population makes their calls using cell phones, and around three billion cell phones are in use worldwide

Once seen as a luxury toy, the cell phone is now regarded by many people as an essential gadget. It took decades to develop and remains at the forefront of today's technology. As well as keeping you in touch via phone or e-mail, the device serves as an organizer, computer, movie camera, still camera, and multimedia player—and it even fits in your pocket.

Cell masterminds

The idea of cell phone communication first came to light in 1947, but it was not until the 1960s and 1970s that the race was truly on to develop a portable phone device that could be taken anywhere. American companies Motorola and Bell Laboratories both sought to become the first inventors of this groundbreaking technology, with Motorola, led by Martin Cooper, eventually masterminding the cell phone in 1973.

Personal data, such as your phone number and your contacts, are stored in a microchip on the SIM (Subscriber Identity Module) card

The SIM card can be moved from one phone to another, enabling the user to transfer all data—without a card, the phone will not work

This icon shows battery strength

A multitouch display gives fingertip control

This icon shows if the phone is receiving a signal

A computer in the hand

Today, we use cell phones for more than just making calls. On the Apple iPhone 3G, the touchscreen serves not only as the display, but also as a "desktop" for scrolling through applications and as a keypad. There are tens of thousands of apps (add-on applications) for the iPhone, such as games, surf reports, news channels, and wildlife spotter guides.

The display can be programmed to show the user's personal choice of icons

The phone can connect with an e-mail account

Apple iPhone 3G

Pressing the home button returns the phone to this home screen

TOMORROW'S WORLD

In the future, handheld phones could be replaced with an invisible device. One possibility is to use a tiny microchip that would be implanted in your tooth. When the secret toothphone "rings," vibrations would travel along the jawbone and deliver sound into your inner ear.

Wired for sound

Bluetooth or WiFi radio technology enables cell phones to connect remotely with other devices such as computers, other phones, and earpieces.

GPS

The latest phones have GPS (Global Positioning System) and satellite navigation software. They can give your location anywhere in the world.

A portable office

A personal organizer offers a diary, phone, e-mail, and other "home office" functions. It tends to be used more for business than for entertainment.

On the move

Like nothing before, cell phones enable us to get more done on the move, combining a wide range of functions that in earlier days tied us to our desks.

SEE ALSO World Wide Web 44 · Microprocessor 98 · GPS 190

Going mobile

It all began with radio. By the 1920s, radio communication sets were widely used in cars, trains, and planes, but because they weren't linked to the telephone network, they were not true cell phones. It was after technological advances during World War II that cell phones were really developed and, as these pictures show, handsets have shrunk over the past 50 years. This downsizing was partly due to space and military requirements: the electronics in your pocket were originally slimmed down to fit inside space rockets and nuclear missiles.

Backseat talk
During the 1920s, police and other emergency vehicles road-tested car radios that were two-way. They allowed both users to talk at once, rather than one after the other.

At the races
In 1947, Douglas Ring and W. Rae Young, engineers at Bell Laboratories, first proposed the cellular network, which lies at the heart of all cell phone systems. However, years passed before Ring and Young's idea became a reality. During the 1960s, Bell Laboratories faced stiff competition from rival company Motorola to be the first to use cellular technology to invent a handheld cell phone. Ring and Young were up against Motorola employee Martin Cooper. While working as project manager, Cooper set up a base station in New York with the first working prototype of a cell telephone, the Motorola DynaTAC. The invention passed various tests as well as a successful public demonstration.

Ericsson MTA 21, 1956
Weighing in at 90 lb (40 kg), Ericsson's MTA phone was huge! It was the first car phone, with batteries stored in the trunk of the car.

Motorola DynaTAC, 1973/1984
Created in 1973, the DynaTAC prototype (left) was the industry's first cell phone. By 1984, the world's first commercially available cell phone, DynaTAC 8000X (right), was on the market. At 10 in (25 cm) tall and costing several thousand dollars, it needed a big pocket and a big wallet.

> ❝ **Joel, I'm calling you from a 'real' cellular telephone. A portable handheld telephone** ❞
>
> Martin Cooper of Motorola, making the world's first cellular phone call to his rival Joel Engel of Bell Laboratories, New York, April 3, 1973

Leading the way

Martin Cooper's Motorola DynaTAC paved the way for all the cell phone technology that followed, from early handsets the size of briefcases to current versions as small as credit cards. In this century, design developments continue at a rapid rate, with today's cell phones capable of much more than their original purpose of making and receiving calls.

Nokia Mobira Talkman, 1984

The Talkman weighed 11 lb (5 kg) but had a long battery life. Like the DynaTAC, it was very expensive but was popular despite the heavy price tag.

Motorola StarTAC, 1996

This was the world's first clamshell cell phone. For its day, its size—less than 4 in (10 cm) long and 3.5 oz (100 g) in weight—was incredible.

BlackBerry smartphone, 2002

The BlackBerry is more of a computer than a phone. It offers e-mail, Internet, and phone functions—plus a tiny keyboard and trackball.

On the Move

There are many reasons to travel—to see new things, to meet new people, or for the excitement of the journey itself. So, for thousands of years, people have been building machines to help them on their way.

Almost every machine with moving parts contains wheels, and it's difficult to imagine what the world would be like without them. No one knows when the first one was invented, or even whether it was part of a cart or used to make pottery. But we do know that wheels were being used before 3500 B.C.E., in ancient Mesopotamia.

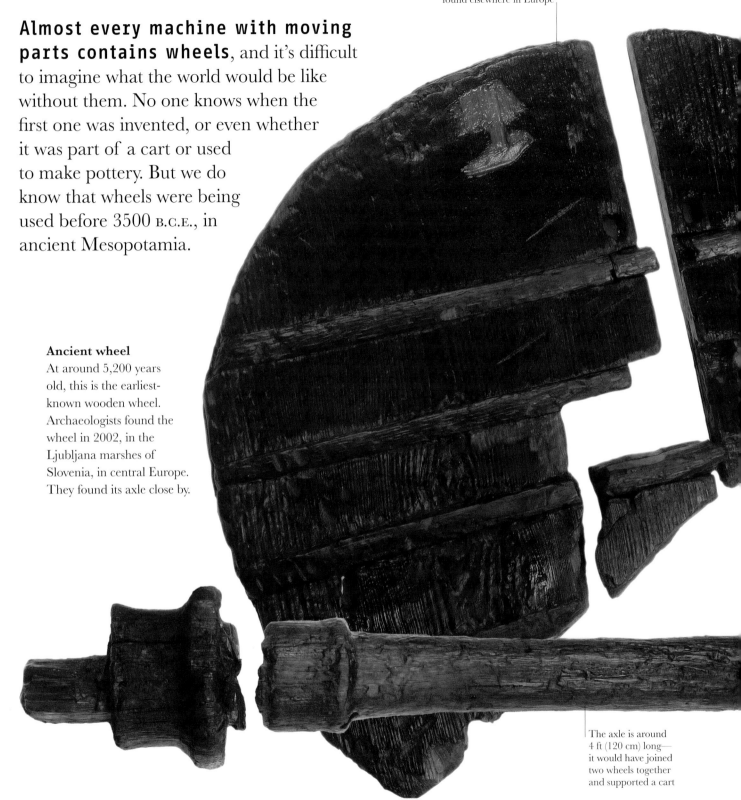

The wheel was technologically superior to later versions found elsewhere in Europe

Ancient wheel
At around 5,200 years old, this is the earliest-known wooden wheel. Archaeologists found the wheel in 2002, in the Ljubljana marshes of Slovenia, in central Europe. They found its axle close by.

The axle is around 4 ft (120 cm) long— it would have joined two wheels together and supported a cart

Wheel

This wheel consists of two wide boards made of ash, held together with four smaller pieces of oak

Spokes make wheels lighter, while keeping their strength. On wooden wheels the spokes push outward, but bicycles have wire spokes that pull inward. The advantage of these is that the wheel can change shape slightly without breaking.

Wheels worldwide

The world is full of wheels of all sizes. Some are too small to see with the human eye, while others are several feet across.

Gear wheels

The teeth on these gears make sure that each wheel drives the next without slipping. We could not have developed mechanical clocks without gear wheels like these.

Well preserved

Usually, wooden objects do not last nearly as long as this wheel has. The muddy marsh waters sealed it away from the living things, such as insects, fungi, and bacteria, that would otherwise have eaten it or caused it to rot.

The wheel is around 55 in (140 cm) across and 2 in (5 cm) thick

Giant wheels

Ferris wheels carry people around with them. This one is called the London Eye. It is 443 ft (135 m) high and takes around 30 minutes to complete a full turn.

There were no wheels in America until the 1400s

A bumpy ride

This wheel probably belonged to a two-wheeled carriage or cart, but no trace of it could be found in the marsh. Without any tires or springs, it must have been a very uncomfortable ride.

To protect them from insects, both the axle and the wheel were probably scorched (burned slightly) when they were made

Oak was used to make the axle

The axle slots into an oblong hole in the wheel

SEE ALSO Pendulum clock 78 · Bicycle 166 · Mars rovers 188

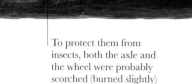

1908

HENRY FORD

When Henry Ford was young, cars were luxuries for the very rich—but Henry had other ideas. He realized that cars were expensive because each one was made differently and took a long time to build. So he set up a factory that quickly made cars of just one type. That type was the Model T, and it was not only affordable, the "Tin Lizzie," as it was known, was also a triumph of design. It was reliable, tough, could handle rough roads, and it ran on any one of three types of fuel.

BRIGHT SPARKS

The world's first car, the three-wheeler Benz Motorwagen designed by German engineer Karl Benz, took to the road in 1886. Its most famous trip was made in 1888, when the inventor's wife drove it nearly 124 miles (200 km) at a top speed of 10 mph (16 km/h).

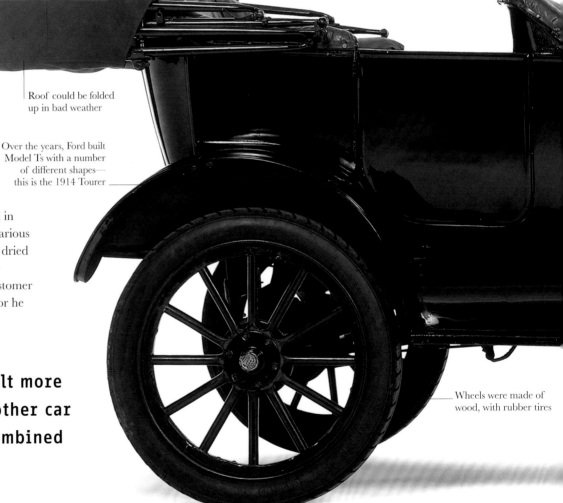

Roof could be folded up in bad weather

Over the years, Ford built Model Ts with a number of different shapes— this is the 1914 Tourer

Why black?
Tin Lizzies were first produced in 1908. They were available in various colors, but because black paint dried the fastest, it was soon the only choice. As Ford put it, "Any customer can have a car painted any color he wants, so long as it is black."

In 1914, Ford built more cars than all the other car manufacturers combined

Wheels were made of wood, with rubber tires

Ford Model T

An adaptable machine

Tin Lizzies were popular with all types of people and were used for all types of things. Some farmers even removed the rear wheels and used the engine to power farm machinery, such as saws and hay lifters.

One problem with today's cars is that they burn fuel, which causes pollution. In the future, many cars may have electric engines, powered by solar panels on their roofs, and the driver would no longer have to find a gas station to stop and refuel.

The car's speed could be controlled either by foot pedals or by levers under the steering wheel—top speed was around 44 mph (70 km/h)

The windshield was hinged in the middle, so that the lower half could be opened for ventilation when the car's roof was in place

Each car came with three oil lamps

Cranky start

Early Model Ts had to be started from the outside, by turning a handle that was inserted just under the radiator at the front of the car.

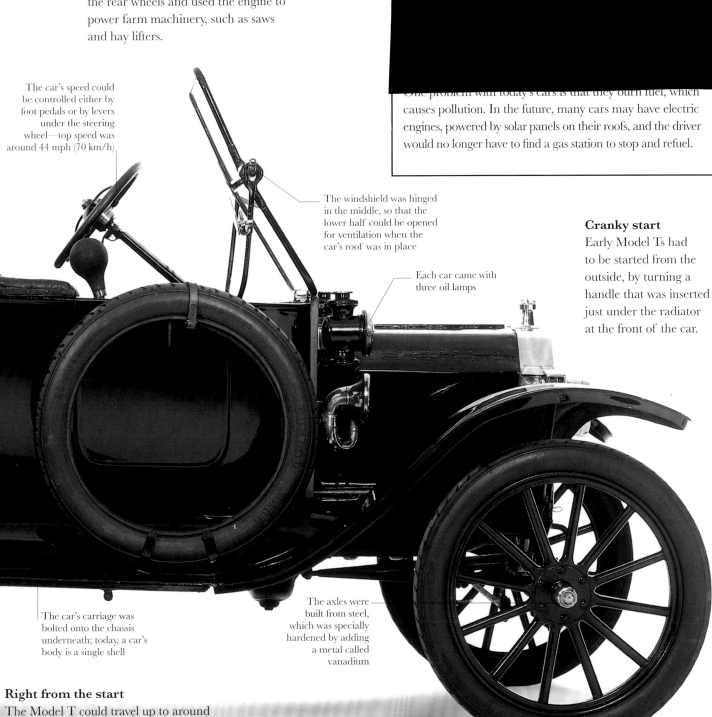

The car's carriage was bolted onto the chassis underneath; today, a car's body is a single shell

The axles were built from steel, which was specially hardened by adding a metal called vanadium

Right from the start

The Model T could travel up to around 25 miles per gallon (10 km per liter). This was true of most cars built in the 1900s, showing how efficient the Ford design was.

SEE ALSO Engine 58 · Cat's eyes 168 · Electric car 172

Ford's model

beginning of the 1900s, each car was made according to the instructions of the person who ordered it, which took a long time and made cars so expensive that hardly anyone could afford them.

Cutting down time

Henry Ford created a completely new way of building cars, called an assembly line. The way that it worked was that the framework of a car moved along a line of workers, each of whom added a new part to it. Stage by stage, the car was assembled until, at the end of the line, it was finished and ready to be driven away. All the cars made in this way were exactly the same. Partly because the workers did not have to spend time moving around the factory and partly because they became very fast at doing the same job over and over again, cars could now be built very quickly. Ford's new method cut the time to make a car from 12 hours to about 90 minutes!

All in one place

To produce cars even more efficiently, Ford decided that every stage of car making should be carried out at the same place. By 1927, the River Rouge plant in Michigan, made almost everything needed to build a car—as well as the cars themselves.

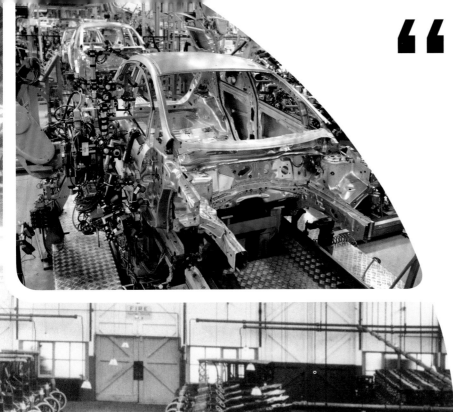

> **" I will build a car for the great multitude. . . constructed of the best materials, by the best men, after the simplest designs that modern engineering can devise "**
>
> Henry Ford, 1922

The way of the future

Soon, Ford's factory was producing them at a rate of more than two per minute, and far more Tin Lizzies were sold than any other car. Since then, the assembly line has been adopted all over the world and not just in car factories. Computers, dishwashers, televisions, and many other machines are made in this way. But today, the workers on production lines are not always human beings—in many cases, robots do the job instead. These changes, started a century ago by Henry Ford, have meant that cars have changed from rare luxuries that most people could only dream of to everyday vehicles that many people can afford. Henry Ford really did make the world a different place.

Henry Ford

The son of a farmer, Ford loved machines of all types; as well as the Model T and many other vehicles, he built a racecar that was the world's fastest at the time.

Sails have been used for thousands of years to harness the wind for travel on the water. Since sails were first attached to the boats of ancient Egypt, sailing ships have been improved through the centuries. During the 1400s and 1500s, western Europeans developed a ship called the carrack, which combined a stern-hung rudder with square and lateen (triangular) sails. This vessel became the standard ship for trade and exploration.

Columbus's carrack

Legendary explorer Christopher Columbus hired the Spanish carrack *Santa Maria* for his first expedition across the Atlantic Ocean in 1492. This was the largest of his three ships and carried a crew of 40 people. *Santa Maria* had a single deck and was constructed from pine and oak trees.

Deep hull

The carrack had a wide, deep hull that made it more stable on the open ocean, particularly in stormy waters. This vessel could carry enough men, food, and other cargo to travel for long periods, whether for trade or explorations. The Portuguese used carracks to move goods to Africa, India, and the Spice Islands.

Sails hung from a pole called a yard

A mainmast, near the centre of the ship, had a square mainsail and topsail

Mizzenmast is the mast aft—or behind—the mainmast; it held a triangular lateen sail

The stern, or rear of the ship, is the area with the steering wheel and rudder—and the officers' quarters

Carrack planking

The deep hull was designed for stability and to carry large cargoes

Sailing ship

Multiple masts

A carrack could have two, three, or four masts. They were kept upright by standing rigging (ropes), which stopped the masts from swaying too much. There were square sails on the foremast and mainmast, and a lateen sail on the mizzenmast.

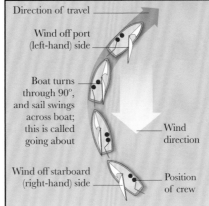

Direction of travel

Wind off port (left-hand) side

Boat turns through 90°, and sail swings across boat; this is called going about

Wind off starboard (right-hand) side

Wind direction

Position of crew

Getting from A to B isn't a straight course at sea. A sailing boat cannot be steered directly into the wind, so sailors use a process called tacking. They steer the boat in a zigzag direction into an upwind position (against the direction of the wind). The crew need to get the boat and its sails into the best position to catch the wind, so that it can move forward.

The foremast was the mast in front of the mainmast

Sails could be decorated to give a vessel its own nautical identity

Stay ropes stopped a mast from falling forward or backward

The bowsprit carried a small, square sail

Super sails

The combination of a triangular lateen sail and square rigged sails made sailing both smoother and faster. The lateen stern sail could make good progress, even when sailing into the wind. As the carrack's design developed, the topsails were added on the mainmast and the foremast.

Santa Maria was around 82 ft (25 m) in length

The bow is the pointed front of a ship

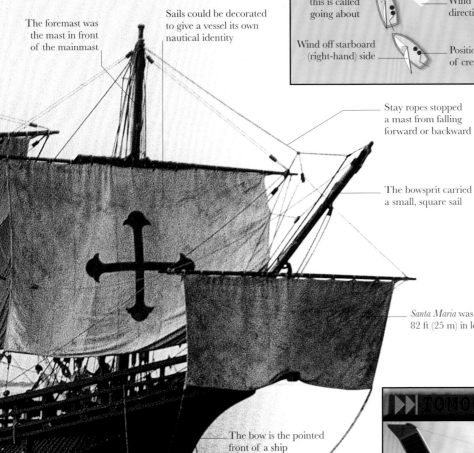

The carrack was one of the most influential ship designs in history

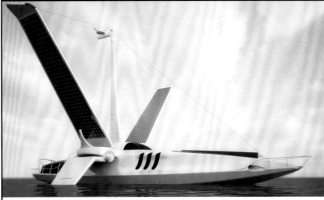

Volitan ("Flying fish") is an innovative sailboat that shows the way future vessel designs can use environmentally friendly features. With its solid solar-panel covered sails, Volitan uses both wind power and solar energy.

SEE ALSO Solar cell 92 · Compass 186

Dutch inventor Cornelius Drebbel built the first submarine in London, England in 1620. He made it from a wooden row boat, which he covered with greased leather to keep out the water. Most submarines built since have been military vessels. Submarines have also been used for marine research and even to take tourists on underwater trips.

Life in modern submarines

Navy submarines are fighting vessels, so there are few luxuries. They are not very spacious—the crew has to fit into the spaces between all the equipment. The submariners have to be able to live and work together in such cramped areas for long periods of time.

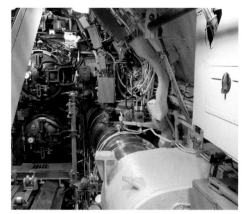

Torpedo room

Military submarines can attack ships and other submarines using torpedoes. These are explosive weapons with propellers to power them toward a target. Torpedoes are launched out of tubes in the submarine.

◀◀ BRIGHT SPARKS

American David Bushnell built the first military submarine. Known as the *Turtle*, it was used in 1776 during America's Revolutionary War, when Sergeant Ezra Lee tried to attach a bomb to a British warship. The attempt failed, but it showed that submarines could be used as weapons of war.

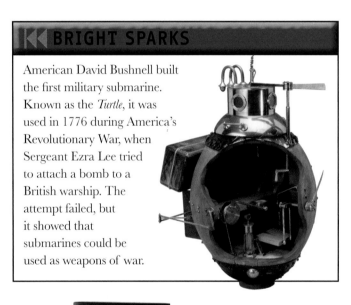

Early submarines

The first submarines were muscle-powered, with the crew turning the propeller by hand. Gasoline or diesel engines cannot be used to power a submarine underwater, because they use up oxygen and produce choking fumes. The modern submarine was not developed until designers struck on the idea of using a battery-powered electric motor.

Driven by steam from the nuclear reactor, machines called turbines turn the propeller at the rear

A nuclear reactor, located within this area, provides the submarine's power by heating water to make steam

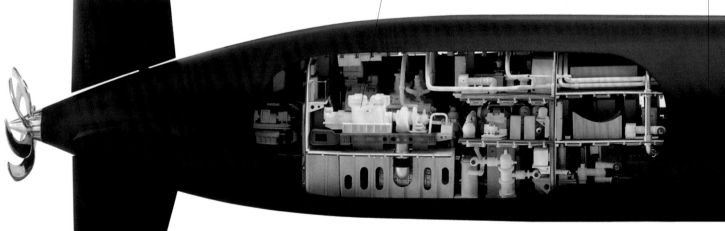

Submarine

Galleys and messes

The submarine's chef prepares food for the crew in the galley. The dining rooms where crew members eat are called messes. Most modern submarines keep food to last 90 days in their store rooms and freezers.

Hot bunking

In most submarines, there are fewer bunks (beds) than crew members. While half of the crew works, the other half sleeps, so two crew members take turns to use each bunk. This is called "hot bunking."

Taking control

Submariners command the vessel from a control room below the sail, sitting in front of an array of computer screens and instruments. Most of the controls for navigating, diving, and fighting are here.

Atom power

Nuclear submarines are powered by the energy given out by splitting atoms. They can stay submerged for several months at a time. Carrying equipment to make both fresh water and air, these submarines only need to come up to the surface to replenish food stocks.

A modern submarine is made from up to 7 million parts and 2,000 engineering drawings

Seeing with sound

Military submarines have no windows, so they use sound to avoid hitting things and to detect nearby vessels. They send out pulses of sound waves and listen for the echoes that bounce back, known as SONAR (Sound Navigation And Ranging).

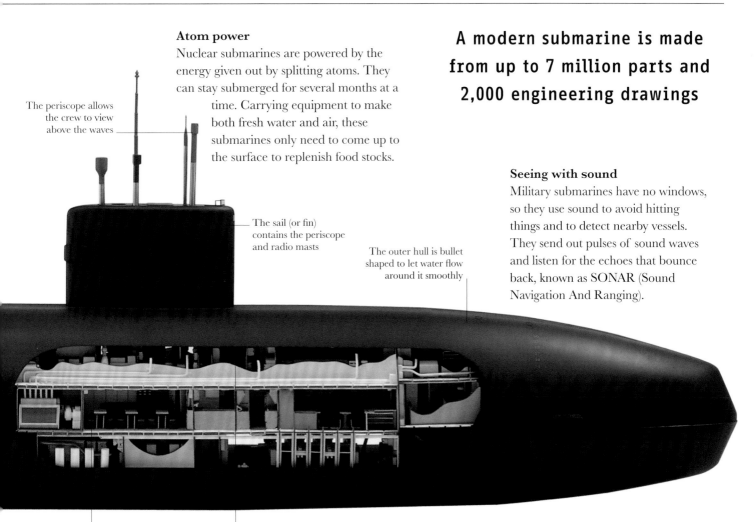

The periscope allows the crew to view above the waves

The sail (or fin) contains the periscope and radio masts

The outer hull is bullet shaped to let water flow around it smoothly

The galley is the submarine's kitchen

The control room is the submarine's command center

SEE ALSO Radioactivity 28 · Electric motor 68

Improvements

It wasn't until the 1930s that better jet engines were developed by Frank Whittle in the U.K. and Hans von Ohain in Germany. In 1939, the He 178 took to the skies. It was built by Heinkel, a German company, and was the first aircraft that flew properly using a jet engine. The He 178 had a metal fuselage (aircraft body) and wooden wings.

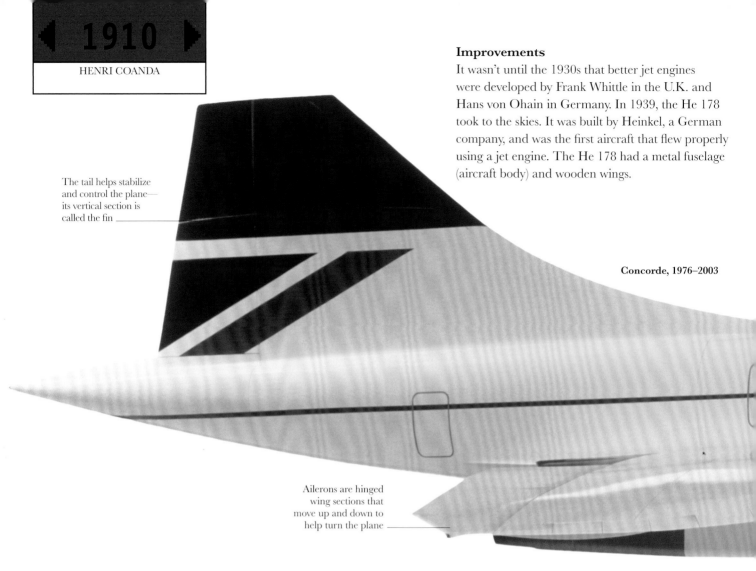

The tail helps stabilize and control the plane—its vertical section is called the fin

Concorde, 1976–2003

Ailerons are hinged wing sections that move up and down to help turn the plane

The first airplanes were pulled through the air by propellers, which meant that they flew relatively slowly. However, the jet engine changed all that, even allowing some planes to fly faster than sound. The groundbreaking Coanda-1910 paved the way for faster jets. Today, jet airplanes carry more people and can fly greater distances, making it easier for people to travel around the world. They also carry huge cargoes.

Coanda-1910

The first jet

The Coanda-1910 was designed and built in 1910 by Henri Coanda, a Romanian engineer. In most respects, the plane looked like any other aircraft of the time, with the pilot sitting in an open-air cockpit behind the engine, exposed to the elements. But the jet's sleek design, innovative motorjet, which was an early type of jet engine, and lack of a propeller made it a first in aviation history and put it way ahead of its time.

Jet airplane

Supersonic travel

It took many years to develop a jet plane with the power, strength, and controllability to fly faster than sound. Concorde was a supersonic passenger jet airliner—the first of its type. Built by French and British engineers, Concorde was a milestone in aviation history.

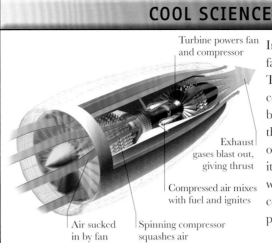
The main body of the plane is called the fuselage

Concorde's fastest speed was Mach 2.2—that's 1,450 mph (2,300 km/h)

The wheels of the landing gear retract in flight and are lowered for landing

Jet engines are fixed under the wing and provide the propulsion to move the plane

Concorde wings were aerodynamically designed in a delta shape to move easily through the air—they were thin and angled back

Turbofans

Today's commercial aircraft use a jet engine called a turbofan. It works by directing low-speed air around the high-speed air that emerges from the engine. This means that the high-speed air doesn't meet the slower air surrounding the engine, which reduces turbulence and makes it a quiet and efficient type of engine.

How wings work

Air moves slower along the bottom of a wing than along its top. Slower-moving air exerts more pressure, creating lift that holds up the plane. The angle of a wing also affects lift. Wing flaps create even more lift for takeoff and landing.

Every year, around two billion passengers travel by jet plane

SEE ALSO Engine 58 · Helicopter 160

The world's only supersonic jet took less than three and a half hours to fly from Europe to New York—this was half the time of other jets

Boom
Like all supersonic jet airplanes, Concorde made a very loud sound called a sonic boom whenever it flew faster than sound. This meant that the plane was forbidden from flying at supersonic speed over land.

A mostly aluminum construction reduced weight, which helped increase speeds

Concorde could carry only 128 passengers

As the plane increased in speed, the center of lift increased in the back of the plane and the nose became heavier, so fuel was moved to the back to balance the lift of the plane, and then forward as speed decreased

The speed during landing was usually around 185 mph (298 km/h)

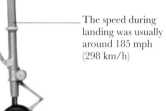

Super jets
The largest jet planes are built for flying people and large containers of goods around the world. The fastest types are designed for different purposes—they are used for battle, surveillance, and research.

X-43A scramjet
The X-43A is a robot plane that is one of the fastest aircraft in the world. It flies at hypersonic speeds, which means that they are at least five times faster than sound.

Stealth fighter
Some military jets are designed to be as difficult as possible to detect. The shape of this Lockheed F-117 Nighthawk, and the material it is made from, make it almost invisible to radar.

Drooped nose

Concorde's long nose was designed for high-speed flight, but its shape made it difficult for the pilots to see the runway during takeoff and landing. The solution was to make it droop when the plane was near the ground.

Though innovative in the 1970s, the analog instruments in Concorde's cockpit would be dated by today's standards

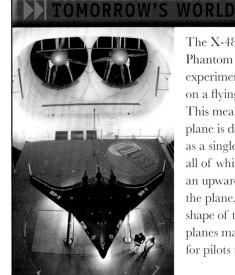

▶▶ TOMORROW'S WORLD

The X-48B Boeing Phantom is a type of experimental plane based on a flying wing design. This means that the entire plane is designed to act as a single huge wing, all of which provides an upward thrust on the plane. However, the shape of these experimental planes makes them difficult for pilots to control.

Concorde was 204 ft 6 in (62.19 m) long and could travel a distance of 3,740 miles (6,020 km)

Disaster

Concorde started to fly scheduled flights in 1976, with no major incidents until 2000, when a crash killed all of the passengers and crew. Three years later, all Concorde flights came to an end, as did the age of supersonic travel.

A probe at the tip of the nose informed the pilot if wind friction was causing the plane to become too hot—the temperature of the nose could reach 260°F (127°C)

Airbus A380

The Airbus A380 is the largest passenger airliner in the world and can carry up to 853 passengers during one flight. Known as the Superjumbo, it has two flight decks, one above the other.

Antonov An-225

One of the largest aircraft in the world, the An-225 is designed for heavy lifting, carrying loads ranging from the Soviet space shuttle *Buran* to supplies to help Haiti recover from the 2010 earthquake.

SEE ALSO Engine 58 · Helicopter 160

Some plants, like maple trees, spread their seeds using natural helicopters

Early development

The invention of the internal combustion engine, at the end of the 1800s, meant that it would be possible to provide enough power to lift a helicopter. In 1907, French bicycle maker and engineer Paul Cornu lifted a twin-rotored prototype helicopter into the air for just a few seconds.

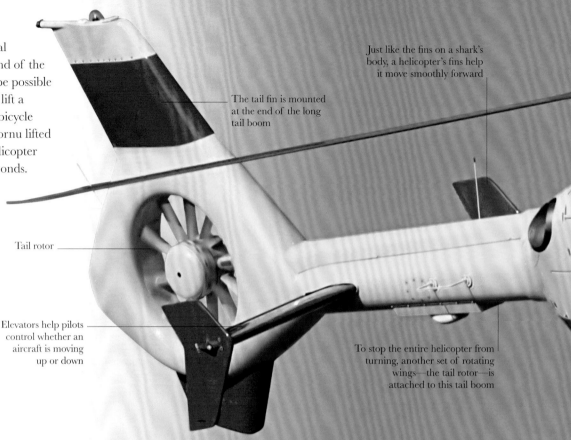

Just like the fins on a shark's body, a helicopter's fins help it move smoothly forward

The tail fin is mounted at the end of the long tail boom

Tail rotor

Elevators help pilots control whether an aircraft is moving up or down

To stop the entire helicopter from turning, another set of rotating wings—the tail rotor—is attached to this tail boom

Helicopters are much more maneuverable than planes. They can also hover and don't need runways. Over the years, a number of people were involved with their creation. But the man who made one that worked well enough to be mass produced was Igor Sikorsky, a Russian-born aircraft engineer. More than 100 Sikorsky R-4 helicopters were built—many more than any previous type. The R-4 was also the first helicopter to be used by both the American and British armed forces.

◄◄ BRIGHT SPARKS

The concept of flight fascinated Italian artist Leonardo da Vinci. More than 500 years ago, he designed a flight machine that resembled a helicopter. Although not practical, Leonardo's design was way ahead of its time. This modern model is based on Leonardo's drawing.

Helicopter

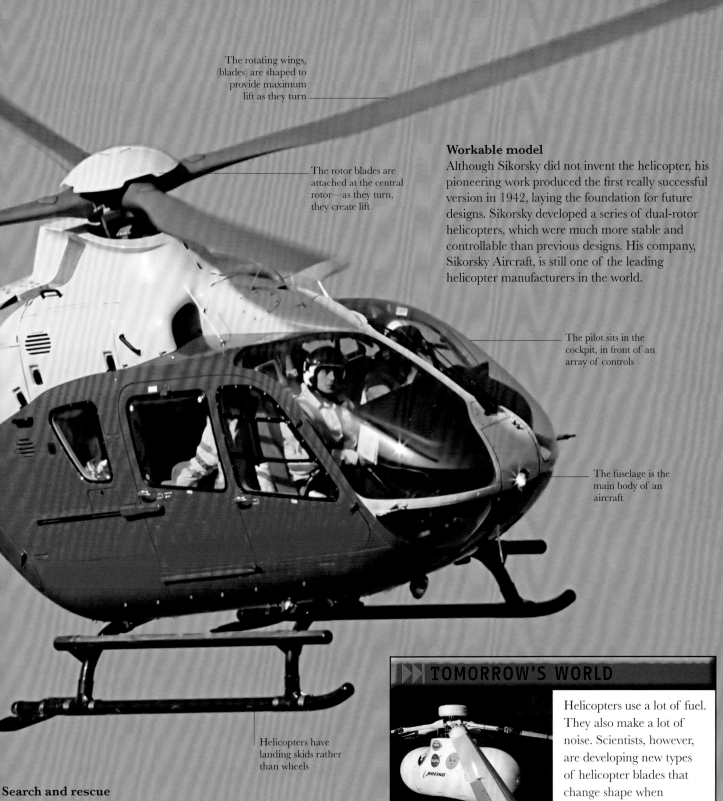

The rotating wings, (blades) are shaped to provide maximum lift as they turn

The rotor blades are attached at the central rotor—as they turn, they create lift

Workable model

Although Sikorsky did not invent the helicopter, his pioneering work produced the first really successful version in 1942, laying the foundation for future designs. Sikorsky developed a series of dual-rotor helicopters, which were much more stable and controllable than previous designs. His company, Sikorsky Aircraft, is still one of the leading helicopter manufacturers in the world.

The pilot sits in the cockpit, in front of an array of controls

The fuselage is the main body of an aircraft

Helicopters have landing skids rather than wheels

Search and rescue

Today, helicopters are used as ambulances where there are no roads or where traffic is heavy. They are also used to rescue people from the sea, and by the police to follow criminals. Piloting a helicopter is an extremely complex skill to master, because these aircraft can not only turn in any direction but also hover and move straight up and down.

▶▶ TOMORROW'S WORLD

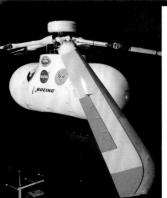

Helicopters use a lot of fuel. They also make a lot of noise. Scientists, however, are developing new types of helicopter blades that change shape when electrical signals are fed to them. This makes them move through the air more quietly, and means less fuel is needed, too.

SEE ALSO Engine 58 · Wind turbine 66 · Electric motor 68

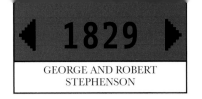

Steam was the force that kept the Industrial Revolution going. Initially used to pump water from mines, steam engines were developed for use in furnaces and factories. Transportation was also transformed by the mid-1800s with the birth of the steam locomotive. Instead of being confined to local areas, people could now travel by steam locomotive, changing economics, trade, and migration forever.

Steaming ahead

Known as the "Father of the Railroads," English engineer George Stephenson established his locomotive works in 1823. He could see the impact that steam locomotives would have on the future of rail travel. Together with his son Robert, he started to build steam locomotives for the U.K. and abroad.

BRIGHT SPARKS

Richard Trevithick built the first steam railroad locomotive in 1803 and many working engines (left). He was a genius, but bad at business, and was bankrupted. Trevithick sailed to South America and returned in 1827, only to discover that other inventors, including Stephenson, had benefitted from his ideas.

Rocket science

The first successful locomotive to launch from Stephenson's factory was *Rocket*. This design was the basis for all steam locomotives to come. One important development was the multitube boiler, boasting 25 copper tubes instead of the usual single or twin pipe, which allowed *Rocket* to travel faster than its rivals.

A tall chimney carried away smoke and fumes

A gauge on the side of the chimney measured the boiler pressure

The boiler had to be well built to withstand the enormous pressure that built up inside

Steam rose and collected at the top of the boiler

Original wheels were made of wood

The piston was connected to a rod that turned the wheels

Rocket

Steam locomotive

Runaway winner

The Rainhill trials were held in Liverpool, U.K., to showcase developing locomotives. In 1829, *Rocket* entered the contest, pulling a load three times its own weight, at 12 mph (20 km/h), and towing a carriage of passengers at 24 mph (39 km/h). This made it the first vehicle to travel faster than a horse. After winning the trials, *Rocket* became one of the world's most famous steam locomotives.

The world's fastest steam locomotive was *Mallard*, which reached 126 mph (203 km/h)

Out of steam

Rocket stayed in service for 67 years. The design was considered a classic, and even the very last steam locomotives built in the U.K. during the 1960s used *Rocket* as the basic model. With the advent of diesel-electric and electric locomotives, this great age had finally run out of steam.

Steam travel

Other vehicles have also been powered by steam, including cars, motorcycles, ships, and paddle wheelers.

Paddle wheeler

This type of ship uses steam power to drive the propellers, or paddle wheels. Steamboats were popular on American lakes and rivers during the 1800s.

Traction engine

Tractors powered by steam were used to pull heavy goods across fields, while smaller vehicles were used to transport lighter loads on public roads.

Heat from the firebox boiled the water to steam

The multitube boiler greatly increased the levels of steam produced

Coal was shoveled into the firebox end of the boiler

The driver and the fireman stood on a footplate

A tender was attached to the engine—it carried coal and a barrel of water

The cylinder converted steam power into movement

Train wheels traveled on metal rails to reduce friction and increase speed

SEE ALSO Engine 58 · Metro 174

Full steam ahead

With the arrival of steam locomotives, the world opened up for trade and travel. Following in the tracks of George and Robert Stephenson's first locomotives, railroads spread across Europe and America during the 1800s. Countries adopted similar designs to the British prototype for their locomotives and networks. Goods were transported across greater distances than ever before. Previously uninhabited regions became populated towns. As railroads gathered steam, landscapes and lives were changed for good.

European progress

Over time, European nations began to modify the original British design and build their own versions of locomotives and rail tracks. Locomotive factories were established in countries across Europe. At first, national rail tracks covered only short distances of up to 62 miles (100 km), but they grew to link up major towns and cities. As a result, rail became the best option for the swift movement of goods and labor, which drove the Industrial Revolution forward.

German production

By 1849, Germany's railroads had expanded to more than 3,100 miles (5,000 km) of track. Local factories assembled new locomotives, such as *Kopernicus* (above), produced near Stuttgart.

French flair

In 1842, the French government passed a law allowing private companies to build railroads connecting Paris with other cities. The main railroad system was born, running numbered locomotives such as *418* (right).

American dream

The railroad had an even greater impact on North America. By the 1830s, America was exporting steam locomotives to Europe and, while Europe merely provided a service between existing cities, American railroads were creating new towns in previously deserted areas. In North America, people were dispersing across the country to set up new communities, which created huge prosperity and progress. By the early 1900s, almost all North Americans lived within 25 miles (40 km) of a railroad.

Heading north

Railroads spread rapidly across North America, with locomotives such as the Great Western Railway's *Essex* (shown here) leading the advance. By 1869, it was possible to cross the entire continent by rail.

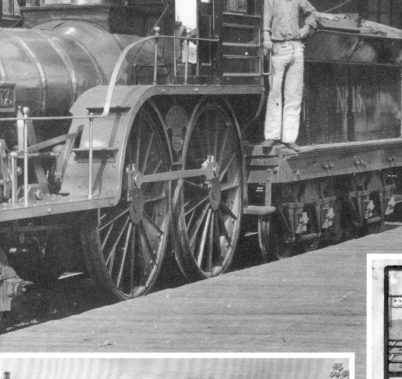

Russian rail

The first steam railroad in Russia connected Saint Petersburg with Tsarskoye Selo and Pavlovsky in 1837 (above). Locomotives could traverse the country's huge expanse and were used to take ore from mines to processing plants, as well as to carry passengers.

Oriental travel

Japan's traditional forms of transportation, such as the horse-drawn carriage, were replaced by the steam locomotive. The country's first steam-run railroad line opened in 1872 and became part of everyday life, as depicted in these three scenes from a 19th-century wood print.

There are more than 800 million bicycles in the world, making cycling one of the most popular modes of transportation. From humble beginnings, the bicycle has developed into an efficient, affordable, and environmentally friendly way to travel. Cycling is a good way to avoid traffic jams in towns and cities, while getting fit at the same time. Today's cyclist is spoiled for choice, with racing bikes, mountain bikes, hybrid bikes, and folding bikes.

BRIGHT SPARKS

First demonstrated in 1818, Baron Karl Drais von Sauerbronn's wooden *Laufmaschine* (running machine) was one of the world's first bicycles. With no pedals, riders pushed their feet against the ground to roll forward.

A bone-shaking ride
The first commercially successful pedal-driven bicycle was introduced by French inventor Pierre Michaux in 1863. Nicknamed the boneshaker, the velocipede became an instant hit in Great Britain and the U.S.A. Special rinks opened so that people could ride a velocipede for a penny a minute.

Chain reaction
In the 1880s, the use of rubber tires and a chain greatly improved bicycle design. The two wheels were now almost the same size, and the chain system turned the back wheel faster than the cyclist rotated the pedals. Safety features, such as brakes and adjustable handlebars, were added later.

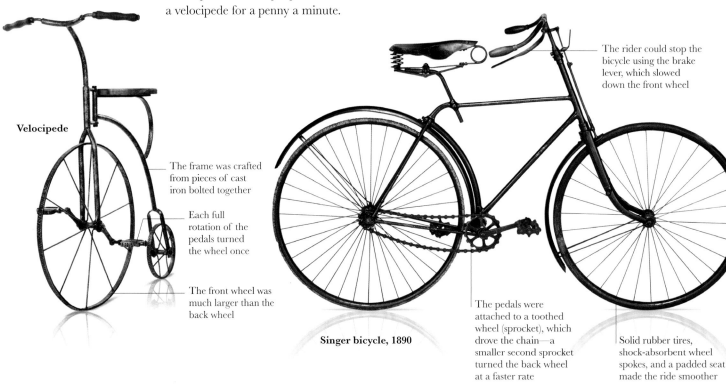

Velocipede

The frame was crafted from pieces of cast iron bolted together

Each full rotation of the pedals turned the wheel once

The front wheel was much larger than the back wheel

Singer bicycle, 1890

The rider could stop the bicycle using the brake lever, which slowed down the front wheel

The pedals were attached to a toothed wheel (sprocket), which drove the chain—a smaller second sprocket turned the back wheel at a faster rate

Solid rubber tires, shock-absorbent wheel spokes, and a padded seat made the ride smoother

Bicycle

The fastest bicycle speed on a flat surface is 83 mph (133 km/h), achieved by Canadian cyclist Sam Whittingham in 2009

Geared for efficiency

Today's mountain bikes have up to 30 gears. Gears make pedalling more energy efficient. When climbing hills in a low gear, a cyclist pedals more, but with less force than when using a higher gear.

Off the road

Cycling enthusiasts in California started the sport of mountain biking in the 1970s. Mountain bikes can traverse steep slopes and rocky terrain. There are now many ways to mountain bike, including cross-country, high-speed, all-day endurance, and slalom.

The rider uses the shift levers to move up or down gears

The frame's triangular shape can withstand extreme pressure

The levers on the handlebars pull wires to work the gears and brakes

The strong rubber tires are pneumatic (filled with air), which helps to cushion the ride

The forks have spring-loaded shock absorbers to help soften the impact from bumpy ground

Derailleur gears move the bike chain across a series of sprockets to "derail" one gear and engage another

A mixture of different-size sprockets produces the bike's gear ratios

Tires with a wide, deep tread provide the best grip on uneven surfaces

Mountain bike

SEE ALSO Wheel 146

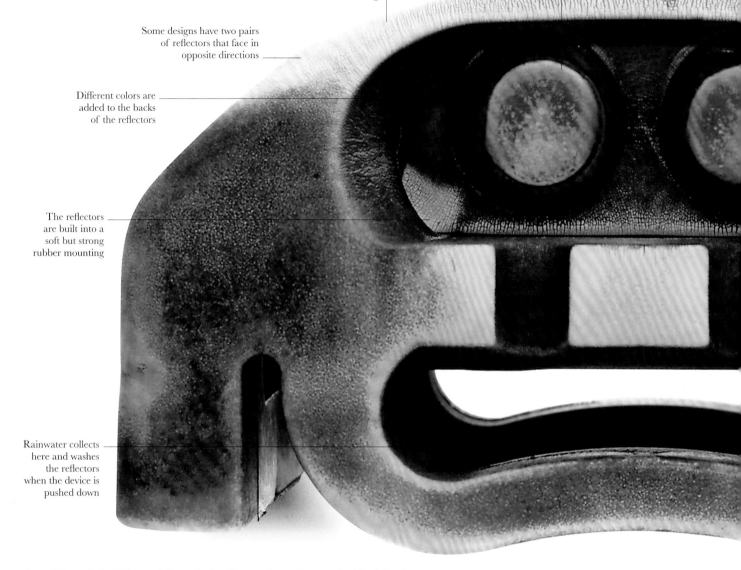

There is a shiny coating at the back of each reflector

When a car runs over the device, it is pushed down into the road to avoid damage

Some designs have two pairs of reflectors that face in opposite directions

Different colors are added to the backs of the reflectors

The reflectors are built into a soft but strong rubber mounting

Rainwater collects here and washes the reflectors when the device is pushed down

In World War II, driving in Great Britain at night was a dangerous business: streetlights were turned off, road signs were taken down, and windows were blacked out, all to make it more difficult for enemy bombers to find their targets. But help was at hand, thanks to Percy Shaw. His road-lighting cat's eyes were simple, durable, cheap—and very reliable. Soon, all over Great Britain, their gleaming points of light were guiding motorists safely home.

Free light
Unlike streetlights, cat's eyes don't need a supply of electricity to work, they simply reflect back the light from cars' headlights. This means that they cost nothing to use.

There are more than 100 million cat's eyes on the world's roads

Cat's eyes

Light from car headlights reflects straight back to the driver

This base is buried in the road surface

The way ahead

There are plans to use flashing cat's eyes as a warning system that could be switched on when there is an accident ahead. There are also plans to use cat's eyes that can turn themselves on when there is mist, drizzle, or ice on the road.

COOL SCIENCE

Percy Shaw's invention really does work just like a real cat's eyes, by using an effect called retroreflection. An ordinary mirror will reflect light in all types of directions. However, a retroreflector will always send light straight back toward its source.

Around the world

Though cat's eyes have been installed in the roads of many countries, they are not the only type of stud warning system in use.

Bott's dots

A different type of warning system is known as Bott's dots: when a car drives over them, the driver can feel a rumble and knows that the car is on the wrong part of the road.

Solar road stud

Unlike a cat's eye, this road marker lights up at night. It gets the power to do this from the Sun's rays, by using the small solar panel built in on top.

Oblong eye

This stud is another type of retroreflector. Oblong eyes are produced in India, and they are used in parts of North America and Australia.

SEE ALSO Solar cell 92 · Ford Model T 148

Percy Shaw

No one is sure where Percy Shaw got his lifesaving idea. Some stories suggest that he was once saved from driving over a dark hillside when the headlights of his car were reflected by the eyes of a cat, while others claim that he simply noticed a road sign with a new reflective coating.

A bright idea

Wherever Shaw got his idea, he knew that it was a good one! He patented his idea in 1934 and in 1935, at just 24 years old, he started his own company to make and sell cat's eyes. At first, he struggled to sell his invention, but in 1937 the U.K.'s Ministry of Transport laid a mixture of cat's eyes and competing designs from other inventors on a 5-mile (8-km) stretch of road to test them. Two years later, the majority of Shaw's cat's eyes were still working, unlike those of his rivals.

Lights in the night

When Shaw was a young man, there was an extensive network of tramlines on the roads linking local towns. He, like other night drivers, relied on the gleam of their rails to stay on the road.

> **The most brilliant invention ever produced in the interests of road safety. . .**
>
> From a British House of Commons statement

A growing business

Shaw's company Reflecting Roadstuds Ltd. started small but eventually grew, with Shaw employing 130 workers and making more than one million cat's eyes per year.

A wealthy man

In 1947, as a result of the increased interest in cat's eyes during World War II, the government launched a massive program to install them throughout the roads of Great Britain. Shaw became rich and famous—he bought himself four televisions and several Rolls-Royces, though he stayed in the house he'd lived in since he was two years old.

Smart move

In 1934, Shaw protected his invention from being copied by patenting it (left). A later patent added a device that enabled the cat's eyes to be self cleaning.

Cat's eyes catch on

Advertising campaigns, using brochures such as this, helped make cat's eyes popular during World War II, when Shaw was receiving orders for 40,000 per week. For a while he wasn't able to keep up with demand, because there was a shortage of rubber.

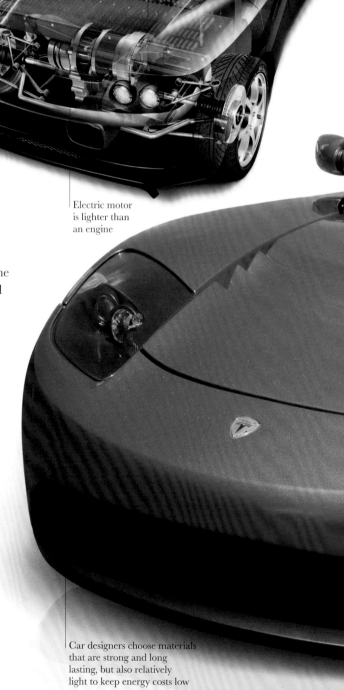

This area controls the electric motor

Video screen shows regenerated power and the number of oil barrels saved

Electric motor is lighter than an engine

Car designers choose materials that are strong and long lasting, but also relatively light to keep energy costs low

Though cars give people freedom, the problem is that they are polluting the atmosphere. Most cars run on gasoline and diesel, two limited and harmful resources. The solution is to design cars that use alternative types of power. The first electric cars were invented as early as the 1830s. These were soon replaced by popular gasoline and diesel vehicles, when little was known about their environmental effects. Electric cars are enjoying a 21st-century revival, and the latest designs replicate the look and performance of modern sports cars.

DarkStar

American car manufacturing Tesla Motors produced the groundbreaking Roadster prototype (right). Nicknamed DarkStar, the Roadster is an all-electric sports car with a top speed of 135 mph (215 km/h). It can accelerate from 0 to 60 mph (95 km/h) in less than four seconds.

The high-performance electric vehicle *La Jamais Contente* ("the never-satisfied") made history in 1899, when it reached 65 mph (105 km/h) in France. Belgian racer Camille Jenatzy had set the new land speed record.

Electric car

Leading the charge

The Roadster doesn't have an engine. Instead it uses an Energy Storage System (ESS), which has a bank of rechargeable lithium-ion batteries (as used in laptops). Like a cell phone, the batteries are charged up by plugging in to an electricity supply. The car has a charging port on one side and a detachable long lead that connects into a standard wall outlet. From a dead battery, the car can be fully recharged within a few hours.

Although they have a reputation for being slow, some electric cars can go from 0 to 100 mph (160 km/h) in less than 10 seconds!

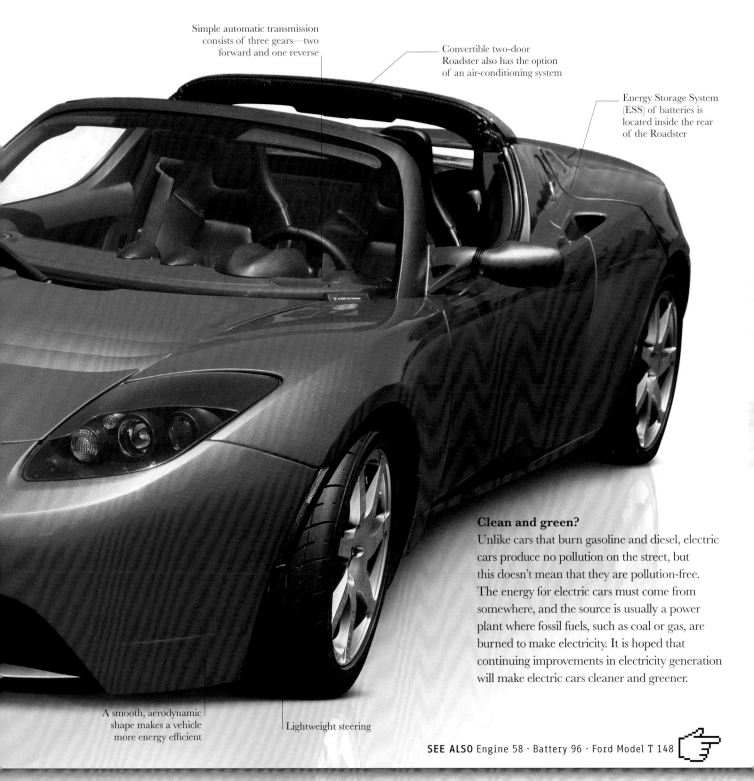

Simple automatic transmission consists of three gears—two forward and one reverse

Convertible two-door Roadster also has the option of an air-conditioning system

Energy Storage System (ESS) of batteries is located inside the rear of the Roadster

A smooth, aerodynamic shape makes a vehicle more energy efficient

Lightweight steering

Clean and green?

Unlike cars that burn gasoline and diesel, electric cars produce no pollution on the street, but this doesn't mean that they are pollution-free. The energy for electric cars must come from somewhere, and the source is usually a power plant where fossil fuels, such as coal or gas, are burned to make electricity. It is hoped that continuing improvements in electricity generation will make electric cars cleaner and greener.

SEE ALSO Engine 58 · Battery 96 · Ford Model T 148

Metro

The London Underground was an innovative solution to traffic problems experienced in the capital city during the 1800s. Vehicle numbers in the city were rising rapidly, and an alternative method of travel was needed in order to ease the growing congestion. The idea of building an underground railroad to link the city of London with mainline stations was first suggested in the 1830s, but it was dismissed as madness by most people. Despite this, English solicitor and underground railroad visionary Charles Pearson was persistent, and by the 1850s, his concept eventually received the necessary recognition and funding. With the initial section opening in 1863, the world's first underground railroad system was operational.

Today, the London Underground has 270 stations and around 250 miles (400 km) of track, making it the world's longest metro system

Electrical advantage

At first, steam-powered trains ran on the London Underground tracks. However, the smoke was damaging and polluted the air. When the City and South London underground line opened in 1890, electric trains were used instead. Electric trains were cleaner, quieter, faster, smoother, and easier to run.

Doors were located at both ends of the train car

Controls and equipment were mounted on both sides of the train car

Logo of engineering company Mather and Platt was displayed on train cars

Three coaches could be hauled behind the driver's car at up to 25 mph (40 km/h)

Nº 10

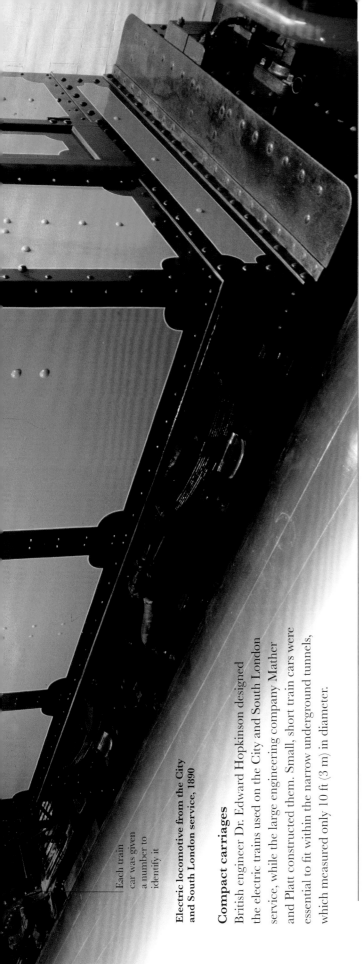

Each train car was given a number to identify it

Electric locomotive from the City and South London service, 1890

Compact carriages

British engineer Dr. Edward Hopkinson designed the electric trains used on the City and South London service, while the large engineering company Mather and Platt constructed them. Small, short train cars were essential to fit within the narrow underground tunnels, which measured only 10 ft (3 m) in diameter.

Global metros

Around 100 major cities around the world now have metro systems. Hidden under busy streets, these thriving underground networks keep people on the move. Multiple lines, stations, and trains ensure a fast flow of passenger traffic.

Mexican museum

During the construction of Mexico City's metro system, a treasure trove of artifacts was uncovered, including ancient Aztec ruins and a 12,000-year-old woolly mammoth. Many of the station logos reflect these fascinating finds.

Moscow splendor

Decorated with dazzling art, marble, mosaics, and chandeliers, the stations of the Moscow metro are the grandest around. Built in 1935 during Soviet rule, this metro system is the world's busiest, carrying at least seven million passengers per day.

SEE ALSO Steam locomotive 162

London Underground

The concept of "trains in drains" was initially difficult for people to grasp in the 1800s. Though a radical idea, key campaigners such as Charles Pearson persevered with their plans. With support and backing, construction began on the first underground railroad. From 1860 onward, many of London's streets were dug up as thousands of construction workers toiled to build the first line of the underground, the Metropolitan Railway.

Going underground

Once street surfaces had been dug up to enable construction, there were temporary problems on the roads as key routes were put out of use. Under the streets, workers laid tracks in trenches and created brick-lined tunnels, before replacing the road surfaces. This was known as the "cut and cover" method. The Metropolitan stretch of line opened on January 10, 1863, measuring 4 miles (6 km).

Charles Pearson

Although Charles Pearson was not directly involved in the running of the Metropolitan Railway, he championed the idea of the London Underground and used his influence to arrange sufficient funding from the City of London Corporation.

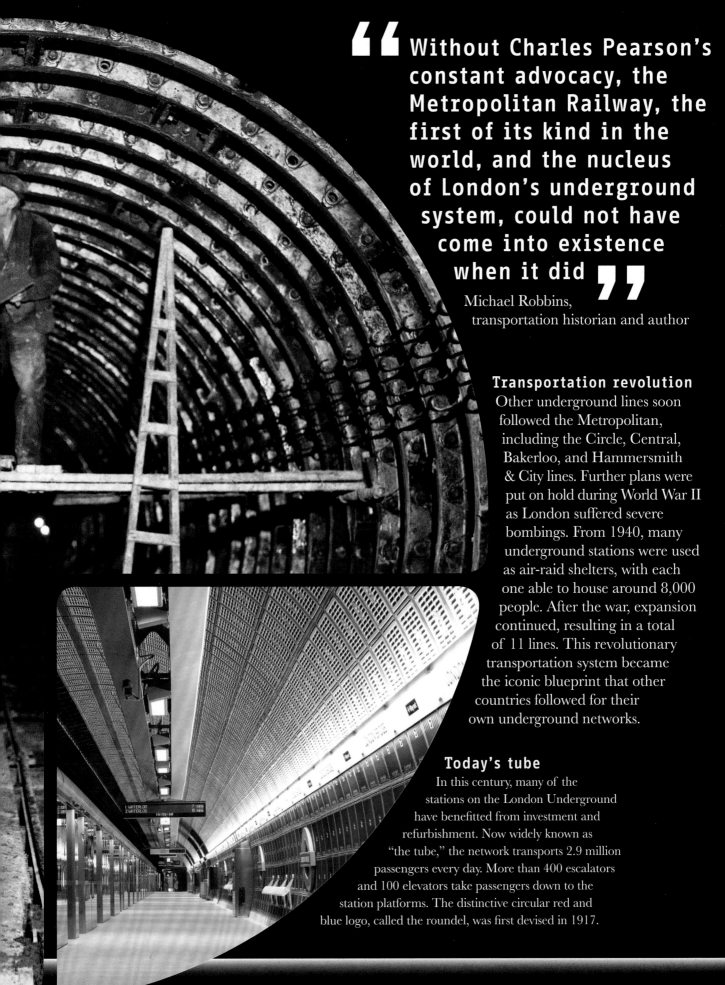

> " Without Charles Pearson's constant advocacy, the Metropolitan Railway, the first of its kind in the world, and the nucleus of London's underground system, could not have come into existence when it did "
>
> Michael Robbins,
> transportation historian and author

Transportation revolution

Other underground lines soon followed the Metropolitan, including the Circle, Central, Bakerloo, and Hammersmith & City lines. Further plans were put on hold during World War II as London suffered severe bombings. From 1940, many underground stations were used as air-raid shelters, with each one able to house around 8,000 people. After the war, expansion continued, resulting in a total of 11 lines. This revolutionary transportation system became the iconic blueprint that other countries followed for their own underground networks.

Today's tube

In this century, many of the stations on the London Underground have benefitted from investment and refurbishment. Now widely known as "the tube," the network transports 2.9 million passengers every day. More than 400 escalators and 100 elevators take passengers down to the station platforms. The distinctive circular red and blue logo, called the roundel, was first devised in 1917.

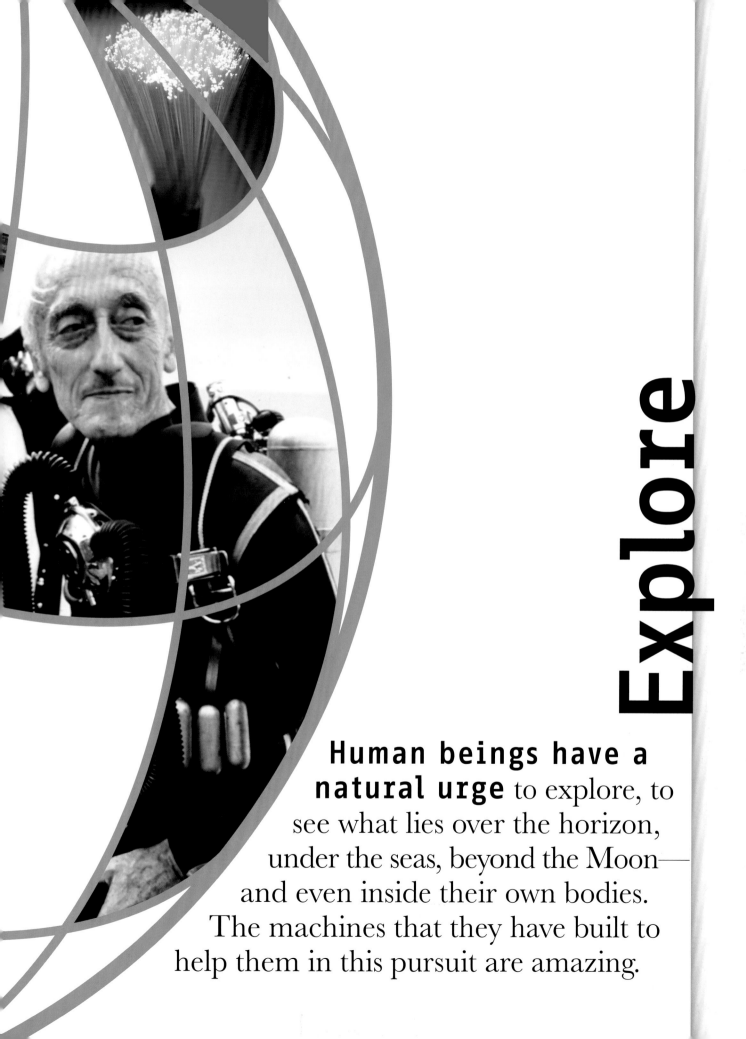

Explore

Human beings have a natural urge to explore, to see what lies over the horizon, under the seas, beyond the Moon—and even inside their own bodies. The machines that they have built to help them in this pursuit are amazing.

The Chinese first created rockets around 800 years ago, using them for fireworks and military weapons. Since the 1950s, space agencies have used much larger rockets to launch satellites and spacecraft. At 363 ft (111 m) tall, NASA's *Saturn V* rockets were the largest of all. Designed to launch the *Apollo* mission spacecraft and send humans to the Moon, they were the most powerful vehicles the world had ever seen.

The *Saturn V* rocket's five first-stage engines were as powerful as 30 jumbo jet airliners

Rockets to the Moon

German-American rocket scientist Wernher von Braun led the scientists and engineers who designed the *Saturn V* rocket for NASA. A total of 15 *Saturn V* rockets were built, and 13 of them were launched between 1967 and 1973.

The Kennedy Space Center on Merritt Island, Florida, was the launch site for the *Saturn V* rockets

Hungry for fuel

Saturn V launch vehicles consisted of three separate rockets (stages) stacked on top of each other, which fired in turn. Together, these weighed 3,300 tons, of which around 3,080 tons was fuel. As the stages ran out of fuel, the rocket discarded them.

Saturn V rockets took off from Launch Complex 39

3, 2, 1, liftoff!

When a *Saturn V*'s engines fired, the ground shook. Seven seconds later, with the engines running at full power, the rocket slowly rose off the launchpad. Around 12 minutes later, the *Apollo* spacecraft that it carried was orbiting Earth.

COOL SCIENCE

Rockets work because they follow Isaac Newton's third law of motion: each force (an action) has an equal force in the opposite direction (the reaction). As the fuel burns, the expanding exhaust gases are pushed backward, and the Newtonian reaction pushes the rocket forward.

Saturn V

In an emergency, the launch escape system could pull the Command Module away to safety

The Command Module was designed to carry the crew to the Moon and back

The Service Module provided oxygen, electricity, and rocket propulsion for the spacecraft

The Lunar Module landed two men on the Moon

The crew walked along the access arm to reach the Command Module

The third stage engine propelled the spacecraft toward the Moon

The first stage engines fired for 2½ minutes, and then the second stage for around six minutes

Space stations

The biggest spacecraft are space stations. Some are so large, rockets can only launch them in pieces and these have to be put together in orbit.

Skylab

Launched by a *Saturn V* rocket in 1973, Skylab tested how well people could cope with living in space. Over six years, three crews visited for a total of 171 days.

Mir

The Russian space station Mir was built in space from seven parts launched between 1986 and 1996. Before its mission ended in 2001, 105 astronauts from 12 countries had visited Mir.

International Space Station (ISS)

The ISS is a huge spacecraft being built in orbit by the space agencies of 16 countries, led by the U.S.A. and Russia.

SEE ALSO Spacesuit 194 · Space helmet 198

Each week, Hubble sends down enough data to fill a shelf of books more than 3,300 ft (1,000 m) long

The big idea

The idea for a space telescope was first suggested in 1923 by rocket scientist Hermann Oberth. He realized that a telescope in space, high above the atmosphere, would have a clearer view of the universe than telescopes on Earth.

The campaign

In 1946, American astrophysicist Lyman Spitzer wrote a paper in which he explained why a space-based telescope should be built. Spitzer campaigned relentlessly, but like Oberth, his idea was still way ahead of the technology that existed.

Space telescopes are astronomical instruments

launched into space to study planets, stars, galaxies, and other cosmic objects. They form sharper pictures and collect more information than telescopes on Earth and have greatly increased our knowledge of the universe. One of history's most important observatories, the Hubble Space Telescope, was also the first space-based optical telescope.

Radio antennae receive instructions from Earth and transmit data back

Astronauts use the handholds when servicing the telescope

Solar panels create electricity from sunlight

Onboard batteries provide power while Hubble is in Earth's shadow

Reflective silver insulation stops Hubble from overheating

Cameras and other instruments (within this area) take pictures and collect data

Hubble

Closing the aperture door protects the telescope from debris and sunlight

Getting the picture

Hubble sends images to Earth as digital radio waves. It uses NASA's fleet of space communication satellites to transmit this data.

Blast off!

It was not until the late 1960s that NASA began its space telescope program and the Hubble Space Telescope became a reality. Spitzer played a key part in both the design and development of Hubble.

Starlight, which forms Hubble's images, travels down this aluminum tube

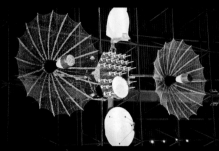

Satellite communications

Around twice a day, Hubble sends data to one of NASA's Tracking and Data Relay Satellites, which orbit Earth. The satellite relays the data down to Earth.

When in use, the light shield stops stray light from entering the telescope

Facts and figures

Similar in size and weight to a big bus, Hubble is the largest and most accurate telescope in space. It orbits Earth around 350 miles (570 km) above the ground. Traveling 5 miles (8 km) every second, it takes around 1½ hours to go all the way around our planet.

Ground station

The radio dishes at a ground station in New Mexico receive the satellite's data and send it on to the Goddard Space Flight Center in Greenbelt, Maryland.

▶▶ TOMORROW'S WORLD

A future space telescope called SIM Lite will search for Earth-size planets orbiting other stars. It will measure the positions of stars with great accuracy, even detecting tiny wobbles caused by the pull of gravity from nearby planets.

Space Telescope Science Institute

The space center forwards the data to the Space Telescope Science Institute in nearby Baltimore. Only there is it finally converted back into images.

SEE ALSO Solar cell 92 · Radio 116 · Cassini 192

183

Hubble in action

Hubble was launched from the space shuttle _Discovery_ on April 24, 1990. Since then, it has sent hundreds of thousands of pictures of the universe down to Earth. These images have helped astronomers find planets orbiting distant stars, understand how galaxies form, and even calculate the age of the universe. With its spectacular images, Hubble has changed the face of modern astronomy.

Hubble gallery

Hubble has whirled around Earth, taking images that no land-based telescope could ever take. It has photographed stars as they are born and in their dying days and has captured distant galaxies colliding with each other. Some pictures show galaxies so distant that the light forming Hubble's images started its journey across the universe more than 13 billion years ago—not long after the universe formed.

The Great Red Spot

Named the Great Red Spot, a huge storm larger than Earth has been raging on the planet Jupiter for at least 340 years. This Hubble image shows the Great Red Spot with a new storm called Red Spot Junior, which appeared in 2006. The smallest red spot, on the left side of the image, is another storm that appeared in 2008.

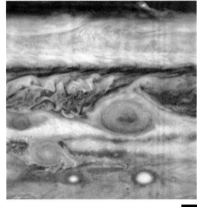

Ice-cold poles

Some images show the frozen white poles of the planet Mars, which grow and shrink with the seasons. Hubble has also photographed dust storms swirling around Mars, the biggest of which engulf the entire red planet.

Repairs in space

With Earth high above his head, astronaut Story Musgrave stands on the end of the space shuttle's robotic arm. During this mission in 1993, astronauts attached devices that helped Hubble focus better—like a pair of glasses! Altogether, there have been five servicing missions to repair and update the telescope.

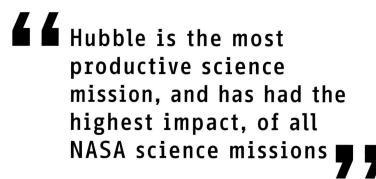

" **Hubble is the most productive science mission, and has had the highest impact, of all NASA science missions** "

David Leckrone, Hubble project scientist

Hubble trouble

The story of Hubble could have been very different. Hubble is a reflector telescope, which uses curved mirrors to focus light. These must be smooth and exactly the right shape in order to form sharp images. But almost immediately after Hubble first went into orbit, scientists discovered a serious problem—its main mirror was the wrong shape. The tiny flaw, amounting to just one fiftieth of the width of a human hair at the mirror's edge, was enough to blur its images. As the telescope was already in space, it had to be fixed by astronauts. Since then, Hubble has worked tirelessly, revolutionizing astronomy.

Clouds of color

Hubble has taken beautiful images that show clouds of gas and dust, which are called nebulae. Some of them were formed by stars exploding; others are places where new stars are forming. Some nebulae are cool and dark, while others glow brightly.

Galaxies

A galaxy is a collection of stars moving through space together. We live in a spiral galaxy called the Milky Way, but there are billions of galaxies, most with hundreds of billions of stars. Hubble has photographed galaxies of all shapes and sizes, including huge spiral galaxies like our own.

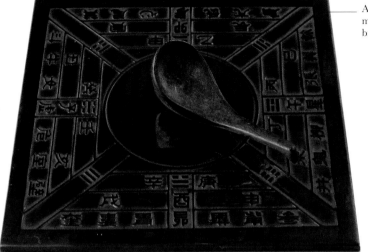

The spoon was made of lodestone, which swivels to point north

A flat plate was made of stone, brass, or bronze

A wooden box protects the compass from damage

A magnetized needle pivots on top of a sharp point

Swiveling spoons

The first direction-finding compasses were made in China around 220 B.C.E., using a flat plate with a spoon-shaped piece of lodestone (a magnetic rock) resting on it. The spoon swiveled until its handle pointed south, because the bigger bowl of the spoon was attracted to the north. This ancient Chinese compass was called a sinan, meaning "south pointer."

The compass was the main means of finding direction on long sea voyages, with records indicating that the Chinese started using compasses for navigation around 1100. They were only improved with the development of radio navigation and satellite navigation in the second half of the 1900s. The great voyages of exploration, discovery, and trade, such as Christopher Columbus's voyages to the Americas in the 1400s, would have been impossible without the magnetic compass to guide ships across the oceans.

Pocket compass

Travelers, explorers, surveyors, and soldiers wanted small compasses that were light and easy to carry. The answer was the pocket compass. By replacing the large piece of magnetic lodestone used by earlier compasses with a small magnetized needle, compasses could be shrunk down to a much smaller size—small enough to fit in a pocket. The compass shown above was used by the American explorers Meriwether Lewis and William Clark in their attempt to find a route across North America in 1804–1806.

Compass

Magnetic compasses don't work correctly within 1,200 miles (1,900 km) of either pole

Liquid compass

Compasses are difficult to read if they are shaken by the pitching and rolling motion of a ship, so ships' compasses were mounted in gimbals—swiveling rings that let a compass stay level when a ship moved. The liquid compass is a further improvement. A magnetic card with north marked on it is sealed inside a glass or plastic bubble that is full of liquid. The liquid steadies the card and makes it easier to read.

Liquid inside the plastic bubble steadies the compass card

A magnetized needle is attached to a card that has degrees marked on it

The card swivels until the zero degrees line points north

SEE ALSO GPS 190

Mars has fascinated people for centuries.

It was once thought to be the home of intelligent creatures, but the first space probes to reach Mars, in the 1970s, found a dry, dusty, lifeless world. Since then, NASA has developed small electric vehicles called rovers to explore the surface of the planet. In 2003, they launched two rovers—*Spirit* and *Opportunity*—which landed safely on Mars in 2004. Designed to last just 90 days, they have been sending data back to Earth ever since.

Spirit and *Opportunity* have sent back more than 260,000 photographs of the Martian surface to Earth

Landing on Mars
When each rover plunged into the Martian atmosphere, huge air bags inflated like balloons around it and rockets fired to slow it down. On landing, the rovers bounced along, inside the bags, before coming to a halt and driving out on to the surface.

Driving on Mars
When scientists instruct a Mars rover to take a close-up look at a nearby rock, it maps the ground ahead and figures out how to safely reach its destination. This means it can avoid other rocks and holes in the way.

Cameras look out at the Martian surface

A tall mast holds the cameras up high

Solar panels turn sunlight into electricity to power the rover

The robotic arm has a rock grinding tool

Mars rovers

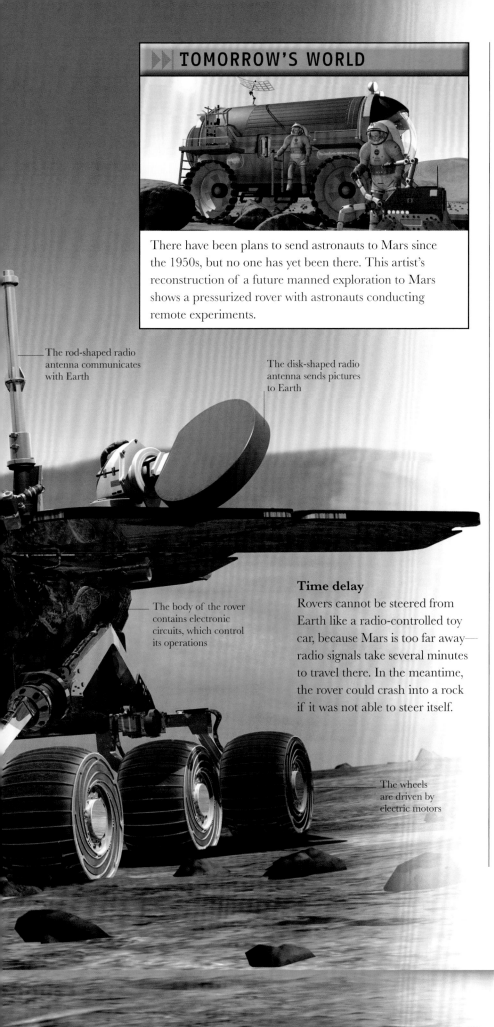

There have been plans to send astronauts to Mars since the 1950s, but no one has yet been there. This artist's reconstruction of a future manned exploration to Mars shows a pressurized rover with astronauts conducting remote experiments.

The rod-shaped radio antenna communicates with Earth

The disk-shaped radio antenna sends pictures to Earth

The body of the rover contains electronic circuits, which control its operations

Time delay

Rovers cannot be steered from Earth like a radio-controlled toy car, because Mars is too far away— radio signals take several minutes to travel there. In the meantime, the rover could crash into a rock if it was not able to steer itself.

The wheels are driven by electric motors

Life on Mars

Mars is like a smaller, colder, drier version of Earth, and scientists want to know if life ever existed there. Water is essential for life, so some of the space probes and rovers have been searching on Mars for water or for signs that it was there in the past.

Under the surface

Spirit and *Opportunity* have cameras and tools to look for rocks that formed in water. At the end of the robotic arm, there is a tool for grinding away the surface of rocks, so scientists can find out what is inside them.

Revealing rocks

Scientists believe that the Gusev Crater on Mars once contained liquid water. Although there is no liquid water on the surface now, it is possible that some still exists underground.

SEE ALSO Robots 74 · Solar cell 92

Former Russian premier Vladimir Putin's dog wears a GPS collar, so that it can be found if it wanders off

Satellite navigation has been used since the 1960s. The first satellite navigation system was developed by the U.S. Navy and called Transit. Today, it is used by millions of drivers, sailors, and pilots to find out exactly where they are and how to reach their destination. The most common system is called GPS—Global Positioning System. It was set up by the U.S. government for its military forces, but everyone can use it.

Submarine navigation
The U.S. Navy developed satellite navigation for its nuclear submarines. To fire their missiles accurately, the submarines needed to know exactly where they were. Out of sight of land, satellite navigation was the answer.

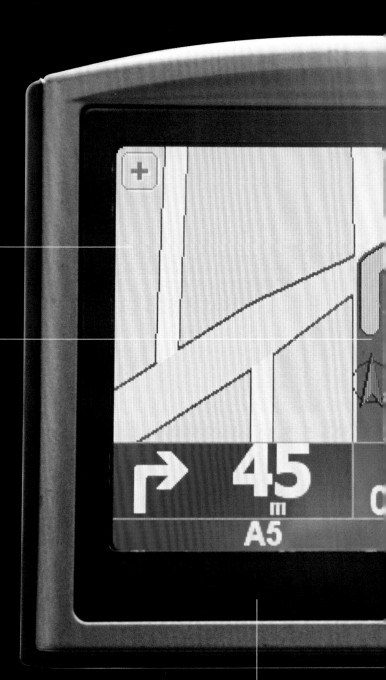

A street map shows the receiver's surroundings

As the receiver moves, the map moves, keeping the receiver's position in the middle of the screen

This receiver is controlled by touching its screen

COOL SCIENCE

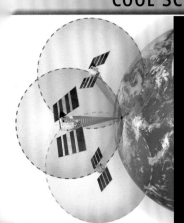

A GPS receiver uses radio signals from GPS satellites to figure out how far it is from the satellites. Knowing how far it is from three satellites tells it where it is on Earth's surface. With a fourth satellite, it can also tell how high it is.

GPS

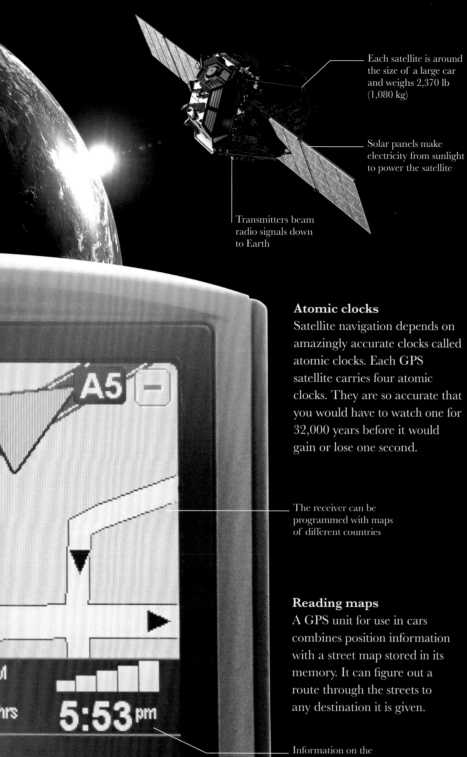

Each satellite is around the size of a large car and weighs 2,370 lb (1,080 kg)

Solar panels make electricity from sunlight to power the satellite

Transmitters beam radio signals down to Earth

Around the world

A satellite navigation system uses more than 20 satellites spread out evenly around Earth. GPS uses 24 satellites. A Russian satellite navigation system called GLONASS has 21. Europe is building a new satellite navigation system, called Galileo, with 27 satellites.

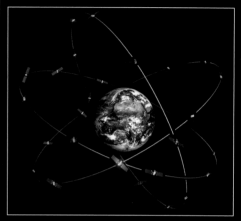

Galileo

Europe's Galileo navigation system will use a fleet of satellites orbiting Earth at a height of 14,430 miles (23,222 km). Three extra satellites will be launched and kept in space in case they are needed to replace faulty satellites.

Atomic clocks

Satellite navigation depends on amazingly accurate clocks called atomic clocks. Each GPS satellite carries four atomic clocks. They are so accurate that you would have to watch one for 32,000 years before it would gain or lose one second.

The receiver can be programmed with maps of different countries

GLONASS

Russia completed its own satellite navigation system, called GLONASS (Global Navigation Satellite System), in 1995. The GLONASS satellites orbit at a height of 11,868 miles (19,100 km), a little lower than GPS satellites.

Reading maps

A GPS unit for use in cars combines position information with a street map stored in its memory. It can figure out a route through the streets to any destination it is given.

Information on the screen includes the time and how much longer the journey will take

The receiver can be powered by a car or by its own battery

SEE ALSO Pendulum clock 78 · Cell phone 140 · Compass 186

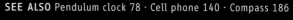

A space probe is an unmanned spacecraft sent to study the Moon or planets. The first space probe was *Luna 1*, a spacecraft launched toward the Moon by the Soviet Union in 1959. It was a metal ball that weighed just 796 lb (361 kg). In 1997, the U.S. space agency NASA launched one of the biggest, heaviest, and most complex space probes ever constructed—*Cassini*. It was named after the Italian astronomer Giovanni Domenico Cassini, who, in the 1600s, discovered four of Saturn's moons as well as a gap in the planet's rings. *Cassini* also carried a mini probe, *Huygens*, built by the European Space Agency (ESA).

The planet Saturn is lighter than water—if there was a bowl of water big enough, Saturn would float in it

COOL SCIENCE

April 1998
Venus flyby

June 1999
Venus flyby

Saturn
July 2004

Sun

Launch:
October
1997

Jupiter
December
2000

Earth flyby
August 1999

Space probes sent to explore the most distant planets use the gravity of the planets that they pass in order to change their speed and direction. As well as helping them travel farther, this saves a lot of fuel. *Cassini* flew past Venus (twice), Earth, and Jupiter on its way to Saturn.

Cassini

Mysterious planet

The rings that surround Saturn are mostly made of chunks of water ice. The main rings are several thousand miles wide but only 33 ft (10 m) thick. They were first seen by Italian astronomer Galileo Galilei when he looked at Saturn through a telescope in 1610—although he didn't know what they were. The *Cassini* space probe was designed to explore this, as well as many other mysteries.

Cassini fires its rocket to slow down and enter orbit around Saturn

The *Huygens* mini probe is housed behind this dish-shaped heat shield

New discoveries

Seven years after its launch, *Cassini* reached the orbit of the planet Saturn. The space probe discovered new moons and rings around Saturn and spotted lakes and sand dunes on Titan, one of its moons. *Cassini*'s mission was planned to end in 2008, but the probe was so successful that its mission has been extended twice. *Cassini* will continue exploring Saturn, its rings, and its moons until at least 2017.

Cassini dwarfs technicians fitting instruments to it prior to the launch

The main radio dish is 13 ft (4 m) across

The cosmic dust analyzer measures the size, speed, and direction of dust particles in space near Saturn

Three rocket thrusters steer *Cassini*

The adapter connects *Cassini* to its launch rocket; two rocket engines are located inside the adapter

Exploring Titan

Cassini sent the mini probe *Huygens* to explore one of Saturn's moons, Titan. This moon, the second-biggest in the Solar System, has interested scientists for many years, because it is the only moon with a thick atmosphere.

Falling through a haze

Huygens, which was named after the Dutch astronomer Christiaan Huygens, had a safe landing on Titan on January 14, 2005. It descended through the hazy atmosphere by parachute and came to rest on the shoreline of a dry riverbed.

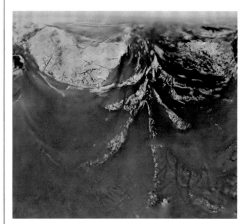

Wind, rain, and rivers

Winds blowing at 280 mph (450 km/h) were measured by *Huygens*, which also photographed a rocky surface shaped by flowing liquid. Titan is too cold for liquid water. Titan's rain, rivers, and lakes are made of liquid methane.

SEE ALSO Saturn V 180 · Hubble 182

There is no air in space. It's colder than a freezer in shadows, and hotter than boiling water in direct sunlight. When astronauts go into space, they travel inside a spacecraft. If they have to go outside their spacecraft, they need to wear a spacesuit. Without one, an astronaut would be dead within seconds. American aerospace company B.F. Goodrich was chosen by NASA to develop a spacesuit that would withstand the challenges of space exploration. In 1959, the design was finalized.

Made to measure

The first spacesuits were made specially to fit each astronaut. Today, the spacesuits worn by Space Shuttle and International Space Station (ISS) astronauts are made of legs, arms, and bodies that come in standard sizes, like store-bought clothes. The parts can be put together in different combinations to fit 90 percent of the population. Each astronaut has one suit for training, and another for the flight itself. The Shuttle/ISS spacesuit weighs 280 lb (127 kg) on Earth, but it is weightless in space.

The U.S. flag is sewn on the arm of all NASA spacesuits

A helmet locks firmly into place with a metal ring

Back on Earth, the suit could withstand up to 24 hours in ocean water

Inner layers included a nylon fabric coated with neoprene (also used to make wetsuits)

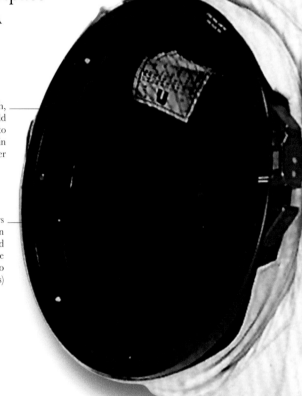

◄◄ BRIGHT SPARKS

American Wiley Post wanted to fly higher than anyone else. The air far above the ground is too thin to breathe, but Post helped to develop a suit that covered his entire body and head and pumped air into it so that he could breathe. In 1935, he flew at a height of more than 50,000 ft (15,240 m).

Apollo 20 mission

The spacesuit shown here was made for Jack Lousma to wear on the *Apollo 20* Moon-landing mission in 1974. He never got to use it, because *Apollos 18–20* were canceled.

The materials were carefully selected to ensure that mold and bacteria would not grow on them

Spacesuit

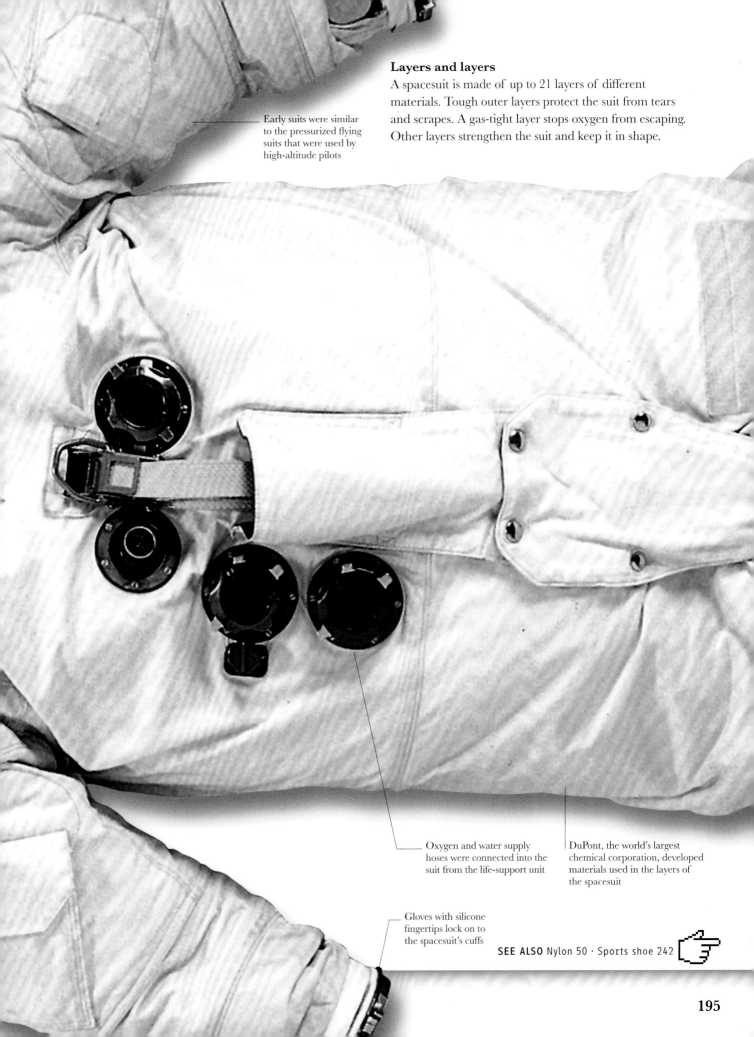

Layers and layers

A spacesuit is made of up to 21 layers of different materials. Tough outer layers protect the suit from tears and scrapes. A gas-tight layer stops oxygen from escaping. Other layers strengthen the suit and keep it in shape.

Early suits were similar to the pressurized flying suits that were used by high-altitude pilots

Oxygen and water supply hoses were connected into the suit from the life-support unit

DuPont, the world's largest chemical corporation, developed materials used in the layers of the spacesuit

Gloves with silicone fingertips lock on to the spacesuit's cuffs

SEE ALSO Nylon 50 · Sports shoe 242

Backpack

The spacesuits worn by Space Shuttle and ISS astronauts for spacewalks have backpacks. A backpack supplies the spacesuit with oxygen for the astronaut to breathe. It also has a radio for astronauts to talk to each other, as well as to their mission controllers on Earth.

Astronaut overboard!

Spacewalking astronauts are always clipped to their spacecraft by a safety line, so they can't drift away into space. If the worst should happen and an astronaut were to become unclipped and float away, the spacesuit has an emergency rescue device. Clipped to the backpack is a device called SAFER (Simplified Aid For EVA Rescue), which is basically a jet-pack. The astronaut can fire jets of nitrogen gas from it to fly back to the spacecraft.

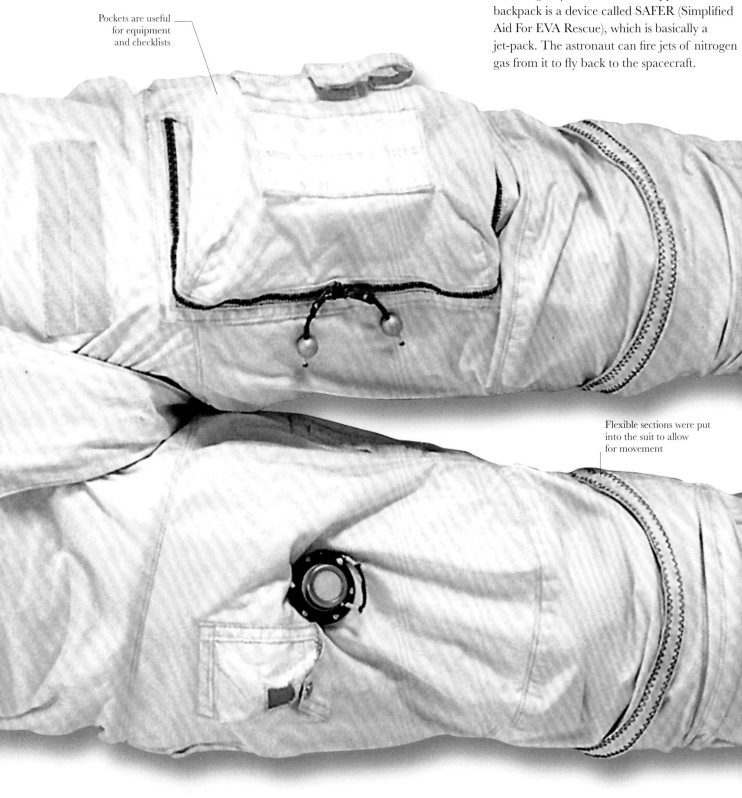

Pockets are useful for equipment and checklists

Flexible sections were put into the suit to allow for movement

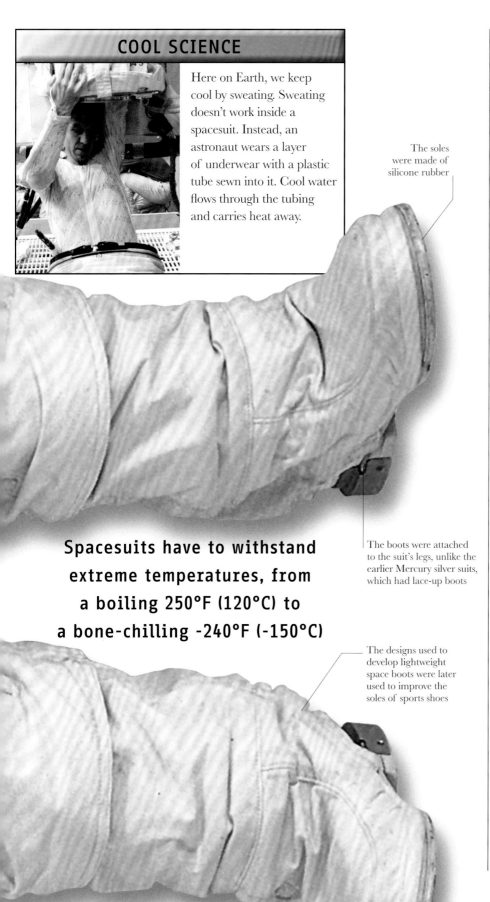

Here on Earth, we keep cool by sweating. Sweating doesn't work inside a spacesuit. Instead, an astronaut wears a layer of underwear with a plastic tube sewn into it. Cool water flows through the tubing and carries heat away.

The soles were made of silicone rubber

Spacesuits have to withstand extreme temperatures, from a boiling 250°F (120°C) to a bone-chilling -240°F (-150°C)

The boots were attached to the suit's legs, unlike the earlier Mercury silver suits, which had lace-up boots

The designs used to develop lightweight space boots were later used to improve the soles of sports shoes

Training for space

Astronauts train for months before a mission. They practice everything that they will do in space, over and over again, until they can do it perfectly.

Training underwater

For each mission, astronauts spend more than 100 hours training underwater in a giant pool. Training underwater feels similar to being in space.

Flight training

Since the 1960s, T-38 jets have been used by NASA to train its pilot astronauts. The pilots fly the jets for 15 hours per month to keep their flying skills sharp.

The vomit comet

Astronauts experience weightlessness in an aircraft nicknamed the vomit comet. As it dives steeply, people inside it float around!

SEE ALSO Saturn V 180 · Sports shoe 242

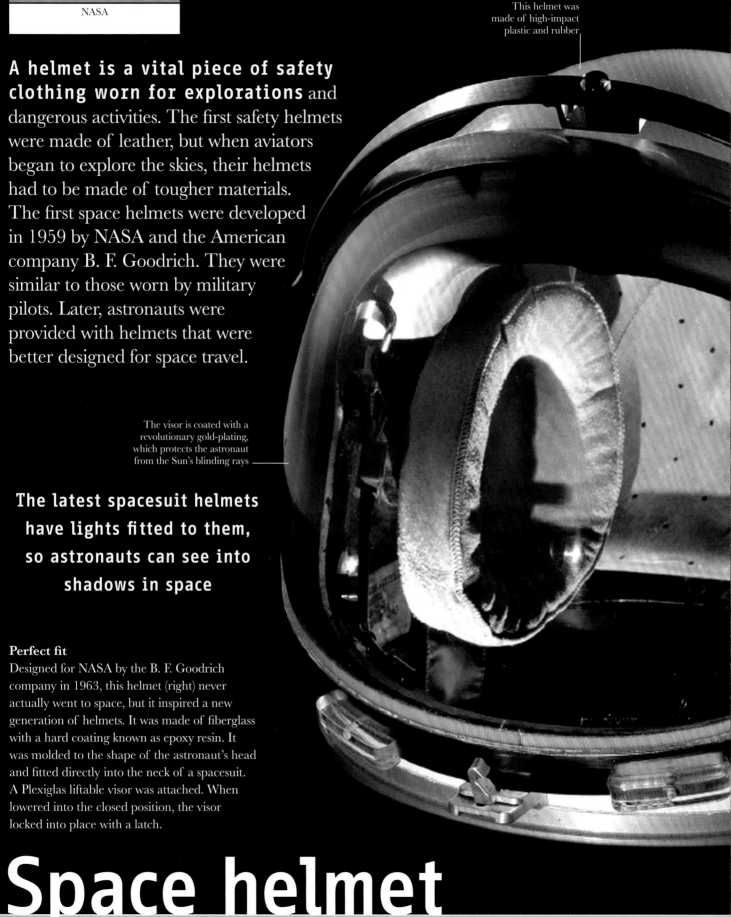

A helmet is a vital piece of safety clothing worn for explorations and dangerous activities. The first safety helmets were made of leather, but when aviators began to explore the skies, their helmets had to be made of tougher materials. The first space helmets were developed in 1959 by NASA and the American company B. F. Goodrich. They were similar to those worn by military pilots. Later, astronauts were provided with helmets that were better designed for space travel.

This helmet was made of high-impact plastic and rubber

The visor is coated with a revolutionary gold-plating, which protects the astronaut from the Sun's blinding rays

The latest spacesuit helmets have lights fitted to them, so astronauts can see into shadows in space

Perfect fit
Designed for NASA by the B. F. Goodrich company in 1963, this helmet (right) never actually went to space, but it inspired a new generation of helmets. It was made of fiberglass with a hard coating known as epoxy resin. It was molded to the shape of the astronaut's head and fitted directly into the neck of a spacesuit. A Plexiglas liftable visor was attached. When lowered into the closed position, the visor locked into place with a latch.

Space helmet

COOL SCIENCE

Early space helmets fogged up when astronauts worked hard: their breath formed a mist on the faceplate. Later helmets used air flow and antifog spray to keep them clear. They also had dark visors to protect astronauts' eyes from the dazzling glare of bright sunlight.

Made to move

The first space helmets fitted snugly, like a motorcycle helmet, and turned when the astronaut's head turned. Later helmets were bigger. They clipped on to a spacesuit's shoulders and didn't turn with the astronaut's head.

Suede headphones held equipment used for radio communication

This helmet was a prototype, which meant that it was the first of its type to be made

Space talk

Early space helmets had built-in microphones and earpieces so that astronauts could talk to each other and mission controllers. Today, astronauts wear a cap with microphones and earpieces inside a plastic bubble helmet.

A drinking water nozzle was provided, to enable an astronaut to drink through the helmet

Head cases

Hard, bony skulls protect brains in everyday life, but they can't withstand the greater impacts suffered when moving at high speed. For this, a helmet is needed.

Ice racers

A four-person bobsled can reach a top speed of 87 mph (140 km/h) on an ice track. The team wears full-face helmets, similar to motorcycle helmets.

Built for speed

The helmets worn by Formula 1 racing drivers are individually made for each person. A helmet is made of at least 17 layers of materials such as carbon fiber.

Cool cyclists

Cycle helmets are light, with slots to keep the cyclist's head cool. They are usually made of polystyrene foam with a hard shell of polycarbonate, carbon, or nylon.

SEE ALSO Saturn V 180 · Spacesuit 194

Submersibles are diving craft that are mainly used by scientists to explore the underwater world. They were developed from the bathysphere, a diving vessel invented by William Beebe and Otis Barton in 1930. While most submarines are large military vessels that operate on their own, submersibles are much smaller craft that have to be transported by a ship to the exploration site. Some submersibles can dive far deeper than any submarine can.

Beebe and Barton

American explorer William Beebe was interested in making deep dives, but in the 1920s there wasn't a diving craft that he could use for this. He teamed up with engineer and inventor Otis Barton, and they created the first bathysphere—a hollow steel ball lowered into the ocean at the end of a cable. In 1934, they dived to a record depth of 3,028 ft (923 m).

Beebe (left) and Barton
with the bathysphere, 1934

Cameras record
whatever the
crew can see

Shinkai 6500

Built for strength

Barton made his bathysphere in the shape of a sphere, or ball, because this is the best shape for withstanding great pressure deep underwater. The crushing force of water pressing in against a sphere is spread evenly all around it. The crew of a modern submersible sits inside a thick-walled sphere called the pressure hull.

Groundbreaking submersible

In 1960, a diving craft called *Trieste* took two men to a record-breaking depth of 35,797 ft (10,911 m). Today, a Japanese submersible called *Shinkai 6500*, is the deepest-diving craft. It can take a crew of three to a depth of 21,000 ft (6,500 m).

Submersible

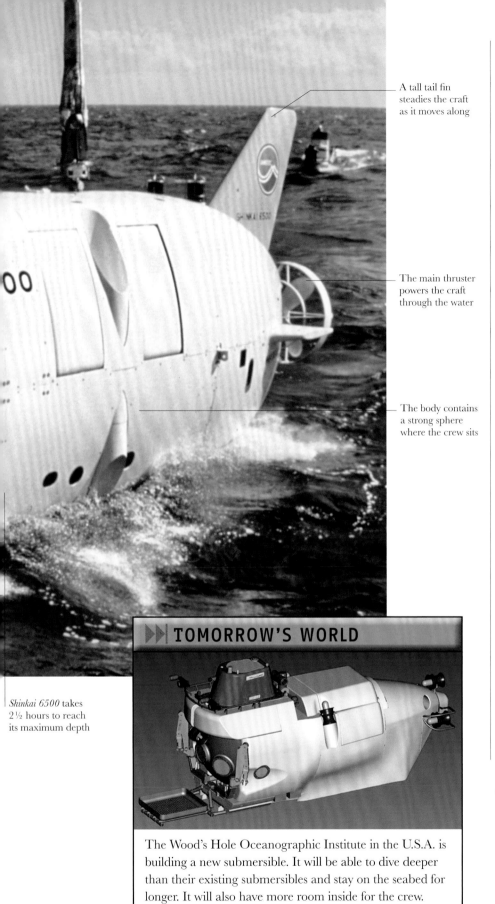

A tall tail fin steadies the craft as it moves along

The main thruster powers the craft through the water

The body contains a strong sphere where the crew sits

Shinkai 6500 takes 2½ hours to reach its maximum depth

Hidden world

More than 70 percent of Earth's surface is covered with water, and yet very little is known about the life that exists in the cold, dark depths. But with the help of deep-diving submersibles, researchers are uncovering some of the hidden gems of the ocean.

Creatures of the deep

Below a depth of 3,000 ft (1,000 m) lies a world of perpetual darkness. This viperfish lives 1,600–8,200 ft (500–2,500 m) below the surface of the oceans. A fierce predator, it has adapted to survive in the harsh conditions.

Hydrothermal vents

Hot water springs called hydrothermal vents were discovered at the bottom of the ocean in 1977. Only a handful of people have ever seen them. Their existence changed our understanding of life on Earth.

Twelve people have walked on the Moon, but only two people have visited the deepest part of the world's oceans

▶▶ TOMORROW'S WORLD

The Wood's Hole Oceanographic Institute in the U.S.A. is building a new submersible. It will be able to dive deeper than their existing submersibles and stay on the seabed for longer. It will also have more room inside for the crew.

The self-contained underwater breathing apparatus (SCUBA) was invented in 1943 by Frenchmen Jacques Cousteau and Émile Gagnan. Until then, divers had to wear heavy, cumbersome suits, and they were tethered to the surface by hoses that supplied the air that they breathed. Scuba gear allowed divers to freely swim around underwater while breathing air from cylinders on their backs. Scuba divers dive to explore the oceans, inspect oil rigs, carry out search and rescue work, or just for fun.

◀◀ BRIGHT SPARKS

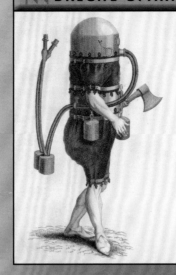

The first diving equipment to be called a diving suit was made by German mechanic Karl Heinrich Klingert in 1797. He made it from a leather jacket and trousers, with a helmet that had small, round glass windows for the diver to look out through. The diver breathed in and out through flexible hoses.

Rebreathing oxygen

One type of scuba device is called a rebreather. It collects the air that a diver breathes out and sends the oxygen that it contains back to the diver to breathe again. Rebreathers are often used on long dives, as they reduce the amount of gas that divers need to carry.

Under pressure

The most important piece of scuba equipment is the regulator. It supplies air from the tank to the diver at the same pressure as the surrounding water. Without it, water pressing against the diver's chest would make it impossible to breathe.

A pressure gauge shows how much air is left in the tank

With fins, divers can swim fast using just their legs

Scuba

An air hose carries air to the diver's mouthpiece

A regulator supplies air at the same pressure as the water

A tank on the diver's back contains compressed (high-pressure) air

A mask lets the diver see clearly underwater

A demand valve opens to let air through when the diver breathes in

A wetsuit keeps a diver warm and protects against scrapes and scratches

Scuba that suits

There are many different types of diving suits and scuba gear. There are super-strong diving suits for making very deep dives to below 2,000 ft (600 m), where water exerts a crushing pressure. There are even diving suits for adventurous pets!

Suits of armor

Atmospheric diving suits let divers breathe air at the same pressure as the air that they normally breathe. The suits have to be strong enough to resist the crushing pressure of water around them—like watertight suits of armor.

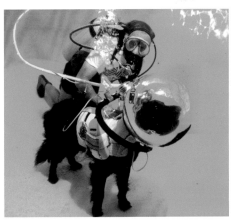

The diving dog

Shadow is a dog who has his own diving suit. He wears a lead-weighted jacket and a helmet, so he can go for walks underwater. Shadow breathes air supplied by a hose linked to his owner's air tank.

The bends

If scuba divers come up to the surface too fast, gas dissolved in their blood forms bubbles. This causes decompression sickness, better known as "the bends," which can be very painful or even fatal. To prevent the bends, divers may make several decompression stops on their way back up to the surface.

Smart diving

There are computers for almost everything today, including diving. A dive computer measures the time and depth of dives and warns a diver who stays down too long or comes up to the surface too quickly.

Leonardo da Vinci designed a diving suit 500 years ago

SEE ALSO Submarine 154 · Submersible 200

Jacques Cousteau

Jacques-Yves Cousteau died in 1997, but he is still known as the world's most famous undersea explorer. Even when he was a young naval officer in the 1940s, Cousteau wanted to show everyone the marvels that he had seen when diving. He spent the rest of his life developing equipment and methods for undersea exploration and filmmaking.

Aqua-Lung

Cousteau worked with engineer Emile Gagnan to develop the diving regulator in 1942. One year later, they began selling the "Aqua-Lung," which was a key part of Cousteau's scuba equipment. After leaving the navy in 1949, he fitted out a ship called *Calypso* as a floating laboratory and used it as a base for exploration and filmmaking all over the world.

Calypso

Calypso, a former minesweeper (a ship that cleared mines from seaways), served as Cousteau's diving vessel for more than 40 years. In 1996, *Calypso* sank in Singapore harbor after a collision with a barge.

An ideas man

Cousteau worked with designers and engineers to produce new machines and vehicles for exploring the oceans. These included underwater scooters and a tiny submersible craft that looked like a flying saucer.

Undersea home

Jacques Cousteau wanted to prove that people could live and work underwater. Between 1962 and 1965, he set up underwater bases called Conshelf I, II, and III. Up to six divers, called oceanauts, could live in a base for up to one month.

Saucers and fleas

Cousteau helped develop the diving saucer: a two-person submarine that could dive down to 1,300 ft (400 m). He also experimented with smaller craft, called Sea Fleas, that could dive to 1,640 ft (500 m).

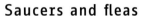

Cousteau's legacy

In his later years, Cousteau widened his work from exploring and studying the oceans to trying to protect them. He was one of the first people to popularize the idea that Earth's oceans are fragile environments. In 1973, he founded the Cousteau Society for the Protection of Ocean Life, which raises funds for education, research, and the protection of the natural world. Although Cousteau himself is no longer at the helm, his work continues.

Undersea movies

Millions of people saw the undersea world for the first time in Jacques Cousteau's movies. He also made a long-running television series.

> **❝ From birth, man carries the weight of gravity on his shoulders. . . But man has only to sink beneath the surface and he is free ❞**
>
> Jacques-Yves Cousteau

BASIL HIRSCHOWITZ

The optical fibers inside an endoscope are strands of glass as thin as a human hair

A fiber-optic endoscope enables a doctor to explore inside a patient's body without cutting it open. It is a technique that has changed surgery, making many operations safer, easier, and cheaper. Each endoscope is a thin flexible tube that contains glass threads called optical fibers. Light travels down the fibers, into the patient, and an image travels back. Instruments at the tip of the endoscope can grip, cut, and take samples.

A better view

In the 1950s, Basil Hirschowitz was a physician at the University of Michigan. He wanted a better way to see inside a patient's stomach and intestines than the metal tubes in use at that time. After reading about fiber-optics, he developed the first flexible fiber-optic endoscope. It was ready for use in hospitals by 1960.

An eyepiece shows the doctor the view from the tip of the endoscope

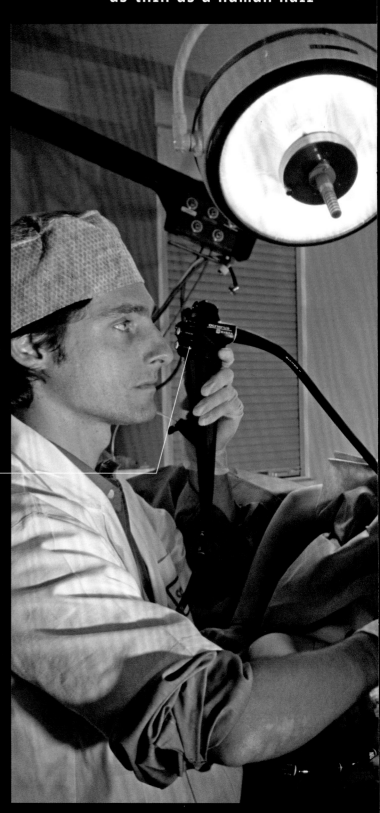

COOL SCIENCE

When light enters one end of an optical fiber, it stays inside the fiber. Even if the fiber is bent or tied in a knot, the light stays inside it and follows it to the end, like water flowing through a bent pipe. Optical fibers have to be made of very pure glass, free from defects, in order to carry the maximum light intensity from end to end.

Fiber-optic endoscope

The image seen by the doctor in the endoscope is often shown on a screen, so others can watch the surgery, too

An endoscope the size of a large pill has been developed. Called a capsule endoscope, it is swallowed by a patient and passes through the body, transmitting pictures on its way. Future capsule endoscopes may be self-propelled and able to carry out minor surgery using a movable arm.

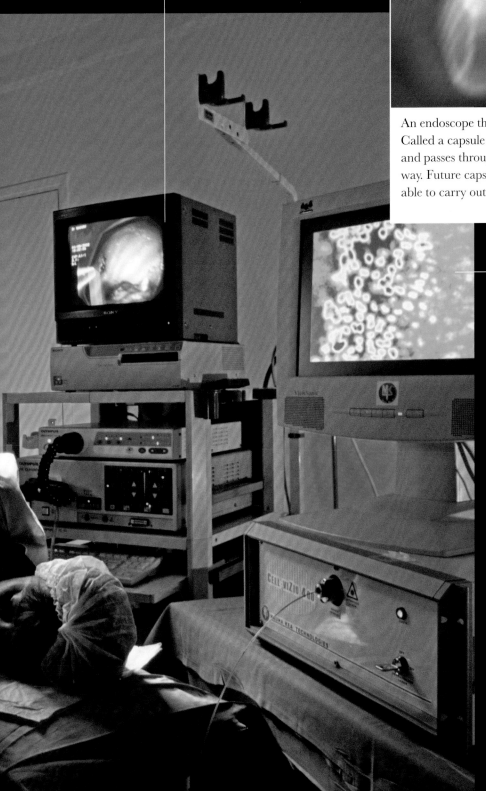

A second screen shows magnified images from this endoscope's built-in microscope

Fine control

A doctor can control an endoscope, turning the tip to point in different directions. This enables a doctor to look around inside a patient's stomach or steer an endoscope through the patient's intestines. Before the fiber-optic endoscope was invented, doctors often carried out major surgery to look inside a patient's body. Such surgery was more dangerous, and it took longer to recover.

Internal explorers

The flexible fiber-optic endoscope wasn't the first endoscope. The endoscope was invented in 1805 by Philip Bozzini in Vienna, Austria. It was a rigid pipe. Rigid endoscopes are still used today to look inside the nose, joints, and other parts of the body where the doctor doesn't have to twist and turn the endoscope.

Groundbreaking developments in imaging technology

have enabled doctors to explore the human body in incredible detail. Imaging devices that use x-rays are very good at showing bones, but not the soft parts of the body, such as muscles, nerves, and organs. Another type of imaging device, called a magnetic resonance imaging (MRI) scanner, is used to explore the body's soft tissues.

Amazing technology

These two examples are among a number of other imaging devices that are used to explore the human body without the need for surgery. One reveals the growth of an unborn baby. Another shows the brain thinking.

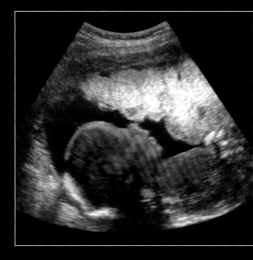

Ultrasound

Unborn babies are scanned using ultrasound—high-frequency sound waves. The sound waves travel through the mother and bounce off the baby. The reflected sound waves are received and processed

Who invented MRI?

In 1970, U.S. scientist Raymond Damadian found that he could detect harmful growths called tumors inside people by using magnets and radio waves, and in 1974 was granted a patent for his magnetic resonance technique. During the 1970s, other scientists, mainly Paul Lauterbur in the U.S.A. and Peter Mansfield in England, invented more advanced MRI scanners that made detailed pictures of the inside of the human body.

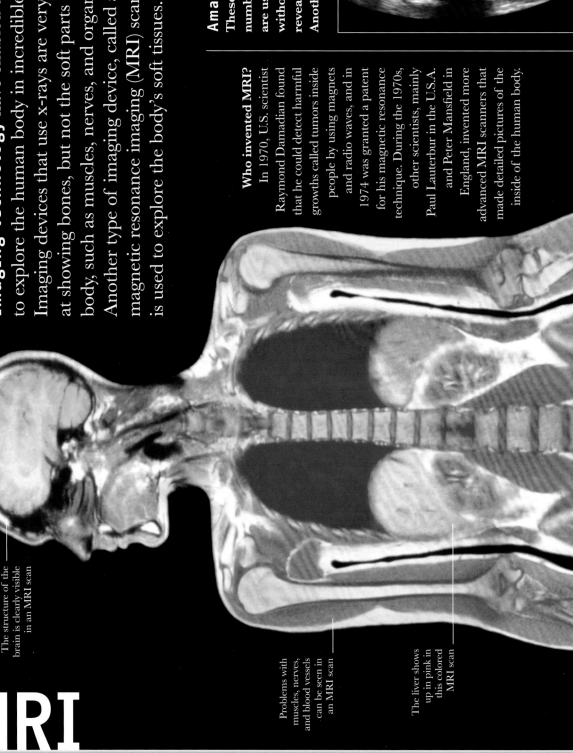

The structure of the brain is clearly visible in an MRI scan

Problems with muscles, nerves, and blood vessels can be seen in an MRI scan

The liver shows up in pink in this colored MRI scan

A number of scans are combined to produce a clear picture of the entire body

MRI

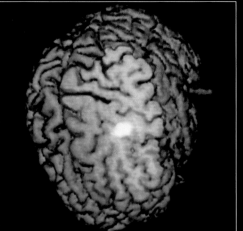

MEG

Magnetoencephalography (MEG) is used to make images of the brain in action. It shows which parts of the brain are working. It works by measuring the tiny magnetic forces produced by electric currents flowing through the brain.

How it works

An MRI scanner uses magnetism and radio waves to produce images. A patient lies on a table inside a powerful magnet. Atoms in the body line up with the magnet like compass needles. A burst of radio waves turns the atoms in a different direction. When they swing back, they send out radio signals, which a computer changes into pictures.

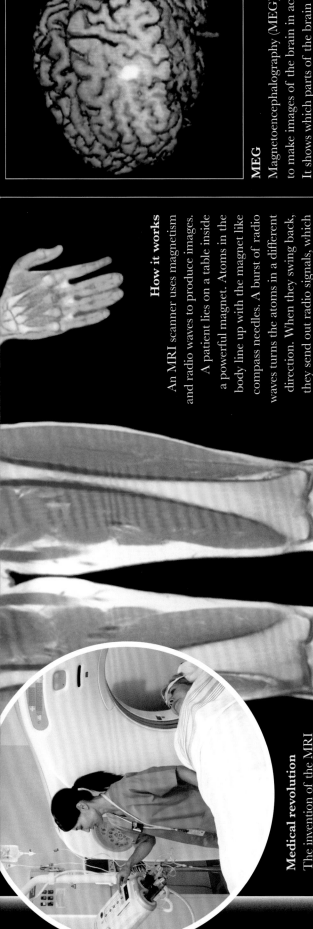

The yellow parts of the image are bones

Medical revolution

The invention of the MRI scanner has enabled doctors to look inside the human body in ways that were not possible before. This has given doctors a new method for finding diseases that other body scanners did not show.

More than 60 million MRI scans are carried out worldwide every year

SEE ALSO X-ray 22 · Fiber-optic endoscope 206

Culture

The lives that we lead today are the result of the ideas and inventions of many people. Some are so vital that we could hardly live without them, but others simply make life more fun!

Cheap and easy to use, the ballpoint pen is now the world's most common writing implement. It was invented by a Hungarian journalist, László Bíró, who was frustrated with the fountain pen that he was using. The ink often leaked from the nib and took so long to dry that it was easily smudged, so Bíró invented a new type of pen with a roller ball instead of a nib. His ballpoint pens first went on sale to the general public in the 1940s, and they were an instant hit. It is estimated that around 15 million ballpoint pens are now sold every 24 hours.

BRIGHT SPARKS

The ancient Egyptians used pens made from thin strips of reed. They shaped the ends to make a sharp nib, which they dipped in ink. Crushed plants mixed with water was used for the black ink. Both the writing tools and the ink were housed in a wooden case.

Sky high

One of the first large orders László Bíró received for his ballpoint pen came from Great Britain's Royal Air Force. The RAF wanted pens that fighter pilots could use at high altitudes—without leaking ink all over the cockpit.

Bíró (seen here using one of his own pens) owed his success in part to the work of his chemist brother György, who developed the thicker, quick-drying ink

Some pen casings unscrew so the ink cartridge can be replaced when the ink runs out

This refillable model was one of the earliest ballpoint pens ever produced and the first to be produced in Great Britain

The ball socket forms the tip of the pen

Appliance of science

Bíró's ballpoint pen had a new pen tip consisting of a small steel ball that could turn in its socket. As the pen was moved across the paper, the ball rolled, picking up ink from the ink cartridge and leaving it on the paper.

Ballpoint pen

The price of popularity

Designed to be thrown away after the ink has run out, the ballpoint has contributed to the notion that everyday things are disposable, and the nonbiodegradable plastic casings litter many landfills.

The pocket clip can be used to attach the pen to clothing

Inside, the thick, quick-drying ink contains colored dye

Gravity forces the ink down the thin, plastic ink tubing, toward the rollerball

The plastic casing is designed for easy grip

Splendid pens

Most ballpoint pens are made of plastic. However, if money is no object, you can buy ballpoints costing thousands of dollars. They are made from precious metals and encrusted with jewels.

21st-century pens

In an age of technology, even the humble pen has been reinvented and would be completely unrecognizable to László Bíró.

Digital pen

Anoto® digital pens contain tiny digital cameras and microprocessors. They are able to convert handwriting or drawing movements into digital signals, which are then displayed on a computer screen as written words or graphics.

Crime-fighter pen

Ultraviolet pens are used to mark property for security identification. The markings are only visible when ultraviolet light is held over them.

COOL SCIENCE

The ball stops the ink in the pen from drying and controls the ink flow. It needs to fit snugly in its socket to stop the ink from leaking, but it must also have enough room to rotate freely so that the ink is deposited on the paper in a smooth, even way.

More than 100 billion ballpoint pens have been sold since 1938

SEE ALSO PET bottles 36 · Microprocessor 98 · Digital camera 112 · Post-its 134

The history of umbrellas stretches back thousands of years to ancient times. In many cultures, ornamental umbrellas were used in religious ceremonies or by rulers. The first umbrellas were parasols, designed to provide shade from the sun. By the 1500s, parasols were a popular fashion accessory, carried by Europe's most stylish women. The Chinese were the first to use umbrellas as rain shields by adding a waterproof wax to the paper canopy. In 1928, German engineer Hans Haupt invented the telescopic pocket umbrella, making it a practical wet-weather protector.

The paper canopy attaches to the underside of the bamboo ribbing

Sun shade
Parasols have been used as sun shades in China for at least 2,000 years. The handle and ribs were traditionally made with bamboo, with oiled paper stretched between the ribbing to form the canopy. Ornate designs were often painted on the paper.

▶▶ TOMORROW'S WORLD

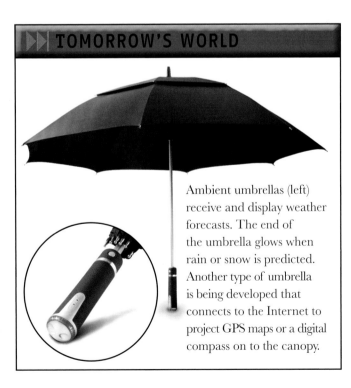

Ambient umbrellas (left) receive and display weather forecasts. The end of the umbrella glows when rain or snow is predicted. Another type of umbrella is being developed that connects to the Internet to project GPS maps or a digital compass on to the canopy.

Handy Hanways
Until the 1700s, umbrellas were considered a women's accessory, so when English traveler John Hanway first carried an umbrella through the rainy streets of London in the 1750s, he was ridiculed. Hanway wasn't deterred and continued carrying an umbrella for the rest of his life. His trendsetting ways soon caught on, and umbrellas were even known as "Hanways" for a while.

More than 75,000 umbrellas are lost each year on London's public transportation network

Umbrella

Metal ribs are slotted into a notch at the top of the shaft

The stretchers are connected to the runner, which slides up and down the shaft

Panels of waterproof nylon fabric are sewn together to form the canopy

The basic design of an umbrella has changed very little over the years

Metal hinges are used to join the stretchers to the ribs

The fabric canopy protects the user from rain and provides a shady cover in sunshine

One spring at the bottom of the shaft locks the umbrella in the closed position

A handle is at the bottom of the umbrella shaft and a finial is at its top

Practical and light

In 1852, Englishman Samuel Fox built a steel-framed umbrella, which was much lighter than the 10-lb (4.5-kg) wood and whalebone frames of the time. German inventor Hans Haupt later developed the Knirp umbrella, which could be collapsed and popped into a pocket.

Modern mechanisms

Most modern umbrellas have canopies made from waterproof nylon. Frames and handles made from Teflon-coated aluminum or fiberglass make them even more lightweight, and some umbrellas have mechanisms that enable them to open and close automatically.

SEE ALSO World Wide Web 44 · Nylon 50 · GPS 190

LEGO® bricks have fired the imaginations of generations

of children. LEGO® parts come in a huge range of shapes and sizes, most have two basic components—studs on the tops and tubes on the insides. Push the studded top of one piece into the tube-filled base of another piece, and the two bricks stick together. The bricks can be built up to create everything from pirate ships and police headquarters to motorized vehicles and programmable robots.

Fun and flexible

LEGO® elements can be used to create any number of designs and structures. There are more than 900 million different ways of combining six eight-stud bricks of the same color.

Features include searchlights and an emergency toolbox (with banana)

Titanium Command Rig is a digging machine

There are around 55 basic granule colors—new colors are made by mixing

Adjustable drilling platform

Double-geared rotating plenary drill

Heavy-duty spiked wheels

The LEGO® Power Miners were designed with working equipment

Melting and molding

At the LEGO® factory in Denmark, granules of plastic are melted at 450°F (232°C). The liquid plastic is injected into brick molds. Once the molded pieces have cooled, they fall on to a conveyor belt for assembly into packs.

LEGO® brick

Standing small

The first posable LEGO® mini figures were launched in 1978. They had hands that could grip accessories, and arms and legs that could move. They were designed to encourage children to use their imagination and create their own stories.

The distinctive hands of the mini figures are designed to grip LEGO® tools and machinery

The toys are designed to inspire creative play

This model can be transformed into a vertical drilling platform

Around 40,000 new bricks are made every minute

COOL SCIENCE

When one brick is pressed on top of another brick, the studs of the bottom piece push between the walls and tubes of the piece above, slotting the bricks tightly together. Friction between the pieces stops the bricks from sliding apart.

Design and build

The first step in designing toys is finding inspiration. Members of the LEGO® design team dream up ideas for stories, models, and new parts.

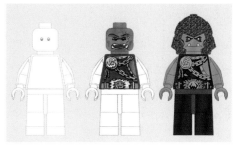

Sketching it out

Each new mini figure character begins as a blank design template. Artists and designers build it up, adding color and features with markers or by using a computer.

Computer models

Engineers and model designers build real models and 3-D computer models to try out their ideas. Some pieces are sculpted by hand before being scanned into a computer.

Model builders

All the parts are checked to make sure that they are child-safe and fit into the LEGO® system, before children test them.

SEE ALSO PET bottles 36

Play well

Since its beginnings as a wooden toy business in Billund, Denmark, the LEGO Group has grown to become the fourth-largest toy manufacturer in the world, selling its famous plastic building bricks in more than 130 countries. The business was founded by master carpenter Ole Kirk Kristiansen in 1932. He named his company LEGO, from the Danish words *leg godt*, meaning "play well."

Plastic fantastic

Ole Kirk Kristiansen first made wooden toys. He designed them to be of high quality and tough enough to pass from one generation of children to the next. When plastic came into use, Ole Kirk moved with the times. In 1947, he bought a plastic injection-molding machine and, two years later, began to develop a new toy—interlocking plastic building bricks that could be used to create anything.

A family business

Three generations were involved with the family business—the founder Ole Kirk, his son Godtfred Kirk, and Godtfred's son Kjeld Kirk. Here, Godtfred and Kjeld are discussing a model car in 1978.

Toy cars

Ole Kirk's son, Godtfred Kirk, joined the company in 1937 at the age of 17. Among his many contributions, Godtfred designed wooden toy cars, producing detailed technical drawings.

Building the future

In the 1950s, the plastic building blocks were branded as LEGO® bricks and the concept of a "System of Play" was developed, enabling a child to create an entire town with endless possibilities. Building on the product's success, the first LEGOLAND® Theme Park was opened in Billund, Denmark, in 1968. Visitors could wander around miniature towns made from LEGO bricks. By the 1990s, programmable brick robots were being made. In its 60-year history, more than 400 billion colorful LEGO bricks have been made.

Play sets

In 1955, the company launched the first set pack—Town Plan No. 1. It contained bricks and materials to create a LEGO® downtown. A young Kjeld Kirk Kristiansen appeared on the packaging.

A model family

The No. 200 LEGO® Family Set was released in 1974 and included a grandmother, father, mother, son, and daughter. It quickly became the biggest selling product at the time.

Robot bricks

The LEGO® Mindstorms® NXT robot was launched in 2006. It can be programmed to walk, hear, and see.

"Only the best is good enough"

Ole Kirk Kristiansen

When Sony's honorary chairman Masaru Ibuka took a tour of the company in late 1978, he had a brain wave that would bring music to the ears of millions around the world. One division had developed a compact tape recorder for journalists called a Pressman. Another part of the company was working on lightweight headphones. But what if the two products were combined? A Sony team worked on the idea, and the new product was shown to Sony's boss Akio Morita. He immediately saw the potential of a personal music player, and in 1979 the Walkman was launched.

Music on the move
The Walkman didn't have a recording function. It was designed purely to listen to prerecorded cassettes and was aimed at a young, music-loving public. It soon became an essential fashion accessory.

The "hotline" button faded the sound so the listener could hold a conversation without stopping the tape

SONY
STEREO CASSETTE PLAYER TPS-L2

STEREO

Inside, a battery-powered, motorized tape spool passed the tape over the tape head

The headphones could be adjusted to fit different head sizes

COOL SCIENCE

A cassette contains plastic tape with magnetically charged particles. The tape passes over a playing head, which reacts to the magnetic particles. This creates vibrations that are converted into sound by the headphone speakers.

The front flap opened so that the cassette could be loaded into place

Walkman

Other names Sony considered for the Walkman included "Stowaway" and "Soundabout"

Handy headphones
The lightweight headphones were perhaps the most innovative features of the Walkman. Headphones at the time covered the entire ear and weighed a hefty 14 oz (400 g). The Walkman's headphones were made with soft foam speakers and an adjustable plastic headband. They weighed just 2 oz (50 g).

The Stop/Eject button stopped the spool motor and flipped open the front flap to release the cassette

There were no separate speakers, only headphones

The headphones were small and covered in soft, spongy foam

Fast-forward
The Walkman had very simple controls, with buttons to Play, Pause, Rewind, Fast-forward, change Volume, and Stop/Eject. Pressing Play triggered the battery-powered motor to turn the tape spools, and pressing Rewind or Fast-forward changed the speed and direction in which the spools turned.

e player was powered
atteries

Wires connected the headphones to the player

Music on the move
Since the days of the Walkman, technological advances have meant increasingly sophisticated personal music players have been developed.

Sony Discman
This portable compact disk (CD) player went on sale in 1984. By the 1990s, CDs had replaced cassettes as the most popular form of music storage.

Minidisk player
Smaller than a CD, minidisks and their players were launched by Sony in 1992. They were popular in Asia but didn't catch on elsewhere in the world.

MP3 players
Modern players, such as Apple's iPod Nano, use digital technology to store thousands of music tracks.

SEE ALSO Electric motor 68 · Battery 96

In the 1950s, Californian surfers, looking for something fun to do when the waves were flat, attached roller skate wheels to wooden boards so that they could street surf. Soon, manufactured skateboards were on sale in surf stores, but skateboarding was seen as a teenage fad rather than as a serious sport. By the 1970s, better boards and wheels had been made—and skateboarders had developed a huge range of tricks and skills to impress the world.

A helmet protects the skater's head if she falls off the board

Elbow pads protect the elbows from injuries

The top of the deck has a special nonslip surface

The truck is a metal device that connects the wheels to the deck and allows the wheels to turn

Polyurethane wheels combine strength with maneuverability and speed

The underside of the board is decorated with skater graphics

Wood and wheels
Skateboards of the 1950s were based on a simple design. A piece of wood was cut into the shape of a miniature surfboard, and two pairs of roller-skate wheels were attached to the bottom. Skateboarding was originally known as "sidewalk surfing."

The deck was made from a single piece of cut wood

Skateboards made in the 1950s used wheels that were originally designed for roller skates

Building boards
Modern skateboards are made from layers of wood that are glued together and placed in a mold. Each board is then pressed and cut into shape. The trucks and wheels are bolted into place, and the board is coated with a waterproof sealant.

Skateboard

COOL SCIENCE

In 1972, Frank Nasworthy revolutionized skateboards by adding polyurethane wheels. These tough, soft plastic wheels greatly improved traction (grip) and paved the way for the development of many new skateboarding tricks.

Tricks and styles

There are many skateboarding styles. Freestyle skaters perform tricks on flat surfaces, and vert skaters use ramps to perform aerial tricks.

Ollies and kickflicks

When skaters perform an "ollie," they make the board look as if it is stuck to their feet. An ollie can be turned into a kickflip (above) by turning the board over in midair.

Keeping control

Typical decks have an upturned nose and tail and a concave shape through the middle to give skaters maximum control. Narrow boards work best on the streets, while wide boards are used by vert (ramp) skaters.

Best foot forward

Regular foot riders keep the left foot on the board and push from behind with the right foot. Goofy foot riders keep the right foot on the board and push from behind with the left foot. Mongo foot riders keep their rear foot on the board while the front foot does the pushing.

Urban skaters

Street skaters perform tricks on street curbs, benches, stairs, and other urban furniture.

Early boards had
simple designs on
the deck

Wheels were bolted
to the deck

From 1977 to 1989, it was illegal to own a skateboard in Norway—they were seen as dangerous for pedestrians

SEE ALSO Wheel 146 · Bicycle 166

People love to know what is happening in the world—to keep in touch with events in their own countries and abroad. Today, there are many ways to do this, such as the Internet and television, but for centuries the only good source of information was the newspaper. It told people about the world around them and how that world was changing. Despite the competition from new types of media, newspapers are still popular and more than one billion people read a paper every day.

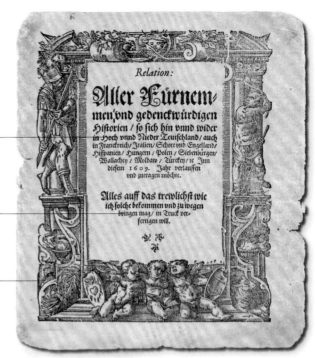

The text was printed in a single column, more like a book

Carolus's paper was written in German

A border decorates the edge of the early printed newspaper—this is dated 1609

First printed newspaper
In 1605, German publisher Johann Carolus produced the world's first printed newspaper, called *Relation*. Beforehand, he had been selling handwritten newsletters. They took so long to write that he bought a printing press.

The newspaper's name appears at the top of the front page

Headlines are printed in large, bold letters to catch the reader's eye

Global spread
The development of newspapers is closely linked with the progress of technology—as printing methods improved in the 1800s, newspapers were one of the first areas to benefit. They became cheaper to produce, and it was soon possible to include photographs in them. As a result, they became more and more popular, and many new ones appeared.

Newspaper

What's inside?

Newspapers are full of articles about current topics of interest, mostly in politics, sports, business, entertainment, and the arts. Some papers focus on local issues, but others describe what is going on in the entire country, along with information about major world events.

Papers are often made from recycled material

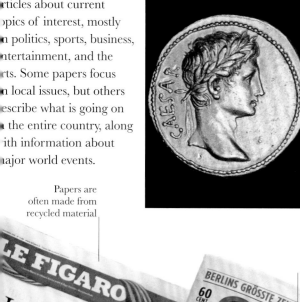

◄◄ BRIGHT SPARKS

Julius Caesar
More than 2,000 years ago, Julius Caesar, a Roman leader, produced a type of newspaper in 59 B.C.E. *Daily Acts*, as it was called, was carved in stone or metal and displayed in public places, so that people could be informed about political and social issues.

Special inks are used that do not come off on readers' hands

Color photographs attract readers

Making a newspaper
Newspapers have to be produced quickly—people want information as soon as possible, preferably within hours of events happening.

Collecting the news
To make a newspaper, first you need to have news stories. These are collected by journalists, who often interview people and then write about what they say.

Printing
Once the information from journalists has been edited together, the newspaper is printed. Often, several "editions" are printed each day as news is updated.

Internet news
Today, there are online versions of most newspapers. These often include more detailed information than the paper editions and video clips, too.

SEE ALSO World Wide Web 44 · Printing press 84

225

In the late 1800s in the U.S.A., there were a lot of difficult jobs around, from gold mining to cattle herding. Tough clothes were just what people needed, and the strong cotton trousers sold by Levi Strauss and Jacob Davis became popular. Cotton was grown in the U.S.A., so they were affordable, too. In the 1900s, jeans were worn by soldiers, pop stars, and film stars, so they were fashionable as well as hard-wearing and comfortable. Today, they are by far the world's most popular clothes and are worn by people of all ages.

Shrinking and fading

Cotton fabrics shrink in hot water, so most jeans are washed before they are sold. You can also buy "shrink-to-fit" jeans. The idea is that you wear them in a bath of water and they shrink to fit your body perfectly. The indigo dye used to color jeans blue fades when they are washed. Sometimes, when jeans are washed at the factory, powdered stone is added to the water to give them a "stonewashed" look.

▶▶ TOMORROW'S WORLD

One day, clothes may remain clean and fresh without washing! Using microwaves, chemicals can be bonded, or fixed, to fabrics to make them repel dirt and kill the bacteria that make them smelly. Clothes that treat skin diseases are also being developed.

Jeans are made of denim fabric, woven from alternate blue and white cotton threads

These are stonewashed jeans

Jeans

Many jeans have
five pockets

War effort
During World War II, factory workers and off-duty soldiers wore jeans, and U.S. soldiers took them abroad. Soon, jeans started to become popular in other countries. Before the war, decorative patterns were stitched on to the pockets of jeans, but this had been stopped to save money. Swirling patterns were painted on to the denim instead.

Orange thread
shows up against a
blue background

Buttons carry the
maker's name
or logo

Rivets are made
of copper

Rebellion!
James Dean was a young American actor, and when he wore jeans in the 1955 movie *Rebel Without a Cause*, sales soared. However, some schools banned jeans because of their link with the movie, which was thought to encourage teenage rebellion.

Each year, around 450 million pairs of jeans are sold in the U.S.A.

Jean styles
The first jeans were loose and baggy and had to be held up by suspenders. Since then, jeans have changed in appearance many times.

1940s fashion statement
Western movies were popular in the 1930s, and the cowboys in these movies wore jeans. So by the 1940s, they were starting to become fashionable throughout the U.S.A.

1950s youth culture
In the 1950s, Elvis Presley and other rock and roll stars wore jeans. They started a trend among teenage music fans that continues today.

1970s jeans for everyone
By the 1970s, jeans were worn by people of all ages and were available in many colors. Other denim clothes, such as jackets and skirts, were also sold.

SEE ALSO Nylon 50 · Zipper 138

Levi Strauss

In 1848, gold was discovered in California, U.S.A., and, over the next few years, hundreds of thousands of people—called gold prospectors—traveled there in the hope of finding more. This "gold rush," as it was called, ended in disappointment and failure for most people—but not for a man named Levi Strauss.

The birth of blue jeans

Levis Strauss was born in Germany in 1829. But, at the age of 18, his family moved to New York, U.S.A., to join his older brothers, who had already made the long journey to seek their fortune. Strauss later moved to San Francisco, California, the largest city in the gold-rush area, to set up a clothing and fabric business on behalf of his family. He hoped that the influx of new people there would ensure its success. Thanks to Nevada tailor Jacob Davis, the company started off very well. Davis was one of Strauss's customers, buying material from Strauss for his own business. He had invented a way of strengthening work pants by using metal rivets and asked Strauss to help get the idea off the ground. Together, he and Strauss started to make the world's first denim jeans.

Moving on
As the Levi Strauss Company grew, it changed offices several times. This is its fifth location in Battery Street, in San Francisco, where it moved to in 1866 and remained for the next 40 years.

Levi Strauss
Strauss insisted that his staff called him "Levi," rather than the more formal "Mr. Strauss" that was usual at the time.

Clothes for workers

As this magazine advert from the 1880s shows, Strauss sold blue denim jackets as well as jeans. At the time, jeans were advertised as tough clothes for working men. It would be many years before they were considered fashionable.

> ❝ **Jeans represent democracy in fashion** ❞
>
> Giorgio Armani,
> Italian fashion designer

Worldwide brand

The business was a great success, and soon Strauss and Davis were making jackets and other clothes out of blue denim and a brown cotton material known as "duck." Duck clothes were not popular, so the company stopped making them. In 1902, Levi Strauss died, and his four nephews took over the business. They continued to work with Davis until his death in 1908. The Levi Strauss company is still highly successful and, though still based in San Francisco, has offices throughout the world.

Labeling Levis

All Levi jeans have a small red label and a larger leather label between the belt loops. The leather label was introduced in 1886, sewn in place with the orange thread that is still used to decorate Levis. The small red label was added in 1936.

Going global

Strauss was not the only 19th-century jeans manufacturer. The Lee Company made them, too, and it also exists today. Jeans are now manufactured and sold by many companies throughout the world. In the U.S.A. alone, people spend more than $10 billion on them every year. They remained cheap until the late 1970s, when more expensive "designer" brands were introduced.

This kinetoscope parlor was in San Francisco, California

Parlors had several kinetoscopes—one for each customer

In the late 1800s, this simple wooden box was the closest thing to a television or a movie screen. Its flickering, silent, black and white images amazed people—because they moved, just like living things. American inventor Thomas Edison came up with the idea for the kinetoscope and gave his employee, William Dickson, the task of building the machine. Although they were soon replaced by movie projectors, kinetoscopes started a craze that led to the birth of the American movie industry.

One of the first arcade movies lasted only around four seconds and showed a man sneezing

Flashing photos

The kinetoscope moved a sequence of photographs, called frames, over a shutter. As each frame moved into position, the shutter opened briefly, allowing light to flash through it. So the user saw a rapid series of still photographs.

BRIGHT SPARKS

Invented in the 1600s, magic lanterns were the first devices to project pictures on to surfaces. In this model, light from an oil lamp shone through a picture printed on a glass plate, reproducing the image on a wall or screen.

Fooling the brain

Kinetoscope movie makers took around 40 frames every second. By showing these in sequence at the same high speed, the kinetoscope could fool the viewer's brain into merging the separate photographs into a single moving image. Today's televisions, movie theaters, and computer games all work in a similar way.

The case was made of wood and sometimes also glass

Kinetoscope

Viewers looked down the peep hole, through a lens that focused the image

The shutter lets light shine upward through each frame in turn

An electric motor turned a system of pulleys and wheels

The film was fed round a set of rollers

The long strip of film moved around in an endless loop

Hundreds of black and white photographs were printed on to the transparent film

The first American movie
The first kinetoscope movie lasted only a few seconds. Called *Monkeyshines, No. 1*, it showed one of Edison's employees doing exercises. Dickson and his colleage, William Heise, made the movie to test the system, so it was never shown to the public.

The first picture house
The first public kinetoscope parlor opened in 1894 on Broadway in New York City. It had 10 kinetoscopes. The movies showed a horse being shod, a trapeze artist, and a Scottish highland dance.

Moving images
In the 1860s, inventors built simple devices that made pictures appear to move. The popularity of these gadgets led to the development of more complex machines.

Lumière cinematograph
Patented in 1893 by the Lumière brothers of France, the cinematograph could project a movie on to a screen so many people could watch a movie at the same time.

Gaumont Kalee projector
By the 1950s, cinema movies had sound and sometimes color. This projector was made by Gaumont, the world's oldest film company, which was founded in 1895.

SEE ALSO Television 88 · Video games 234

What is 3-D?

The world around us is three-dimensional (3-D), which means that a solid object has height, width, and depth. But images in books, and in most movies, have just two dimensions: height and width. Movie makers have found ways to make movies seem more realistic, and exciting, by using techniques that give the appearance of three dimensions—we call them 3-D movies.

Brilliant brains

Humans have two eyes, and each one sees and sends a slightly different image to the brain. Our brains combine the information from each eye to create a 3-D moving image, which enables us to judge distance and speed. This remarkable ability is called binocular vision, and without it, we would not be so good at figuring out how far away something is or how close things in the distance are to one another.

Goofy glasses

A simple way to give movies depth is to project one version of a film in red and the other in green or blue. Two-tone tinted glasses let each eye see just one of the colored views. The brain then puts the two views together, creating 3-D color images.

Stunning effects

Most 3-D movies today, such as *Avatar*, use more complex technologies than their predecessors. These include polarization—special filters are used in projectors, and movies are beamed on to silver screens.

3-D illusions

Our brains are so used to figuring out 3-D shapes from pairs of images that it is quite easy to fool them. For a long time, people have made toys that use pairs of pictures drawn or photographed from two slightly different angles to create the illusion of 3-D. Inventors like John Logie Baird did the same thing with moving images. The problem is in finding a way of showing one image to the left eye and another to the right eye—for a single viewer it's easy enough to arrange, with one viewing tube for each eye. Doing something similar for a whole cinema audience is a challenge being met by modern movie makers.

> **" With digital 3-D projection, we will be entering a new age of cinema "**
>
> James Cameron,
> who made the 3-D movie *Avatar*

3-D in the 1950s

In the 1950s, 3-D movies were very popular. A number of movies, including thrillers and monster movies, were released in 3-D versions.

3-D cameras

Camera operators use special cameras with two lenses to record a 3-D movie. The lenses are the same distance apart as human eyes, so the differences in the scenes they film are very similar to the differences we would see ourselves.

Viewing 3-D movies

Audience members still need to wear special glasses that work with modern 3-D technologies, or they see a fuzzy-looking movie. In the future, it may be possible to watch movies without the two-tone glasses.

In the 1970s, video gaming took hold of the public's imagination with the launch of Atari's Pong. Originally an arcade video game, the success of Pong led to the birth of the home video gaming industry when Atari lauched a home version in 1975. This simple game of tennis was an instant success. Since then, video games have moved on from the bat-and-ball graphics of Pong to complex online virtual worlds, where gamers from all over the world can play and even communicate with each other.

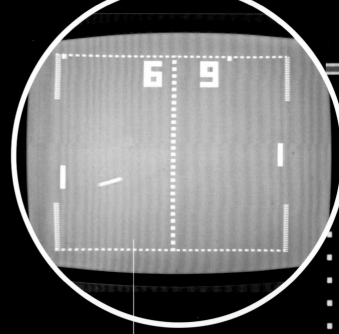

The simple graphics of Pong allowed players to bat a ball across the screen court

379 million video games were bought in 2009

BRIGHT SPARKS

Thomas T. Goldsmith and Estle Ray Mann are credited with inventing the first interactive electronic game, using a cathode ray tube. Players used controls to aim and fire a pretend missile at a target. The game was inspired by the radar displays that were common during World War II.

Pong

In 1973, Atari released Pong—an arcade video game based on Ping-Pong (Atari first developed the prototype in 1972). By moving a paddle vertically across the screen, a player hit a ball back to their opponent's side. If the opponent failed to return the ball, the player earned a point. The simple, two-dimensional game was an instant hit with the public, and Atari decided to modify it for home use. In 1975, the company launched the first successful home video games console.

The game of Pac-Man became a cultural icon of the 1980s

Cutting edge

Early games consoles look old-fashioned now, but when they were launched they contained the most high-tech computer chips in consumer products, and the games featured cutting-edge color graphics and sound effects. Pac-Man was a hugely successful arcade game that was launched in 1980.

Video games

Pac-Man must avoid capture by the four ghosts that haunt the maze

Pac-Man loses a life if touched by a ghost, and when all lives are lost it is "game over"

The player can score extra points by guiding Pac-Man to eat a power pellet

Big business
Every year thousands of video games are published, tapping into current trends and setting new ones.

Sonic the Hedgehog
This platform game was launched in 1991 and spawned many successful sequels. The popular character even starred in a spin-off cartoon series.

Tomb Raider
Starring the character of Lara Croft, Tomb Raider was one of the first video games to feature a heroine and became one of the bestselling video games of all time.

Second Life
This groundbreaking interactive environment allows players to live in a virtual 3-D world. They can design their own characters (avatars), socialize with other players, and do business.

As the player guides Pac-Man through the maze, it eats pac dots

Console development
By the 1990s, companies such as Nintendo, Sony, and Sega had entered the home console market. Joysticks and keypads were replaced with gamepads with multidirectional controls and action buttons. Simple two-dimensional graphics made way for 3-D worlds, motion sensors, fitness challenges, and ever-more interactive experiences.

SEE ALSO Television 88 · Kinetoscope 230

Emperor Nero is believed to have worn polished gems over his eyes to protect them from the Sun's harsh glare when watching gladiator fights in ancient Rome. Judges in 12th-century China wore smoky quartz glasses to hide their facial expressions from witnesses. But it wasn't until 1929 that sunglasses designed to protect the wearer's eyes from the Sun's rays were developed by American Sam Foster. By the 1930s, movie stars and musicians were wearing them, changing sunglasses from humble eye protectors to fashion accessories.

Light filters

When sunlight hits water, the light is reflected in one direction, rather than being scattered. If it gets into your eyes, it produces a dazzling effect called glare. Fortunately, glare like this can be filtered out by sunglasses with polarized lenses. The lenses are coated with a film made up of molecules that work like a filter to block light reflected from horizontal surfaces.

"Doggles" are sunglasses that have been designed for dogs that are bothered by glare

UV protection

Good sunglasses protect the eyes from the Sun's strong ultraviolet (UV) rays. UV is separated into two categories based on the wavelength of the light: UV-A and UV-B. The eye's cornea (clear outer covering) absorbs all UV-B and most UV-A light, providing natural protection, but a small amount of UV-A can enter the eye and, over time, cause eye diseases. The lenses in sunglasses have a special coating that blocks harmful UV rays from reaching the eye.

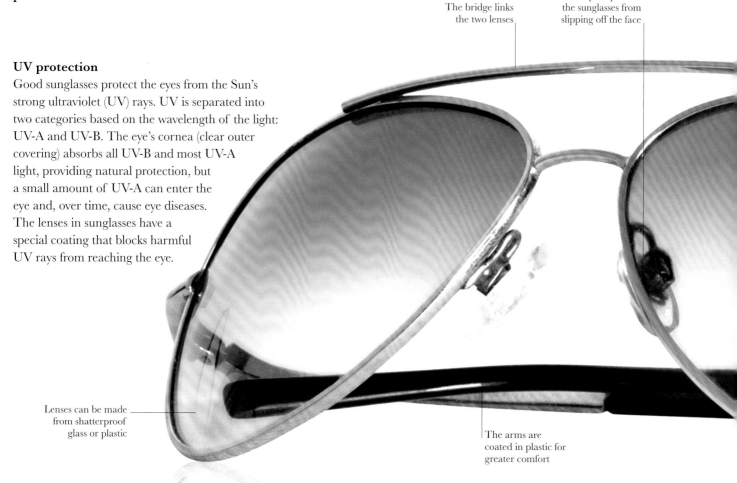

The bridge links the two lenses

Nosepads prevent the sunglasses from slipping off the face

Lenses can be made from shatterproof glass or plastic

The arms are coated in plastic for greater comfort

Sunglasses

COOL SCIENCE

Some sunglasses have photochromic lenses, which contain chemicals that darken and absorb visible light when UV light hits them. When the wearer goes indoors, the reaction is reversed and the lenses turn pale again.

Colors and tints

Sunglasses lenses come in a variety of colors. The color of the tint determines the parts of the light spectrum (red, orange, yellow, green, blue, indigo, and violet) that are absorbed. Gray tints protect against glare. Purple and rose tints are good for contrasting objects against a blue or green background. Yellow and gold tints block out some blue light, while amber and brown tints absorb some blue and violet light.

Some glasses have more tint near the top of the lens than at the bottom

A wire frame holds and protects the lenses

Hinges allow the arms of the sunglasses to fold down

Sports sunglasses

Some sports require special eye protection. Goggles need to be securely attached to the head and are designed to cope with extreme conditions.

Surf goggles

Used by water-sport enthusiasts, surf goggles are shatterproof, attached to the head with a strap, and have a nose cushion to help keep them in place.

Ski goggles

Two layers of lenses inside ski goggles prevent the insides from becoming foggy. A tint protects the eyes from the glare of the Sun on the snow.

Glacier goggles

Sunlight reflecting off ice can cause snow blindness. Glacier goggles have very dark, round lenses and leather blinders at the sides to block out the Sun's rays.

SEE ALSO Laser 46 · Glasses 114

The tone knob
changes the strength
of overtones—sounds
that are higher than
the main note

The electric guitar revolutionized 20th-century popular music. Like its acoustic cousin, it has six strings, which run down a long neck over metal strips called frets. But rather than having a hollow body to make the sound louder, most electric guitars are solid. Electromagnets change the strings' vibrations into electrical currents, which are then amplified (made louder) electronically. Rickenbacker Electro Instruments produced the first electric guitars in 1931. But electric guitar playing really caught on in 1949, with the simple, rich-sounding Fender Telecaster. Musicians started using this to play a new type of music called rock and roll.

A guitar's shape does
not affect its sound, but
curved edges make it
more comfortable to play

Fender Telecasters
have bodies made of
solid ash wood

Bodies

Known as the Rickenbacker frying pans, the first electric guitars had metal bodies. But as with most modern electric guitars, the Telecaster is made from wood. Experts agree that guitars made from heavier materials make better sounds. Some musicians believe that they can distinguish between the sound quality from different types of wood.

◄◄ BRIGHT SPARKS

The tomb of Djeserkaraseneb—an Egyptian official who died in around 1400 B.C.E.—shows women playing a guitarlike instrument called a lute. Modern guitars were developed in Europe in the 1700s and 1800s.

A guitar for everyone

Radio repairman Leo Fender designed his Telecaster for mass production in 1949. With the neck simply bolted to the body, it could easily be assembled and repaired. Players could create different notes using the frets along its neck and turn knobs to control its volume and tone.

Electric guitar

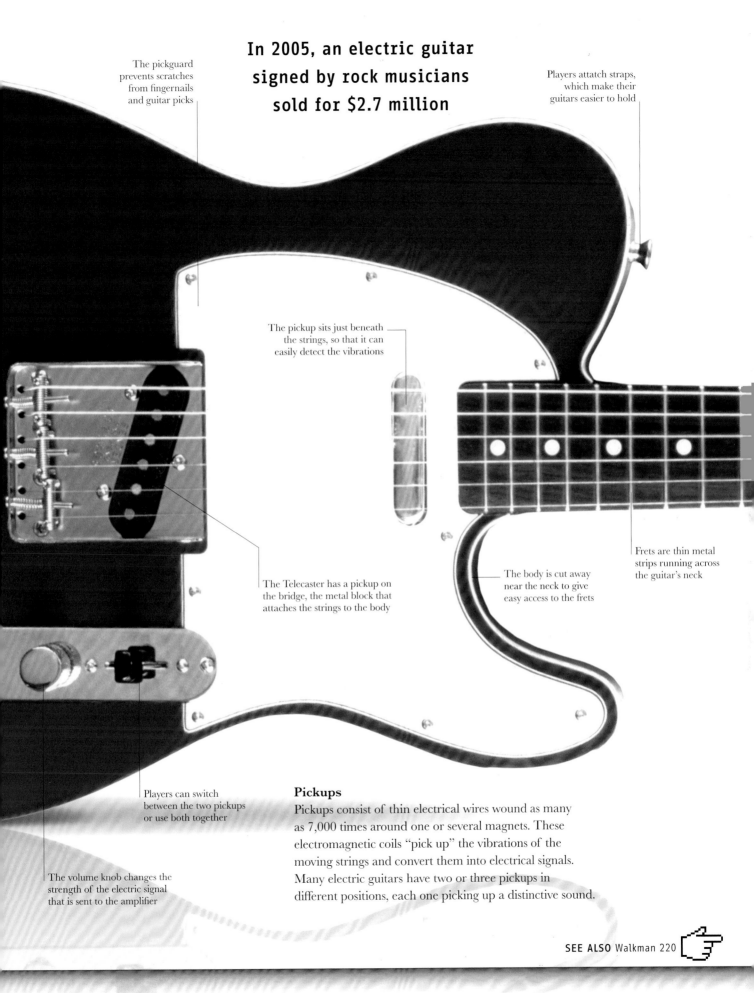

In 2005, an electric guitar signed by rock musicians sold for $2.7 million

The pickguard prevents scratches from fingernails and guitar picks

Players attatch straps, which make their guitars easier to hold

The pickup sits just beneath the strings, so that it can easily detect the vibrations

Frets are thin metal strips running across the guitar's neck

The Telecaster has a pickup on the bridge, the metal block that attaches the strings to the body

The body is cut away near the neck to give easy access to the frets

Players can switch between the two pickups or use both together

The volume knob changes the strength of the electric signal that is sent to the amplifier

Pickups

Pickups consist of thin electrical wires wound as many as 7,000 times around one or several magnets. These electromagnetic coils "pick up" the vibrations of the moving strings and convert them into electrical signals. Many electric guitars have two or three pickups in different positions, each one picking up a distinctive sound.

SEE ALSO Walkman 220

Which guitar?

There are different types of guitars that can be amplified electronically, depending on the sound that musicians want to produce. Good guitar players sound even better on high-quality instruments, so they choose their guitars carefully.

Martin acoustic guitar
Pickups are added to acoustic guitars to amplify their sound electronically. For soft, acoustic tones, many professionals choose Martin guitars.

Gibson Les Paul electric guitar
In the 1950s, legendary jazz guitarist Les Paul helped the Gibson guitar company to develop this classic guitar. It is still hugely popular today.

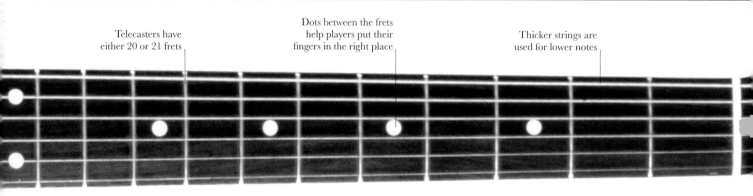

Telecasters have either 20 or 21 frets

Dots between the frets help players put their fingers in the right place

Thicker strings are used for lower notes

The Who's Pete Townshend was the first rock star to smash his guitar on stage—in 1964

Necks

Electric guitars have six steel strings. Carefully spaced along the neck beneath the strings are the thin metal frets. Pressing a string down on a fret effectively makes it shorter, so it vibrates faster and produces a higher note.

COOL SCIENCE

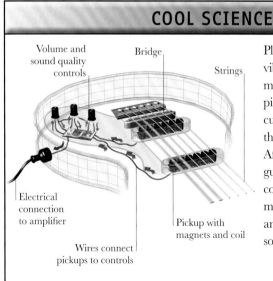

Volume and sound quality controls

Bridge

Strings

Electrical connection to amplifier

Wires connect pickups to controls

Pickup with magnets and coil

Plucking a string makes it vibrate. By disturbing the magnetic field above the pickups, this makes electric currents flow in the wires that coil around the magnets. After passing through the guitar's volume and tone controls, these currents are made stronger by an amplifier and then converted back into sound by a speaker.

Jimi Hendrix plugged his guitars into this Uni-Vibe effects pedal to distort their sound

Effects pedals are connected to both a guitar and an amplifier

Rickenbacker bass guitar

Bass guitars have only four strings and make lower notes than electric guitars. This one is made by the company that made "frying pans."

Tuning involves turning pegs to make the strings looser or tighter

The headstock, or peghead, holds the guitar strings

Amplifiers

On its own, an electric guitar is pretty quiet and the electric current from a pickup is very small. It is the amplifier that makes the guitar sound loud—by magnifying the current until it produces a loud enough sound from the speaker.

Speakers

Speakers also contain electromagnets. These turn the electrical signals from the amplifier back into vibrations that we can hear. Larger currents make the speaker cones vibrate more, making a louder sound. When bands play concerts, they often play through huge "walls" of speakers.

Guitar legend Jimi Hendrix used this Marshall amplifier in the 1960s

The amplifier has controls for tone, volume, and other effects

Speaker cabinets can contain several speakers

Marshall's amplifier with combined speaker

SEE ALSO Walkman 220

Intended as a flexible alternative to leather, the rubber-soled sports shoe was developed by the U.S. Rubber Company in 1892. In 1917, U.S. Rubber set up a company called Keds to manufacture and market their sports shoes, or "sneakers." Today, around 350 million pairs of sneakers are sold every year in the U.S.A. alone. Modern sneakers are designed to maximize sporting performance, with cushioning systems to absorb shock. They are also a fashion staple, with competing labels and designs moving in and out of style.

Vulcanized rubber

In 1839, Charles Goodyear invented vulcanized rubber, which doesn't melt in the heat or turn brittle in the cold. It proved to be useful for the manufacture of many products, including tires and shoe soles.

TOMORROW'S WORLD

Barefoot running causes fewer injuries than running in shoes, because different points of the foot hit the ground first. Research is being carried out to develop a new line of sneakers that copy the benefits of barefoot running.

The first trainers

Keds was the first company to sell the new lightweight, flexible rubber-soled sneakers on a mass scale. They had a high top covering the ankle, a vulcanized rubber sole, and a plain brown canvas upper. The shoes became known as "sneakers" because the rubber sole was so quiet you could sneak around without making a noise.

The seams are stitched together

Canvas is lightweight and allows air to circulate

Basketball shoes sold in the 1980s could be pumped up with air, like bicycle tires

Sports shoes

COOL SCIENCE

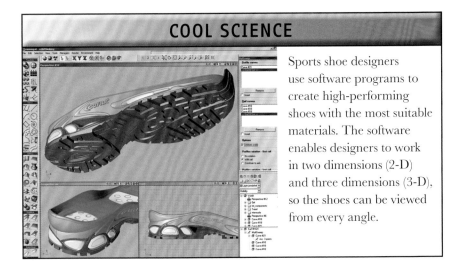

Sports shoe designers use software programs to create high-performing shoes with the most suitable materials. The software enables designers to work in two dimensions (2-D) and three dimensions (3-D), so the shoes can be viewed from every angle.

Shoes to suit

In the 1920s and 1930s, sports shoe companies started to design sneakers to suit different sports, such as sprinting and soccer. By the 1950s, sneakers were also being worn as leisure footwear. Companies began using famous athletes in their advertising campaigns in the 1980s, and sneakers quickly became objects of fashion.

The laces can be tightened to ensure a comfortable fit

The laces feed through metal eyelets (holes)

Thick rubber soles can bend with the foot

Sports shoes

Trainer companies develop shoes to help athletes maximize their performance, but different sports have different footwear needs.

Soccer cleat

Studs can be screwed into the base of a soccer cleat to aid grip. Different studs can be used, depending on how hard or soft the field is.

Cycling shoe

Many cycling shoes have clips, which are also called cleats, on their bases. Cleats can be slotted into bicycle pedals to stop the shoes from slipping.

Sprinting shoe

Athletes' shoes have spikes to increase grip with the running surface. The same idea is used by cheetahs, which run with their claws outstretched.

SEE ALSO Soccer 244

The covering of thick leather was strong and hard-wearing

Played and watched by billions of people, soccer is the most popular team sport in the world. Versions of the modern game were played in medieval Europe, when hundreds of players would roam the streets kicking a ball between them. The modern sport is based on rules drawn up in 1863 by the English Football Association (soccer is called "football" in many parts of the world) in an attempt to standardize the various forms of the game played in England. The aim of soccer is simple: two teams compete to dribble, pass, or head a ball across a field and into their opponent's goal.

World's oldest soccer ball

This soccer ball was discovered in the ceiling rafters in what was once the bedroom of Mary Queen of Scots, in Stirling Castle, Scotland. Experts believe that it dates from the 1540s, making it one of the oldest known soccer balls in the world.

◀◀ BRIGHT SPARKS

Cuju is a ball game that was first played in China around 2,500 years ago. The ball was made from leather and a type of rubber and stuffed with feathers. Two teams played against one another to score points, and a referee ensured that the game was played fairly. A similar game was also played in Japan and Southeast Asia.

Its dry weight was just 4 oz (125 g), less than one third of most modern soccer balls

The leather absorbed water, so it became very heavy when wet

Soccer

Three leather panels were stitched together to create a spherical shape

The stitching was visible where two panels join

A pig's bladder inflated inside the leather panels gave the ball shape and bounce

Only 5.5–6 in (14–16 cm) across, this ball was much smaller than modern soccer balls

The leather cracked from old age

Rules for the rowdy

For a long time, soccer fans and players have had a reputation for being boisterous. In 1314, the English King, Edward II, banned the game from the streets of London because players were fighting each other and damaging property. But the threat of imprisonment didn't make the sport any less popular!

Heavy on the head

Early soccer balls were made by blowing up pigs' bladders and stitching leather panels around them. In wet weather, the balls became extremely heavy as they soaked up a lot of water. So heading the ball on a wet day could be dangerous—sometimes even fatal. Nowadays, soccer balls are made of synthetic leather with a waterproof coating.

240 million people around the world regularly play competitive soccer

Types of modern soccer balls

More than 40 million soccer balls are made every year. Panels are stitched together, but one seam is left open so that the rubber bladder can be inserted. Once the final seam is sewn, the bladder can be inflated with air through a pump valve.

Popular panels

The most common panel pattern—the truncated icosidodecahedron—is a mix of 20 hexagons and 12 pentagons. Designed for the 1970 World Cup, Adidas's Telstar had white hexagons and black pentagons.

New shapes

The 2006 World Cup soccer ball had just 18 curved panels. Rather than stitching these, Adidas bonded them together to create a smoother shape. The ball performed the same way no matter where it was kicked.

SEE ALSO Skateboard 222 · Sports shoes 242

A time line of inventions featured in this book.

c. 3500 B.C.E.
Wheels are in use in Mesopotamia.

c. 650 B.C.E.
The ancient kingdom of Lydia is the first civilization to use stamped coins.

c. 515 B.C.E.
The ancient Greeks use cranes to lift heavy objects.

c. 220 B.C.E.
China developss the first magnetic compasses.

c. 1100s
A version of the modern game of soccer is widely played in Europe.

c. 1200s
Glasses with magnifying lenses are invented.

c. 1440
Johannes Gutenberg revolutionizes communication with the printing press.

c. 1450s
Western Europeans develop the carrack, ancestor of the modern sailing ship.

1590
Hans and Zacharias Janssen invent the compound microscope.

1596
John Harington invents the first modern flushing toilet.

1605
Johann Carolus produces the world's first printed newspaper.

1620
Cornelius Drebbel builds the first submarine.

1642
Galileo Galilei designs a clockwork mechanism.

c. 1656
Christian Huygens makes the first working pendulum clock.

1759
John Harrrison designs his chronometer.

1764
James Hargreaves invents his spinning jenny, greatly increasing the speed with which yarn can be spun.

1796
Edward Jenner discovers the technique of vaccination to prevent smallpox.

1800
Alessandro Volta builds the first battery.

1810
Peter Durand creates tin cans by dipping sheets of metal in molten tin.

1821
Michael Faraday invents a simple electric motor.

1824
Joseph Aspdin discovers Portland cement.

1829
George and Robert Stephenson build the first modern locomotive, known as the *Rocket*.

1830
Joseph Henry discovers the essential principle of the electric telegraph.

1840
Rowland Hill's sticky postage stamp goes on sale.

1852
Elisha Otis demonstrates the first elevator equipped with a safety device.

1860
Étienne Lenoir builds a successful internal combustion engine.

1863
The world's first underground railroad system opens in London, England.

1863
Pierre Michaux introduces the first commercially successful pedal-driven bicycle.

1866
Alfred Nobel invents dynamite, the first powerful explosive that is safe to handle.

1870
Zénobe Gramme builds the first generator.

1870
Levi Strauss manufactures denim jeans.

1876
Alexander Graham Bell patents his telephone.

1877
Claus Boerdine develops the single stapler.

1879
James Ritty invents the cash register.

1881
Joseph Swan and Thomas Edison invent the commercial lightbulb.

1883
Charles Fritts builds a solar cell.

1887 James Blyth and Charles Brush both use a windmill to generate electricity.

1888
Heinrich Hertz detects radio waves.

1888
Thomas Edison and William Dickson make the kinetoscope.

1892
The U.S. Rubber Company manufactures rubber-soled sports shoes, or sneakers.

1893
Whitcomb Judson comes up with the idea of a zipper.

1895
Wilhelm Röntgen discovers and experiments with x-rays.

1896
Henri Becquerel discovers radioactivity.

1901
Guglielmo Marconi uses radio waves to send a message across the Atlantic Ocean.

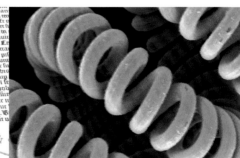

Timeline

1908
Henry Ford designs his Model T, the world's first affordable motor car.

1910
Henry Coanda designs an early type of jet engine.

1913
Harry Brearley develops stainless steel.

1925
John Logie Baird gives a public demonstration of the television.

1927 Christian Steenstrup designs an affordable refrigerator.

1928
Alexander Fleming accidentally creates the first antibiotic, penicillin.

1928
Hans Haupt invents the telescopic pocket umbrella.

1929
Sam Foster designs sunglasses to protect wearers' eyes from the Sun.

1930
William Beebe and Otis Barton invent the bathysphere, a device for underwater exploration.

1931
Rickenbacker Electro Instruments make the first modern electric guitars.

1934
Percy Shaw invents cat's eyes.

1935
Wallace Carothers and DuPont produce nylon.

1938
László Bíró invents a new type of pen with a rollerball, the ballpoint pen.

1942
Igor Sikorsky makes the first helicopter to be mass-produced.

1943
Jacques Cousteau and Émile Gagnan invent scuba gear.

1947
Percy Spencer's microwave oven goes on sale.

1949
Joseph Woodland and Bernard Silver file a patent for their bar code system.

1949
Ole Kirk Kristiansen and his son Godtfred Kirk create plastic LEGO® bricks.

1950
Diners' Club Inc. introduces the first credit cards.

1950s
Californian surfers attach wheels to wooden boards to create skateboards.

1953
Frances Crick and James Watson discover the chemical structure of DNA.

1955
George de Mestral designs Velcro.

1957
Gordon Gould designs the first laser.

1959
NASA develops a spacesuit to withstand the new challenges of space exploration.

1959
NASA, with the help of B. F. Goodrich, develops the space helmet.

1960
The U.S. Navy develops a satnav system called Transit.

1960
Basil Hirschowitz makes the first fiber-optic flexible endoscope.

1961
George Devol and Joseph Engelberger invent Unimate, the first industrial robot.

1967
James Fergason discovers the type of liquid crystal used in modern LCDs.

1967
Werther von Braun and NASA launch the *Saturn V* rocket.

1969
Willard Boyle and George Smith invent the CCD.

1971
The first microprocessor goes on sale.

1972
Atari develops the Pong prototype.

1973
Nathaniel Wyeth designs a plastic bottle strong enough to hold carbonated drinks.

1973
Motorola's Martin Cooper develops the first working cell phone.

1974 Art Fry, Spencer Silver, and 3M produce Post-it® Notes.

1974
Raymond Damadian, Paul Lauterbur, and Peter Mansfield create the MRI scanner.

1976
Steve Wozniak and Steve Jobs launch the Apple I and revolutionize home computing.

1979
Masaru Ibuka and Akio Morita launch the personal music player, the Walkman.

1989
Tim Berners-Lee invents the World Wide Web.

1990
NASA launches a space-based telescope, Hubble.

1997
NASA launches the *Cassini* space probe.

2003
NASA develops two rovers to explore Mars.

2008
Tesla Motors produces an all-electric sports car.

Acoustic
A type of guitar that makes sound from a hollow wooden body, without electric amplification.

Aerodynamic
Shaped to minimize air resistance (friction from the air). Aerodynamics plays an important part in the design process, helping engineers achieve the best levels of safety and performance.

Allies
The countries that fought against Germany, Italy, and Japan in World War II, including Great Britain, the U.S.A., and the Soviet Union.

Alternating current (AC)
An electrical current that changes direction many times per second.

Antibiotic
A medicine that slows down, or stops, the growth of bacteria.

Assembly line
A series of workers and machines in a factory. They each have a role in putting together, or assembling, an object. The assembly line was pioneered by Henry Ford in the early 1900s.

Atmosphere
The gases that surround a planet or star.

Atom
The basic unit of a chemical element, made up of a tiny dense nucleus, which is positively charged, and surrounded by a cloud of negatively charged electrons.

Bacteria
A group of single-celled microorganisms, commonly known as germs. Some cause diseases such as typhoid; others can be helpful, such as those that aid digestion.

Battery
A portable power supply that generates electricity when chemical reactions happen inside it.

Blood vessel
A tube, such as an artery or vein, that carries blood through the body.

Boer War
The Boers are people descended from a group of Dutch travelers who settled in southern Africa in the 1600s. During the Boer Wars (1880–1881 and 1899–1902), they fought with the British, who mostly controlled the region at that time.

Carrack
A large oceangoing ship with three- or four-mast sails. Carracks were used in the 1400s and 1600s by Portuguese and Spanish explorers.

Cathode ray tube
A tube with a vacuum inside, in which cathode rays produce an image on a screen—used mainly in televisions and computer screens.

Charge-coupled device (CCD)
An electronic device that converts an image into an electrical signal. CCDs are used in telescopes and digital cameras.

Cholera
An infectious bacterial disease that is often caught from infected water supplies.

Chromosomes
Threadlike structures present in all body cells that have a nucleus. They carry the genetic code for the formation of the body. A normal human body cell carries 46 chromosomes arranged into 23 pairs.

Cistern
A tank for storing water, especially for a flushing toilet.

Convex lens
A lens that is shaped like the curved outside of a sphere (a concave lens has a surface that curves inward, like the inside of a sphere).

Deoxyribonucleic acid (DNA)
A chemical with a double helix structure that carries genetic information in the form of a chemical code. DNA is stored in the nucleus of cells and is a chief component of chromosomes.

Direct current (DC)
An electrical current that flows in one direction only.

Dynasty
A family that rules a country over a long period of time.

Electromagnet
A core of soft iron that is turned into a magnet when electric currents are passed through a coil that surrounds it.

Glossary

Electromagnetic radiation
A type of radiation, including radio waves, visible light, and x-rays.

Electron
A negatively charged particle that forms part of an atom—electrons carry electricity in solid materials.

Element
A substance of a single type, such as gold or iron, that cannot be broken down into simpler substances.

Endoscope
An instrument that can be put into a body, so that internal organs and other parts can be viewed.

Fluorescence
Light, or another type of radiation, that is emitted by certain substances when x-rays or ultraviolet light shine on them.

Galaxy
A collection of billions of stars, clouds of gas, and dust that move together through space.

Gecko
A type of lizard that is most active at night and has particularly sticky feet, enabling it to run along smooth surfaces.

Gene
A distinct section of a chromosome that is the basic unit of inheritance. Each gene consists of a segment of DNA containing the code that governs the production of a specific protein.

Generator
A machine that converts mechanical energy into electrical energy.

Genetic fingerprinting
The analysis of DNA from samples of body tissue, such as blood, that can be used to identify people (apart from identical twins, every person's DNA is unique).

Genetics
Study of inheritance and transmission of genes from one generation to the next.

Hologram
A 3-D image formed by light beams, such as laser beams. Holograms can also be produced as photographs.

Hypersonic
Traveling at least five times faster than the speed of sound.

Incandescent
Emits light as a result of being heated: a lightbulb becomes incandescent when an electric current flows though the filament.

Industrial Revolution
A revolution in the way that people lived and worked that started in Great Britain around 250 years ago before spreading throughout the western world.

Inheritance
In genetics, the way that characteristics, such as eye color or flower shape, are passed from one generation of living thing to the next generation.

Internet browser
Also known as a "web browser." This is a software program that allows a computer to search for, find, and view information using the Internet.

Laser
A device that emits, or produces, an intense beam of light in which the waves all travel in step.

Limestone
A type of rock that is mainly formed of calcium carbonate. It is used as a building material and to make cement. Chalk is a type of limestone.

Magnetic field
A region where magnetic forces can be detected.

Mesopotamia
The area between the Tigris and Euphrates rivers in what is now Iraq.

Methane
A gas made from carbon and hydrogen, which is colorless, odorless, and flammable (able to burn).

Microchip
A slice of a special material called a semiconductor that incorporates, in miniature, all the components found on a circuit board, made up of separate electronic parts, such as transistors. The components are an integral part of the semiconductor material.

Microorganism
A living thing that is too small to be seen with the naked eye.

Microprocessor
The brain of a computer, combining the functions of many microchips on a single unit and capable of carrying out hundreds of millions of operations every second. A typical microprocessor chip contains around 300 million transistors.

Molecule
The smallest amount of a chemical compound that can exist. When atoms of one or more elements are bonded together, this is called a molecule.

Moon
A planet's natural satellite (a smaller body that orbits another, more massive one).

Morse code
A code in which letters are represented by combinations of long and short signals (of sound or light).

Motor
A machine that provides power for a vehicle, or other device with moving parts, to work.

NASA
America's National Aeronautics and Space Administration. It was established in 1958 to spearhead space research and exploration, such as the Apollo Moon landings and the Space Shuttle missions. NASA also undertakes scientific research.

Nebula
A cloud of gas and dust in space.

Nobel Prize
An international award given annually for outstanding achievement in the following fields: physics, chemistry, physiology, literature, and peace. Set up at the request of the scientist Alfred Nobel, it was first awarded in 1901.

Nucleus
The control center of a cell that contains its DNA.

Orbit
The path of a satellite, planet, or other body as it moves around a more massive body in space.

Organ
Body part, such as the kidney or brain, with a specific role or roles that is made up of two or more different types of tissues.

Oxygen
A gas that makes up around one-fifth of the air and is essential for animal life.

Patent
A type of legal protection that gives an inventor or organization the sole right to make, use, or sell an invention for a fixed period. It prevents others from profiting from an inventor's ideas. In return the inventor discloses full details of the invention so that anyone can make it once the patent has expired.

Penicillin
A group of antibiotics produced naturally by a mold called *Penicillium chrysogenum*. Antibiotics can also be created in a laboratory or factory.

Piston
A tightly fitting disk that is driven back and forth inside a cylinder to create motion or to pump fluids.

Pixel
A tiny region of a display screen or camera sensor—many pixels are required to make up an image.

Polarized
A type of light that has been passed through a filter so its waves move in only one direction.

Pollution
Anything added to the natural environment that is harmful to living things.

Pressure (water)
A force that presses against something. Water pressure is caused by the weight of water above, so water pressure increases with depth. The deeper a submarine or submersible dives, the stronger it must be to resist water pressure.

Prototype
The first type or model of something, especially an invention.

Pyramid
A large monument with a square or rectangular base and four triangular sides. Pyramids served as tombs in ancient Egypt and as both temples and tombs in Mesoamerica (a region stretching from modern-day Mexico down to Guatemala).

Radiation
Energy that is transmitted as electromagnetic waves—for example, heat, light, and electricity.

Radioactivity
The emission, or releasing, of radiation or particles caused by an atom's nucleus disintegrating.

Scuba
An air-supply system used by divers. The word scuba stands for Self-Contained Underwater Breathing Apparatus.

Semaphore
A system of sending messages by using the arms, flags, or two poles put into certain positions to indicate letters of the alphabet.

Sewer

An underground drain that carries away waste from a house; sewers connect to make a sewage system.

Silicon

A nonmetal chemical element found in quartz and beach sand.

Solar array

A panel-like arrangement of solar cells that converts sunlight into electricity.

Solar cell

A device that is used to convert energy from the Sun (solar radiation) into electricity.

Space probe

An unmanned craft that is used to explore space. Probes send information about their environment back to scientists on Earth.

Space telescope

A device that is used to view objects, such as planets, in space. It operates in space and is controlled from Earth, so its views are not affected by Earth's atmosphere.

Stage (aerospace)

A section of a launch vehicle that burns its fuel and then separates and falls away from the rest of the vehicle.

Star

A luminous globe of hot gas that makes energy. Stars vary in size, temperature, color, and brightness.

Submarine

A large watercraft that can dive underwater and operate independently of other vessels. Most submarines are military craft.

Submersible

A small watercraft that can dive underwater. Some submersibles can dive to a great depth. Unlike submarines, submersibles have to be transported to their dive site by a ship.

Supersonic

Traveling faster than the speed of sound—that is more than 770 mph at 70°F (1,240 km/h at 20°C).

Synthetic

Artificial or man-made; synthetic things do not occur in nature.

Three-dimensional (3-D)

An object that has three dimensions can be measured in three ways because it has length, breadth, and depth (or height, width, and depth). Two-dimensional objects can only have their length and breadth measured, because they have no depth.

Ultrasound scan

A scanning technique that uses high-frequency sound waves to produce images of the inside of the body, including those of a developing fetus.

Vaccination

This is the process whereby a vaccine is injected into the bloodstream to stimulate the body to produce its own antibodies against a disease. It is also called immunization.

Vaccine

A substance that can be used to stimulate the body to create antibodies. Our bodies naturally make antibodies to fight diseases, so vaccines can prevent us from developing full-blown diseases.

Vacuum

When the air has been removed from a container, a vacuum has been created.

Valve

A device that controls the movement of fluid through a pipe or current through a wire, sometimes allowing movement only in one direction.

Virus

Infective nonliving agents, much smaller than bacteria, that invade cells and cause diseases such as the common cold and measles.

Wavelength

The distance between the peak of one wave and the peak of the following wave.

Wind turbine

A large device that uses wind power to turn a turbine, generating electricity.

World War I

An international conflict between the Allied Powers (Great Britain, France, Russia, Italy, Japan, and the U.S.A.) and the Central Powers (Germany, Austria-Hungary, and Turkey). The war lasted from 1914 to 1918.

World War II

A war that lasted from 1939 to 1945, during which a group of countries, including Germany, Italy, and Japan, was defeated by the Allies—a group of countries that included the U.S.A., Great Britain, and the Soviet Union.

X-ray

A type of radiation that reveals bones when projected through the body on to a photographic film.

Index

DK would like to thank: Jackie Brind for the index, Sarah Owens for proofreading, Ed Merritt for the globe artwork, and Andrea Mills, Matilda Gollon, and Ashwin Khurana for editorial assistance.

Credits